Agile Office 365

Successful Project Delivery Practices for an Evolving Platform

Haniel Croitoru

Apress®

Agile Office 365: Successful Project Delivery Practices for an Evolving Platform

Haniel Croitoru
Toronto, ON, Canada

ISBN-13 (pbk): 978-1-4842-4080-9 ISBN-13 (electronic): 978-1-4842-4081-6
https://doi.org/10.1007/978-1-4842-4081-6

Library of Congress Control Number: 2018962019

Managing Director, Apress Media LLC: Welmoed Spahr
Acquisitions Editor: Joan Murray
Development Editor: Laura Berendson
Coordinating Editor: Nancy Chen

Cover designed by eStudioCalamar

Cover image designed by Freepik (www.freepik.com)

Distributed to the book trade worldwide by Springer Science+Business Media New York, 233 Spring Street, 6th Floor, New York, NY 10013. Phone 1-800-SPRINGER, fax (201) 348-4505, e-mail orders-ny@springer-sbm.com, or visit www.springeronline.com. Apress Media, LLC is a California LLC and the sole member (owner) is Springer Science + Business Media Finance Inc (SSBM Finance Inc). SSBM Finance Inc is a **Delaware** corporation.

For information on translations, please e-mail rights@apress.com, or visit www.apress.com/rights-permissions.

Apress titles may be purchased in bulk for academic, corporate, or promotional use. eBook versions and licenses are also available for most titles. For more information, reference our Print and eBook Bulk Sales web page at www.apress.com/bulk-sales.

Any source code or other supplementary material referenced by the author in this book is available to readers on GitHub via the book's product page, located at www.apress.com/9781484240809. For more detailed information, please visit www.apress.com/source-code.

Printed on acid-free paper

This book is dedicated to my wonderful wife and best friend, Keren, who has and continues to support me through all my seemingly endless endeavors, and my beautiful children, Maya, Neta, and Eden, for reminding me every day that you never stop learning.

Table of Contents

About the Author

Haniel Croitoru is a seasoned SharePoint and Office 365 consultant, international speaker, and Microsoft Office 365 MVP with over 15 years of experience leading initiatives for both public and private sectors. Since 2003, he has focused on Office 365 and SharePoint, delivering solutions and contributing as a consultant, solution architect, project manager, business analyst, and trainer. In addition to his professional tenure, Haniel has always been a big proponent of sharing knowledge and giving back to the community through presenting at numerous conferences and networking meetings. Haniel holds a Master of Science degree in Computer Science with a specialty in Computer-Assisted Orthopedic Surgery from Queen's University and a Master's Certificate in Project Management from the prestigious York Schulich School of Business. He is a Project Management Professional (PMP) since 2007 and an Agile Certified Practitioner since 2013. When he is not working on client engagements or community activities, he enjoys spending time outdoors with his wife and three agile daughters.

About the Technical Reviewer

Fabio Claudio Ferracchiati is a senior consultant and a senior analyst/developer using Microsoft technologies. He works at BluArancio S.p.A (`www.bluarancio.com`) as Senior Analyst/Developer and Microsoft Dynamics CRM Specialist. He is a Microsoft Certified Solution Developer for .NET, a Microsoft Certified Application Developer for .NET, a Microsoft Certified Professional, and a prolific author and technical reviewer.
Over the past ten years, he's written articles for Italian and international magazines and co-authored more than ten books on a variety of computer topics.

Acknowledgments

Writing a book is no easy feat. Doing it for the first time as a single author is even more challenging. Without the unparalleled support and patience from my family, I would not have been able to achieve this goal. Thank you for being there and for your understanding of the many hours and late nights that went into it.

I also want to thank my countless friends I have gained over the years in the SharePoint and Office 365 communities around the world. The many technical and thought-provoking conversations we had helped fuel my knowledge for this book.

Finally, I would like to thank the Apress team, mainly Gwenan Spearing, Nancy Chen, Joan Murray, and Laura Berendson, and my technical editor, Fabio Claudio Ferracchiati, for your insights and guidance through the entire process from start to finish. When deadlines needed to be shifted due to events which were out of my control, you were flexible and allowed the schedule to shift while gently pushing me towards the finish line. Besides the overall management of the publishing process, the feedback you provided was instrumental in the quality of this book, for which I'm very grateful.

Introduction

Agile project management has been surging in popularity since the birth of the Agile Manifesto back in 2001. Despite some sceptics, the basic principles have and continue to be adopted by many organizations that engage in software development to deliver quality software with higher value and in less time.

More recently, in 2010, Microsoft released its own cloud computing platform called Office 365 (as a successor to the Business Productivity Online Services) to provide users with a path to move away from the traditional hardware-centric infrastructure to a more lightweight Software as a Service model.

While managing software development or integration projects requires specific skills, a heightened technological aptitude is required when leading an Office 365 project using an agile project management methodology to ensure successful implementation that the project manager will be proud of and the client will be happy with.

Agile Office 365 was created to provide you with the knowledge and tools to help you embark on this exciting journey with all the twists and turns that accompany it. Following an introduction to Office 365 and an overview of agile project management, this book will provide you with practical approaches you can leverage throughout the project lifecycle. It will also highlight common pitfalls that are often faced by the inexperienced project lead and ways to avoid them.

Who This Book Is For

Agile Office 365 is meant to provide useful insights for project managers, business analysts, IT managers, and other individuals who are involved in managing the Office 365 environment and delivering solutions for an organization. Although there is no need to have previous experience in either agile project management methodologies or Office 365, it will definitely help in grasping some key concepts in the topics discussed.

How This Book Is Structured

The book has been structured to follow a process typically used to deliver software projects using agile methodologies. The chapters have been broken down into the following sections.

Part I: Overview

Even if you've worked with Office 365 before or are familiar with the agile project management methodology called Scrum, it is a good idea to provide an overview and fill any knowledge gaps. This section will also show how agile Scrum is applied to Office 365 projects.

Part II: Project Conception

Part II is a series of chapters guiding the reader through the process of gathering all the necessary information to meet the project's objectives. Business outcomes drive the project and need to be carefully articulated and prioritized. A successful team composed of business and technical members needs to be assembled and agreements need to be reached during the start of the project.

Part III: Execution

Now that all the planning has been completed, it is time to get busy. The next two chapters focus on identifying how the solution will be built (or sourced). Testing Office 365 is also discussed because it requires some decision making to maximize the ROI of the testing.

Part IV: Deployment

Prior to deploying Office 365 into production, the organizational readiness needs to be assessed and proper transition to operations is required. As well, a final round of training is always a good idea.

Part V: Overarching Activities

Some activities don't fall into a specific phase of the project but rather are ongoing for the entire duration. Some activities extend even beyond the project.

Part VI: Tools for Managing Office 365 Projects

This final section of the book explores how Office 365 out of the box can be used as a tool to manage Office 365 deployments and other types of projects.

PART I

Overview

CHAPTER 1

Introduction to Office 365

As a consultant delivering Office 365 solutions, I often get asked the question "What is Office 365?" The ***marketing*** answer to this question is that Microsoft Office 365 is a collection of cloud-based productivity software products that are licensed through a monthly or annual subscription model. This answer is often received with a glazed look and a follow-up question of "So what exactly is Office 365 and why do I need it?" My usual answer is "What problems are you trying to solve?" While that may sound flippant, the reality is Office 365 can be positioned in many ways depending on the problem it is selected to help solve.

In this chapter, I provide you with a high-level overview of the family of products known as *apps* (applications) that make up the Office 365 offering. By the end of this chapter, you should have an understanding of how Office 365 may be used to solve specific problems within your organization.

Moving to the Cloud

Office 365 is a collection of integrated apps and services that are hosted in a number of Microsoft data centers across the globe. Today's apps, collectively known as *Software as a Service*, or *SaaS*, are available in a mix of desktop, mobile, and browser-based versions. Due to the increase in mobile usage, Microsoft is making big investments in ensuring that Office 365 will be easily accessible from anywhere, anytime, and on any device.

When you register for one of the Office 365 subscriptions, you get a *tenant*. Think of it as renting a room or apartment with others (Figure 1-1). You, as a tenant, are responsible for paying your bills on time and acting in an orderly fashion that is not disruptive to your neighbors. Your landlord (Microsoft) in turn ensures that you receive the services you signed up for and informs you of any issues or updates you need to know.

H. Croitoru, *Agile Office 365*, https://doi.org/10.1007/978-1-4842-4081-6_1

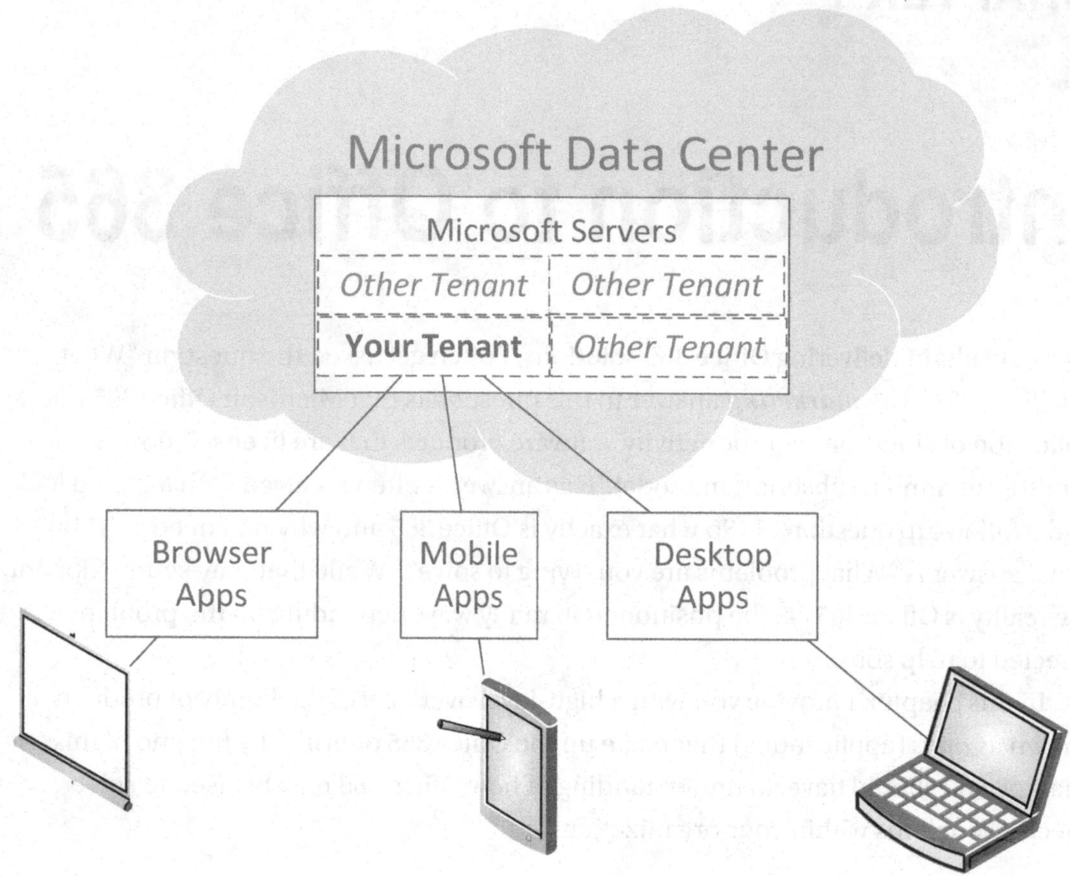

Figure 1-1. *Sharing the Office 365 Cloud tenant with others*

Being part of a tenant has many advantages. You have an army of support staff available 24/7 to deal with issues as they arise. Their sole purpose is to ensure that all systems are performing as they should. This is great when you consider the time and cost needed to support your own infrastructure. In many cases, even with a dedicated internal technical support team, the response may not be as fast.

On the flip side, since you are renting your space in a shared environment, your ability to control global changes are very limited. Going back to my example about renting an apartment, when was the last time a landlord asked for your permission or opinion on what color of wallpaper to use in the hallways (in all honesty, they probably should...)?

It is these pros and cons of being part of a shared environment that are one of the key concepts I based this book on.

A New Service is Born

Office 365 started out as the Microsoft Business Productivity Online Suite (MSBPOS) when it was first launched in late 2008. This was Microsoft's first attempt to position itself as a cloud-based SaaS provider. In its humble beginnings, MSBPOS was designed for smaller businesses with its Exchange 2007, Office Communications Server 2007, SharePoint 2007, and web versions of the productivity tools (Outlook, Word, Excel, and PowerPoint). In October 2010, Microsoft released a limited beta and in April, 2011 a full public beta of what we know today as Office 365. Since that time, Microsoft never looked back and is continuously improving the apps and adding new ones to enhance productivity and user experience. To that end, Office 365 is being positioned as an enterprise SaaS, unlike its MSBPOS predecessor.

Subscription Models

To maintain a presence in various market segments, Microsoft offers Office 365 via a number of subscription models. The subscriptions are divided into the following five groups.[1]

Office 365 for Individual Use

Office 365 for Individual Use is the most basic of the subscription models and is geared towards individuals or families who are looking for the latest Office applications on multiple devices, such as Windows, Apple, and Android.

The Office 365 Personal and Home subscriptions also come with one OneDrive account per user, where you can safely store your documents in the cloud as well as Skype with some credit to allow you to make calls to mobile phones and land lines.

Office 365 for Businesses to Enterprises

This tier of subscriptions is divided into Business and Enterprise groups, and introduces a mix of content collaboration, enterprise communication, and productivity apps. Some of the more popular tools in this category include SharePoint Online, Yammer, Skype for Business, Power BI, and eDiscovery and Compliance.

[1]To find out more about the specific plans and prices, visit `https://products.office.com/en-ca/` and `https://technet.microsoft.com/en-us/library/office-365-plan-options.aspx`.

Office 365 for Educational Institutions

Academic institutions qualify for special discounts for students, faculty, and staff. The tools available in this tier focus largely on communication between faculty and students, and provide a way to share documents between them.

Office 365 for Nonprofit Organizations

Nonprofit organizations wishing to leverage Office 365 can benefit from subscribing to the Office 365 Nonprofit plans, assuming they hold a recognized charitable status in the country in which they sign Microsoft's non-discrimination policy.

The various subscriptions types in this tier are similar to the Business and Enterprise ones, but at heavily discounted prices.

Office 365 for Governments

Like nonprofit organizations, government organizations need to be confirmed for eligibility by Microsoft. Once that has been done, you can leverage a number of subscriptions that are similar to the Enterprise plans, but at a reduced price.

If you haven't done so yet, I urge you to take a moment and visit `https://technet.microsoft.com/en-us/library/office-365-plan-options.aspx` to familiarize yourself with what's included in the subscription you currently have or are looking to get.

Note Make sure to check back on Microsoft's subscription site (`https://products.office.com`) as changes are made quite often when new apps and services are introduced to the Office 365 family.

The Apps Family

Now that you had a chance to review the various subscription models, let's have a look at what all these apps are and how you can best leverage them. At the time of writing of this book there are about two dozen apps in the Office 365 family, as shown in Figure 1-2, with new ones being released every few months. There's a lot that can be said about the apps I discuss here. In fact, there are entire books written on each of them. My goal is to provide you with a high-level overview of what each tool is and its purpose.

Note You may notice some inconsistencies in the names used in the book and what you experience online, since Microsoft occasionally rebrands their products.

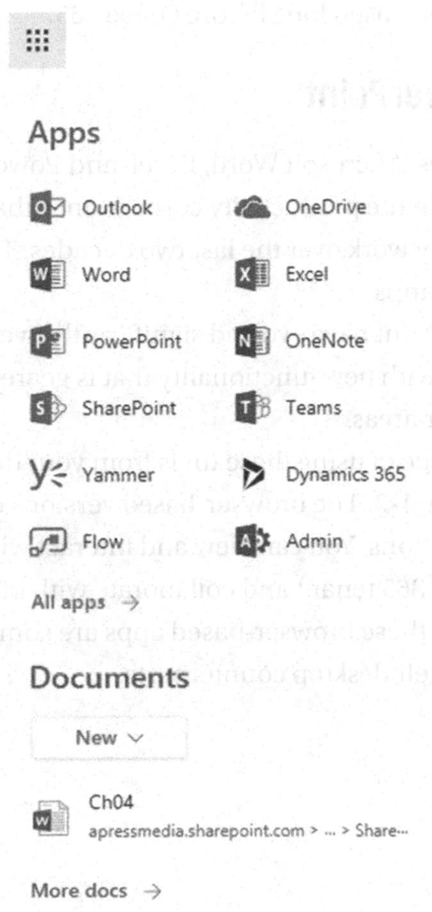

Figure 1-2. The Office 365 Apps Launcher showing the various app tiles

Based on my experience, I have divided the apps into five groups: Productivity, Communication, Collaboration, Business Process Automation and Analysis, and NextGen Portals. You may choose to group them differently.

Productivity

Productivity, as the name suggests, are the apps you and your peers use to get your work done. This includes creating documents, project plans, reports, and notes. I elected to include Outlook in this category because it has been one of the key supporting applications that organizations used long before Office 365.

Word, Excel, and PowerPoint

Let's begin with the easy ones. Microsoft Word, Excel, and PowerPoint need little introduction because they are the productivity cornerstones that many of us have come to rely on heavily for our daily work over the last two decades. They are available as desktop and browser-based apps.

Word, Excel, and PowerPoint have evolved significantly over the years and continue to do so to meet your needs with new functionality that is geared towards the cloud and mobile devices, among other areas.

Today, you have the choice of using these tools from your desktop or directly from a browser, as shown in Figure 1-3. The browser-based versions of these three apps are available with most subscriptions. You can view and interact with your documents that are stored in your Office 365 tenant and collaborate with others inside or outside your organization. However, these browser-based apps are somewhat limited in their functionality compared to their desktop counterparts.

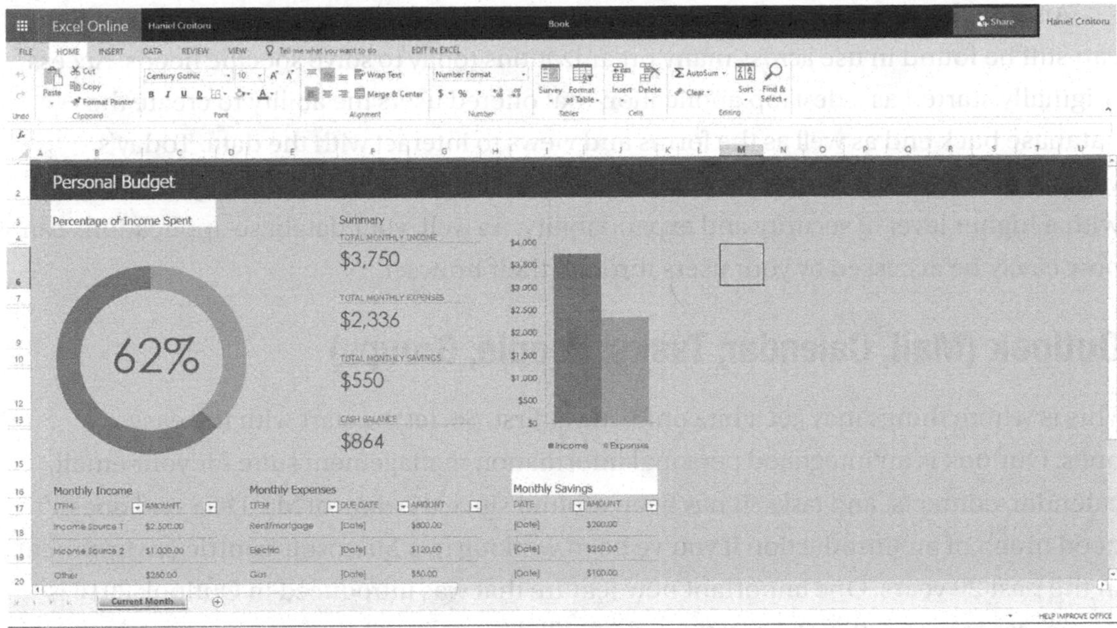

Figure 1-3. The Office 365 apps family

The desktop versions provide you with full functionality. One key differentiator is that using the desktop version of the apps does not limit you from using documents that are stored in your tenant.

Visio, Publisher, and Access

Visio is used to create various types of diagrams such as flow charts, organizational charts, network diagrams, and architectural plans. Its versatility makes it a great addition to the standard tool sets when you need to ensure that your diagrams will maintain a crisp look when scaled up or down.

Like its Word, Excel, and PowerPoint relatives, you can view Visio diagrams directly from within your browser.

If your organization needs to publish content, but doesn't have the budget or dedicated resources for creating such materials, then Microsoft Publisher is a great alternative to some of the mainstream applications like Adobe InDesign and QuarkXPress. It lets you work with a large number of formats, including Corel Draw.

Another long-time favorite of mine is Access. This lightweight database application can still be found in use across many organizations today to solve specific needs. Access originally started as a desktop application that offered users the ability to create the database back end as well as the forms and views to interact with the data. Today's version of Access has its data residing in a relational SQL database, which provides you with a higher level of security and expandability. As well, your database applications can now easily be accessed by your users through their browser.

Outlook (Mail, Calendar, Tasks, People, Groups)

This is where things may get a bit confusing at first. So, let me start with the easier ones. Outlook is an integrated personal information management suite for your email, calendar, contacts, and tasks. It has been around since the days of MS-DOS and doesn't need much of an introduction if you've been working in a Microsoft-centric environment in the past 20 years. One important new feature that was introduced in Outlook 2016 is the access to your Office 365 Groups, which I'll discuss shortly.

The browser-based version of Outlook is feature-rich to the point where some users prefer it over the desktop version. Don't get confused by the separate tiles in the Office 365 App Launcher for Mail, Calendar, People, and Tasks. Opening any of them will take you to the specific part of Outlook.

Microsoft has also released mobile app versions for Outlook for the Windows Phone, iPhone, and Android. However, you can always use your other favorite mobile apps to access your personal content.

OneNote

OneNote has become popular because it allows your users to easily collaborate on free-form content. It captures typed or handwritten notes, images, screen recordings, or audio segments. Unlike traditional word processors such as Word, OneNote lets you add content anywhere on the page. Furthermore, saving occurs automatically as content is added (that's right, no more lost changes when you kick the power bar switch). To organize information logically, OneNote saves information into *pages* that are organized into *sections* within *notebooks*. OneNote lets users search images for embedded text-content, "electronic ink" annotations as text, and phonetical searches of audio recordings on text keys.

OneNote integrates nicely with your email, tasks, and Skype for Business by including meeting information, listing attendees, including information from Skype meetings, and sending the minutes to attendees by email. It even goes as far as providing you word-based searches directly from with the application.

Figure 1-4 shows an example of meeting details pulled into OneNote that were then followed up with a recording, image, and some annotations.

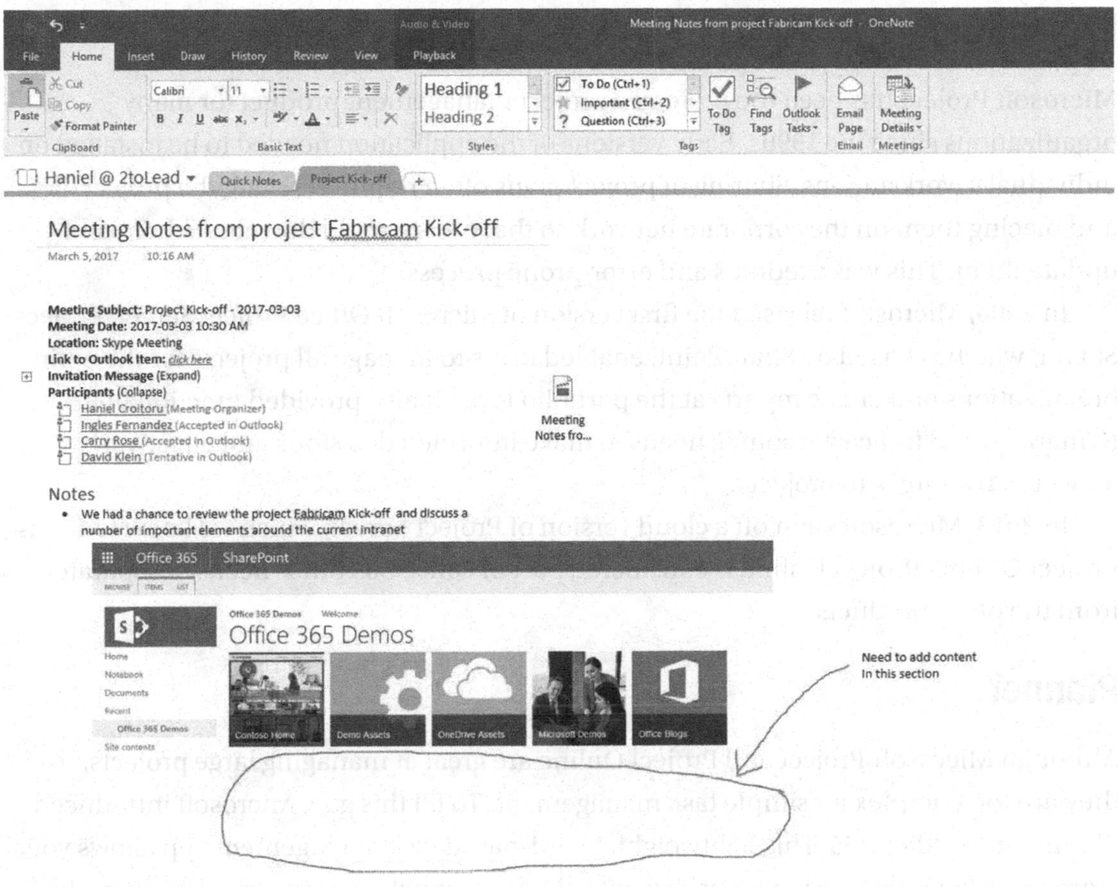

Figure 1-4. OneNote Desktop app capturing meeting minutes with images, drawings, and video

OneDrive for Business

OneDrive for Business is an app that lets users store and share their personal files. By default, each user has a limit of 1TB, which in my opinion is plenty. You should adopt a strategy for your OneDrive for Business which limits what content gets store there versus other collaboration apps (discussed later). This will reduce overall organizational content clutter and ensure that all users are accessing a single source for any document.

A common source of concern I often hear from users who are moving to OneDrive for Business is changing their old habits for storing documents in folders. In reality, this is a non-issue because OneDrive for Business lets you synchronize your documents across multiple locations and devices.

Project Online

Microsoft Project has been the preferred project management product for many organizations since the 1990s. Early versions of the application needed to be installed on individual's workstations. Sharing of project plans often required saving the project files and placing them on the corporate network so that others could download them and update them. This was a tedious and error-prone process.

In 2000, Microsoft released the first version of Microsoft Office Project Server. Project Server, which is based on SharePoint, enabled users to manage all projects for the entire organizations and create reports at the portfolio level. It also provided functionality to manage and forecast resource needs to make informed decisions and effectively allocated resources to projects.

In 2013, Microsoft spun off a cloud version of Project Server, which we know today as Project Online. Project Online is considered part of Office 365 but is licensed separately from the other products.

Planner

Although Microsoft Project and Project Online are great at managing large projects, they are too complex for simple task management. To fill this gap, Microsoft introduced Planner into Office 365. This lightweight, board-based task management app allows your team to assign tasks to each other, organize them into buckets, and even discuss each activity. Each task is represented by a card, which includes all the information about the task, such as name, who is assigned to it, due date, attachments, and conversations about it. Figure 1-5 shows a task card with a checklist.

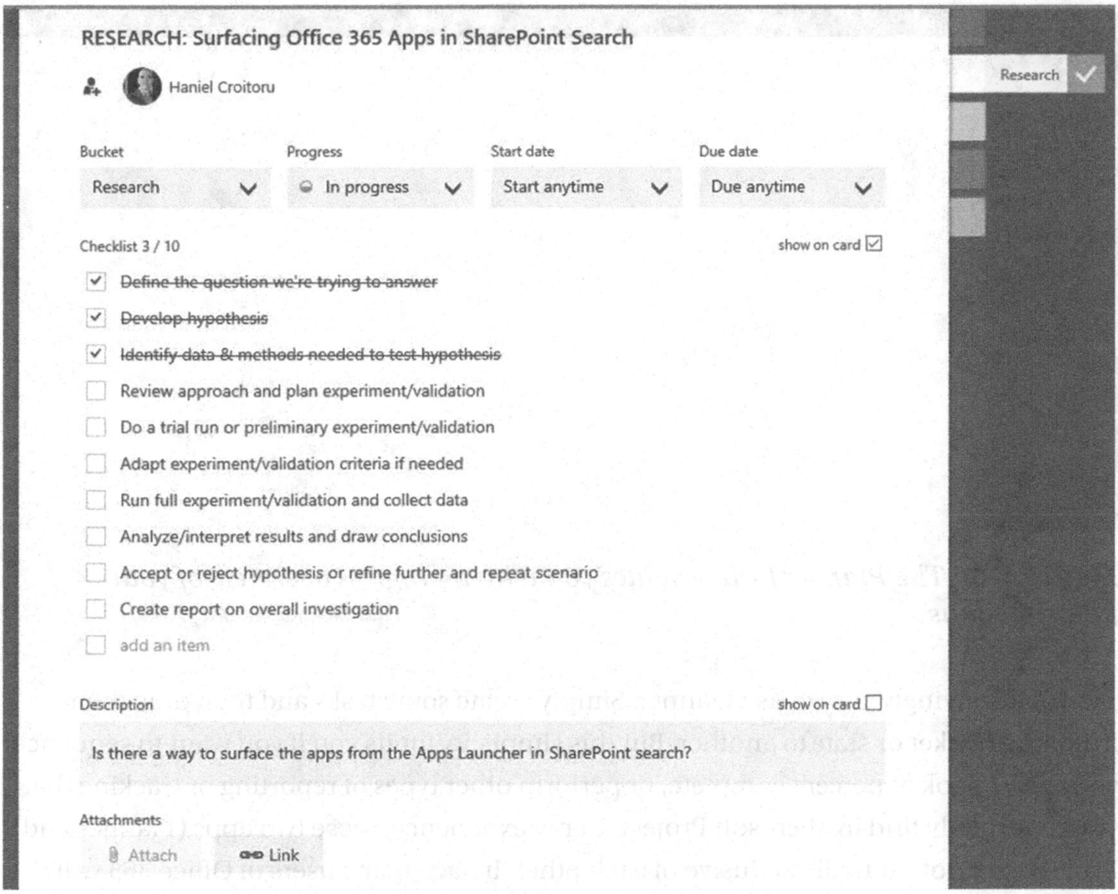

Figure 1-5. *Each Planner card contains information related to the task, such as the task owner, due date, attachments, and conversations*

Planner also provides a quick snapshot on the progress of tasks within each board, called the *Planner hub* (Figure 1-6).

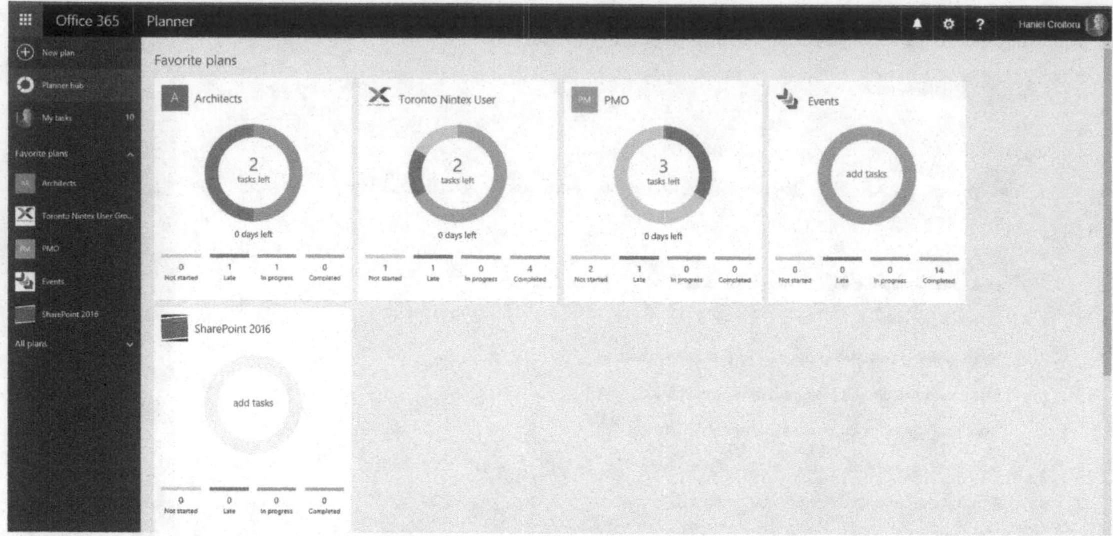

Figure 1-6. *The Planner hub provides you with a progress overview of your favorite plans*

It's deceivingly easy to use Planner. Simply create some tasks and then drag them from one bucket or state to another. But this simplicity limits you if you want to sequence your tasks, look at percent complete, or perform other types of reporting or tracking that you'd normally find in Microsoft Project. In my experience, these two apps (Planner and Project) are not mutually exclusive of each other. In fact, many users of Office 365 will use them in tandem, where project-specific work is captured in Project and ad-hoc type activities live inside Planner.

Communication

Communication comes in several media: written printed, written electronic, audio, and video. For electronic communication, we need to look at peer-to-peer vs. group communication. The apps discussed here are the main ones in the Office 365 family used for communication (including Outlook).

Skype for Business

Skype for Business (formerly known as Microsoft Lync and Microsoft Office Communicator) is the main communication tool used for instant messaging, videoconferencing, and voice over IP (VOIP) calls. During a Skype for Business call, you can use whiteboarding and create annotations, present PowerPoint slides, capture polls, and share the screen for various desktop applications. Due to its integration with other Office 365 apps, you can see your colleague's availability and instant message or call them using Skype for Business directly from other apps (Figure 1-7).

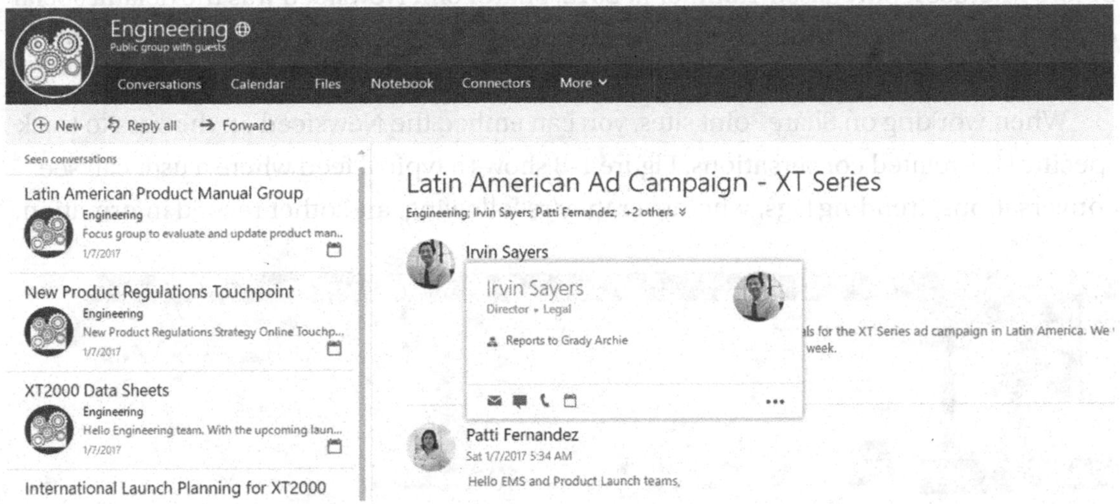

Figure 1-7. *Skype for Business integration with other Office 365 apps enables instant messaging and calling users without leaving the app you're currently in*

Skype for Business allows you to record your conversations and play them back later, making it a great auditing tool.

Yammer

There are two enterprise-level social communication apps available in Office 365. With the purchase of Yammer and its integration into the Office 365 service offering, Microsoft has invested heavily in favor of the currently existing social networking tools available in SharePoint.

Yammer is often seen as a Facebook-like communication feed that allows your users to share information, including links, videos, and documents. To keep conversations organized, Yammer lets you create specific groups and make them private to only specific users. Keeping track of all the chatter in Yammer can be daunting. To make it easier, you can follow people, groups, or specific topics and get notified via email when there is a new, interesting thread for you to read.

Newsfeed

Before Microsoft purchased Yammer in 2012, SharePoint Newsfeed was the default social experience tool in Office 365 for sharing company-wide discussions. Newsfeed lets your users follow people, documents, and tags in SharePoint.

When working on SharePoint sites, you can embed the Newsfeed on the sites to track specific site-related conversations. Figure 1-8 shows a typical feed where a user can see conversations, trending tags, whomever they're following, and other related information.

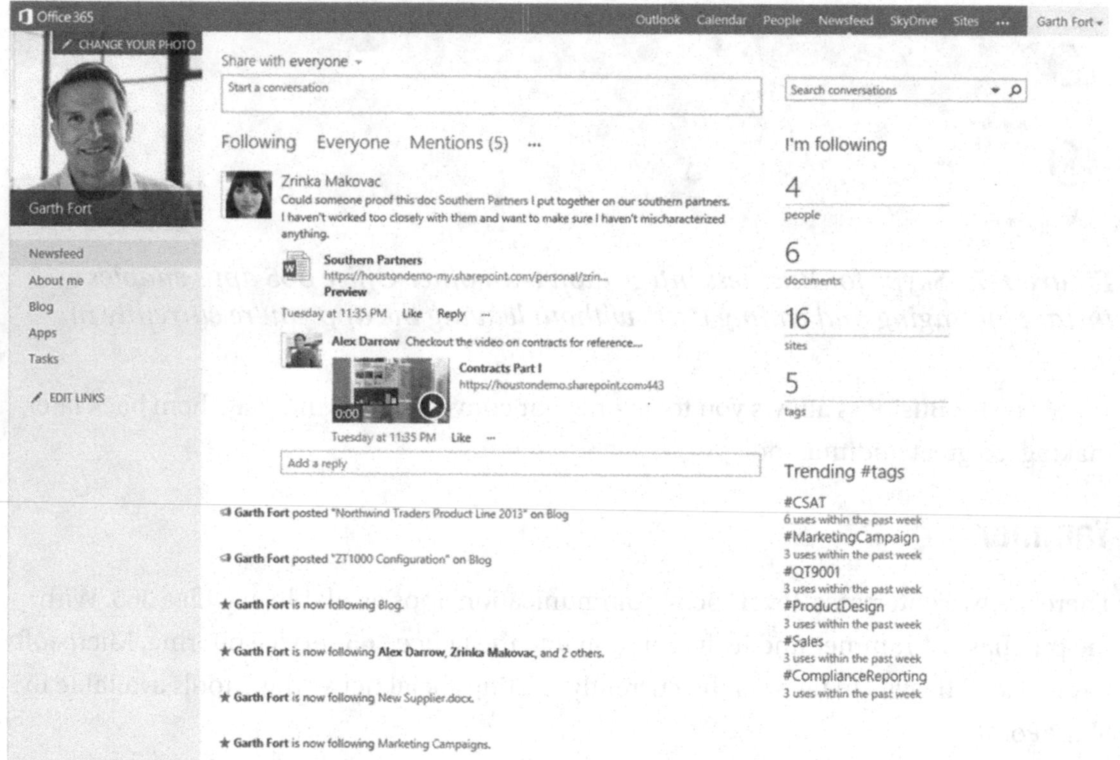

Figure 1-8. *The Newsfeed app showing user activity and tagging*

In the past couple of years, Microsoft slowly retired several SharePoint Online features relating to the Newsfeed and continued to enhance Yammer. With the roll-out of the Modern SharePoint sites, Microsoft has reintroduced the concept of Comments, which are page-specific feeds.

Teams

Microsoft Teams is a new chat-based app. Through private or team conversations, meetings, email threads, and multi-person audio and video conversations, you can stay abreast of what is happening. Teams connects to Office 365 Groups, SharePoint, OneNote, Planner, Power BI, and a growing number of third-party applications to provide you all the information you need from a single location.

Figure 1-9 shows an example of a Microsoft Team conversation. On the left side is the list of all the teams and their associated channels to which the user has access.

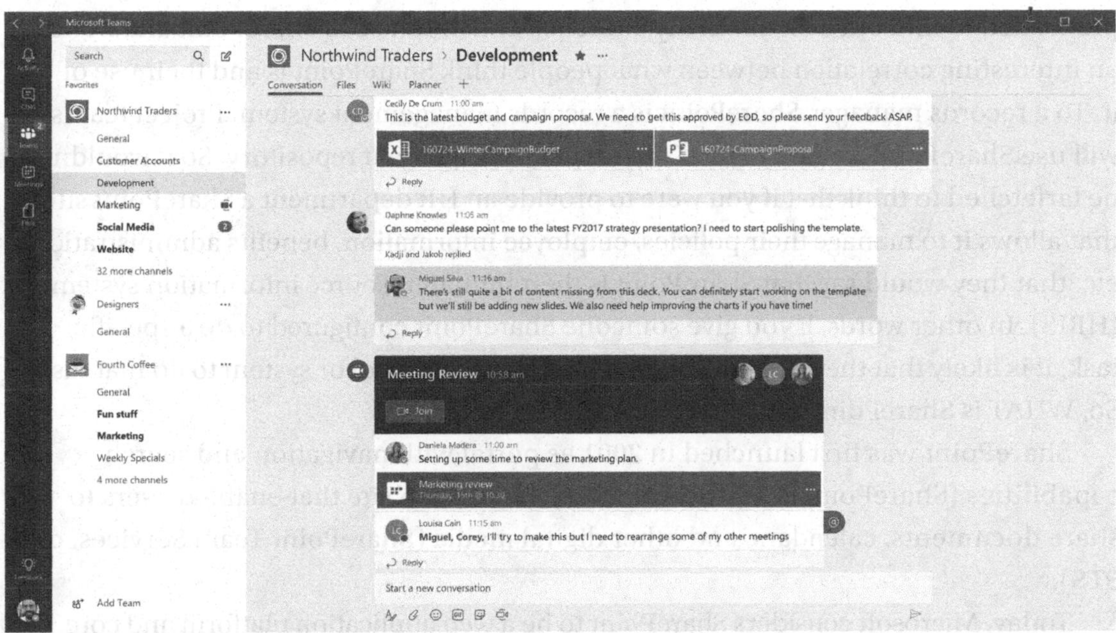

***Figure 1-9.** Communicate and collaborate with your teams from a single location using Microsoft Teams*

Collaboration

Working teams need to collaborate on content effectively in order to succeed. Imagine a scenario where each team member creates their own documents and nothing gets shared. This would be very inefficient, inaccurate, and risk-prone. Like communication, collaboration lies at the heart of a well-structured project team. With Office 365, the concept of working on content together is taken to the next level, where SharePoint and Groups can help organize and control who can access the content.

SharePoint Online

If you search for the definition of SharePoint on your favorite search engine, you will find a plethora of definitions. While the results may differ, they are for the most part correct. I've often heard SharePoint referred to as an 800-pound gorilla, and rightfully so. To many users, the answer to what SharePoint is will be nested in their needs.

I recently gave a presentation to a local Project Management Institute chapter and started my talk with that same question: What is SharePoint? The answers I got included document management system, intranet, website, team sites, and more. I proceeded to find out a bit about my audience and their use of SharePoint and noticed an interesting correlation between what people think SharePoint is and their use of it. To a records manager, SharePoint is a records management system. Project teams will use SharePoint as their central document management repository. So it wouldn't be farfetched to think that if you were to provide an HR department a SharePoint site that allows it to manage their policies, employee information, benefits administration, etc. that they would say that SharePoint is their human resource information system (HRIS). In other words, if you give someone SharePoint configured to do a specific task, it is likely that they will tell you that SharePoint is a tool or system to do that task. So, WHAT is SharePoint?

SharePoint was first launched in 2001 as portal with navigation and search capabilities (SharePoint Portal Server 2001) and a team site that enabled users to share documents, calendars, and other digital media (SharePoint Team Services, or STS).

Today, Microsoft considers SharePoint to be a web application platform and core component of the Office 365 service. Since the first release, much has been added by way of integration with other Microsoft technologies, acquisitions, and developments.

Out of the box SharePoint Online can provide intranet and extranet portals, document and records management, collaboration and social networks, search and eDiscovery, workflow automation, and business intelligence. An example of a fictional intranet page is shown in Figure 1-10.

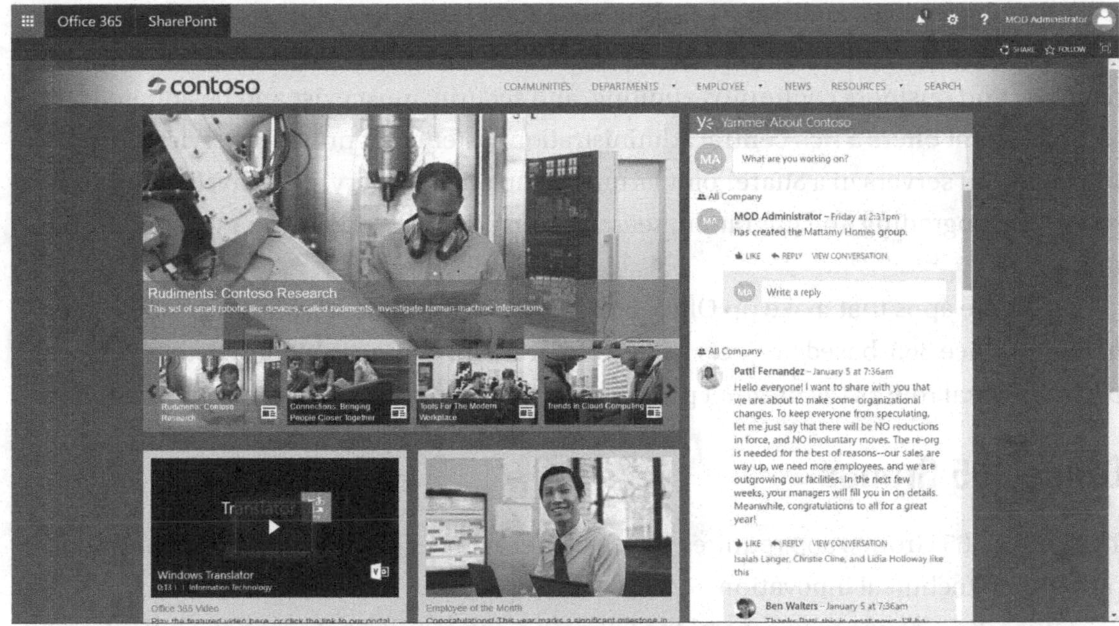

***Figure 1-10.** Home page of Microsoft's fictional company, Contoso Ltd*

SharePoint has been tightly integrated into Microsoft Office and other Microsoft products and is considered to be part of the Office suite. Classing SharePoint sites use the Microsoft Office ribbon menu system, which shortens the learning curve for people already familiar with the ribbons from other Microsoft Office products. Recently, with the roll-out of the Modern SharePoint sites, the menu system has changed, but is still simple to learn. Other benefits of the tight integration with other Office 365 apps allow for a more feature-rich and streamlined user experience such as user account management through Active Directory services or online presence and communication via Skype for Business.

SharePoint's integration capabilities enable easy integration with other enterprise line-of-business (LOB) applications systems. Due to its popularity in the enterprise marketplace, many software product companies have chosen to build connectors to integrate their products with SharePoint.

Since 2013, several important changes were introduced to the way that customizations are built for SharePoint. First, developers can use the skills they've developed using other programming languages, such as PHP, JavaScript, HTML, or others to develop solutions in any development environment. Second, these apps don't run inside the SharePoint environment but are hosted by a third party, such as Microsoft Azure.

All of the features and functions discussed above are important to meet the business needs. However, to effectively function as part of an organization, governance, disaster recovery and business continuity, auditing, and security must exist and be adhered to. SharePoint offers a rich central administration system that provides services for managing all servers in a SharePoint farm, backup and recovery, security, logging and reporting, upgrading and migration, search configuration, workflow management, and more.

Of all the apps that make up Office 365, SharePoint Online is by far the usual center of many Office 365-based projects because SharePoint Online is highly customizable and plays a pivotal role as the intranet portal and collaboration site in many organizations.

Office 365 Groups

The Office 365 Groups app requires a special mention because of its strategic position rather than technical innovation.

Office 365 Groups span several the Office 365 app family, including an Outlook email distribution group, Outlook Calendar, OneNote, Office 365 Planner, and SharePoint-based file sharing through an integrated experience. The goal of Office 365 Groups is to give your team and collaborators from outside your organization a simple way to communicate and collaborate on specific topics. At the core of each Office 365 Group is a SharePoint site that is used to manage the content (Figure 1-11).

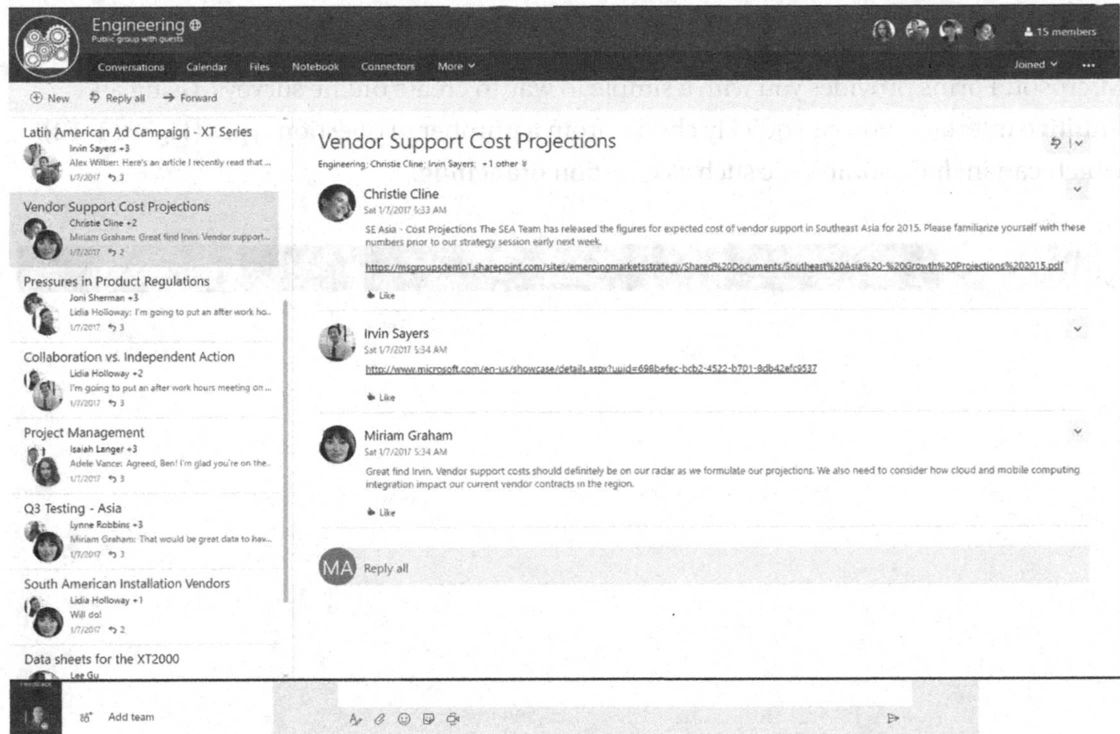

Figure 1-11. If your project team's communication and collaboration needs are simple, then you should consider Office 365 Groups

Recently, Connectors were also introduced to the groups to enable your team to keep current with content and updates from numerous other SaaS providers.

Business Process Automation and Analysis

One of my passions lies in analyzing existing business processes and trying to find ways to simplify them as much as possible. When an organization decides to embrace digital business process automation, it will not only save time; it will also save money by eliminating tedious, mundane tasks, reduce risk of errors associated with such manual processes, and allow employees to focus on activities that will help grow the business. I include Microsoft Forms, PowerApps, and Flow here, which are forms and workflow apps. As well, I include Power BI, which can help you automate the creation of dashboards and reporting for your projects or other information.

Forms

Microsoft Forms provides you with a simple to way to create online surveys. Using an intuitive interface, you can quickly choose from a number of question types (Figure 1-12), which can include some logic such as question branching.

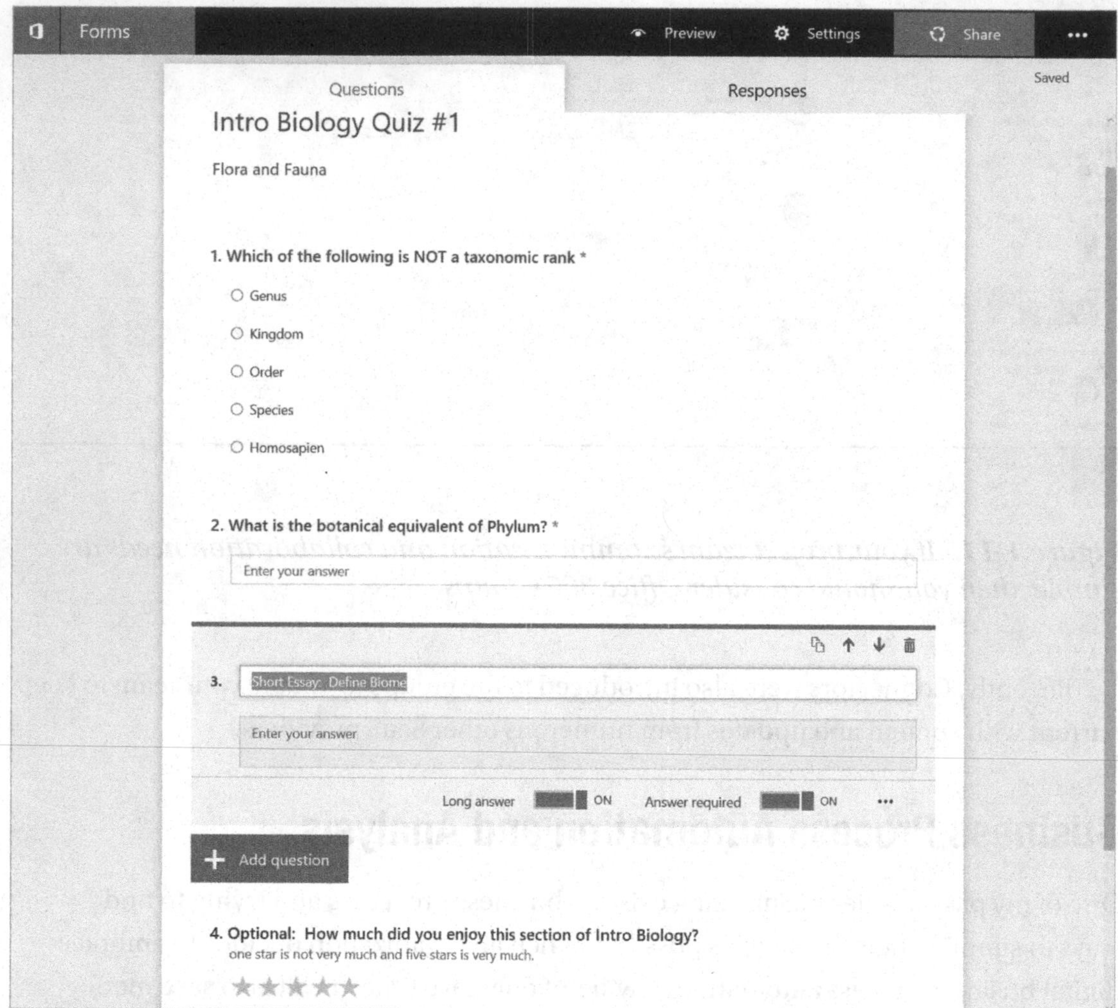

Figure 1-12. *Microsoft Forms allows educators to quickly construct online test, share them, collect the results, and automatically grade them*

Survey responses can be retrieved using Excel or by leveraging the Microsoft Flow workflows (discussed later).

PowerApps

PowerApps lets you build highly customizable apps for your desktop, tablet, or mobile devices using content from numerous Office 365 and other third-party services using over 240 connectors. You can create dashboards, item lists, and forms within a short time and without writing a line of code (Figure 1-13).

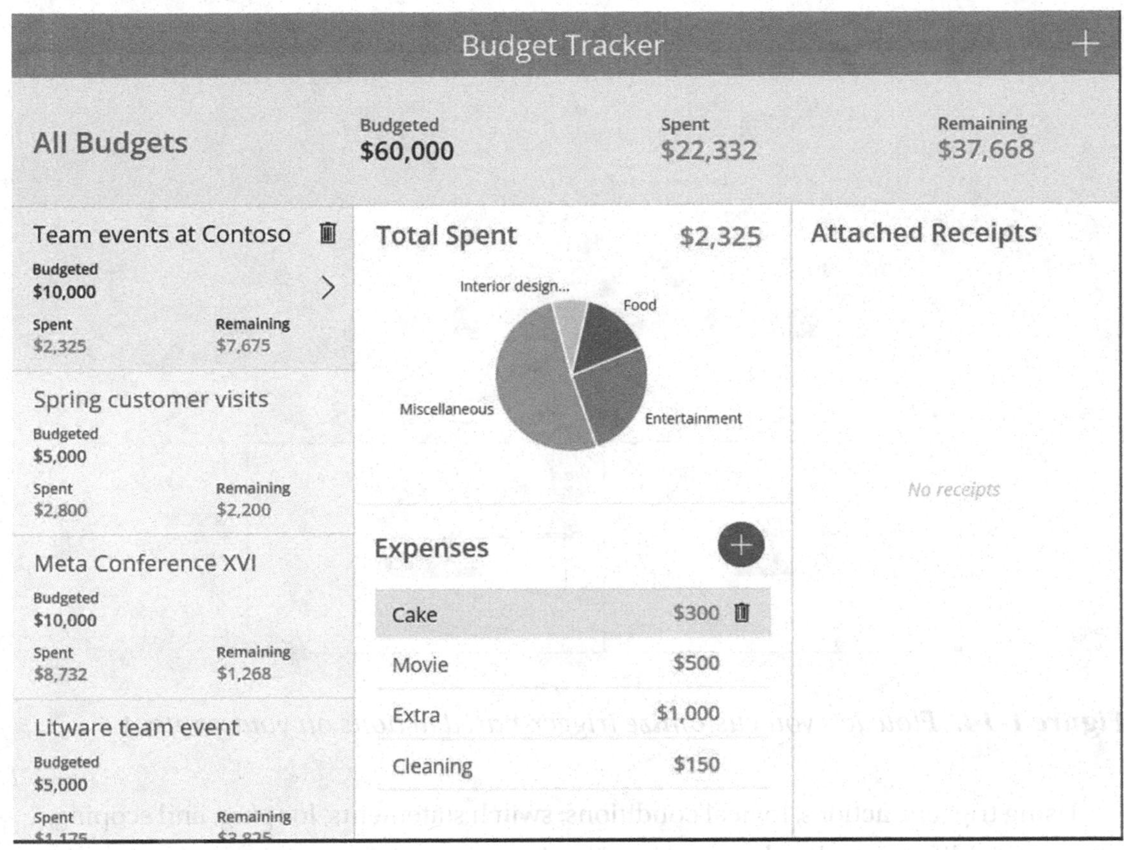

***Figure 1-13.** Sample dashboard that connects to a SharePoint list PowerApp*

When a user launches a PowerApp, the app will limit the user's capabilities based on their permissions. PowerApps can greatly increase productivity for your team by enabling your mobile workforce to access and submit content from anywhere. Once a PowerApp is deployed, you can set it up to appear just like any other app on a tablet or phone.

Flow

Flow is a close relative of PowerApps and they work well hand-in-hand. If you think of PowerApps as your access point to the content, then Flow is the engine that does a lot of the work behind the scenes. Like PowerApps, Flow can connect to over 240 services to create, alter, and delete content (Figure 1-14).

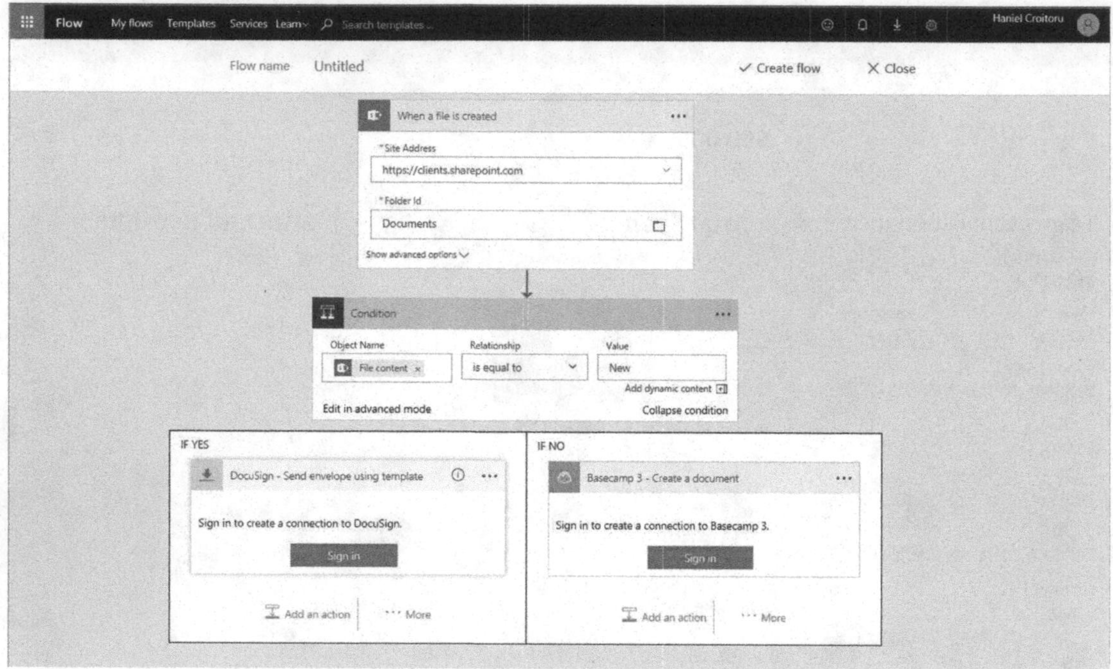

Figure 1-14. *Flow lets you customize trigger-based actions on your content*

Using triggers, actions, logical conditions, switch statements, looping, and scoping, you can simplify manual and paper-based business processes on your content.

Power BI

As a project lead, you may be tasked with creating reports on project progress, issues, costs, and other data. It's not so bad if all your information resides in one place. But what if it doesn't? What do you do if the data you need is dispersed across numerous apps and services and you need to create accurate, real-time reports or dashboards to answer important questions?

Using Power BI, you can create a visually-rich presentation of your organization's data (Figure 1-15). In 2013, Microsoft added natural language query capabilities to Power BI. This addition lets you ask questions of your data using questions and phrases.

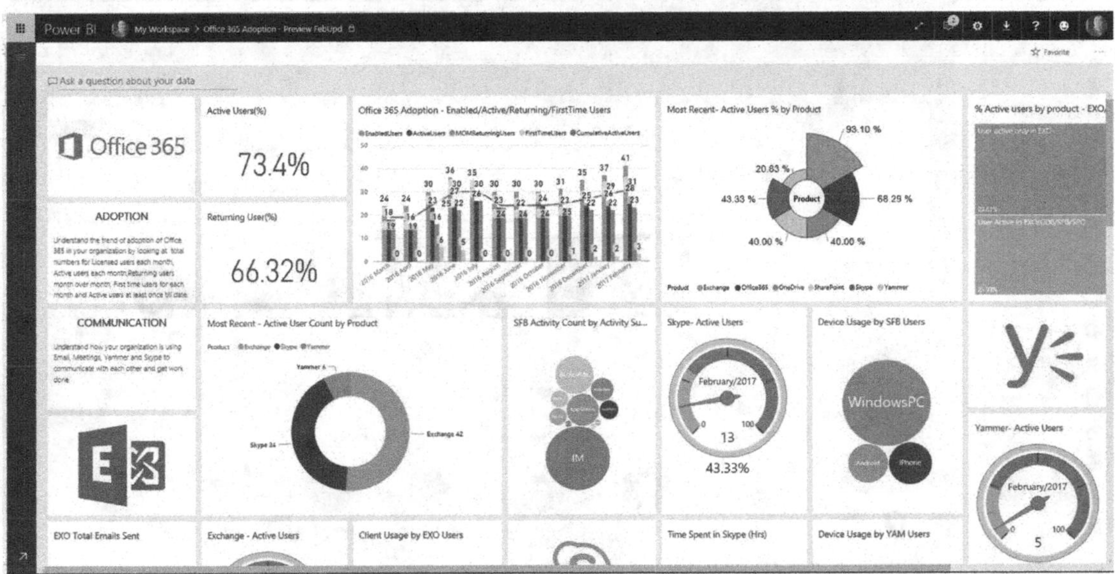

***Figure 1-15.** Using Power BI, you can generate custom dashboards and reports from your data across numerous services*

NextGen Portals

If you took a month to talk to various organizations about how they manage their content, you'd be surprised at how much commonality there exists even across different verticals and geographic locations. Some of the usual suspects include departmental portals, knowledge management, multimedia, and search.

By leveraging several of the core Office 365 apps, including SharePoint Online, Office Graph, and Skype for Business, Microsoft has started rolling out several portals to address specific user needs. Below are a few that are already available to you, depending on your subscription.

Delve

It's great to be able to search for information when you know what it is you're looking for. But have you ever stumbled upon a document or overheard a conversation that you found valuable but had no idea it existed? This type of passive content discovery is where

Delve comes in. Delve helps you discover information that you may find useful across Office 365 (Figure 1-16).

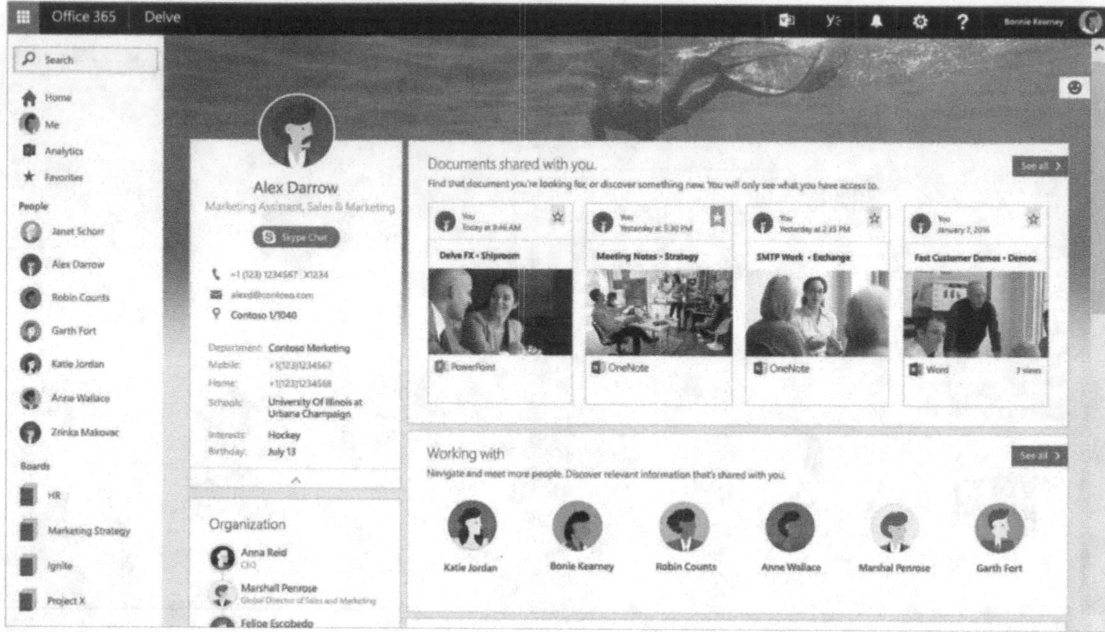

Figure 1-16. *Delve helps you discover information based on your interaction with peers and previous content you've accessed or created*

To determine personal usefulness, Delve relies on one of the cornerstones of the Office 365 platform called *Microsoft Office Graph*, which uses machine learning to analyze organizational interactions and content use.

Office Graph also offers a rich application development interface (API) that can be used to query and update information for the various apps. I'll discuss this topic in more detail later in the book.

Microsoft Stream

If a picture is worth a thousand words, just imagine what a video can do! Videos are one of the most powerful communication media forms today. YouTube® and Vimeo® are two common services that organizations use to share corporate content. Although access can be limited, there is a lack of total control over the content. As well, the integration and discoverability of such videos within Office 365 is very limited.

Microsoft Stream offers your organization a secure company-wide place for discovering, posting, and sharing video content (Figure 1-17).

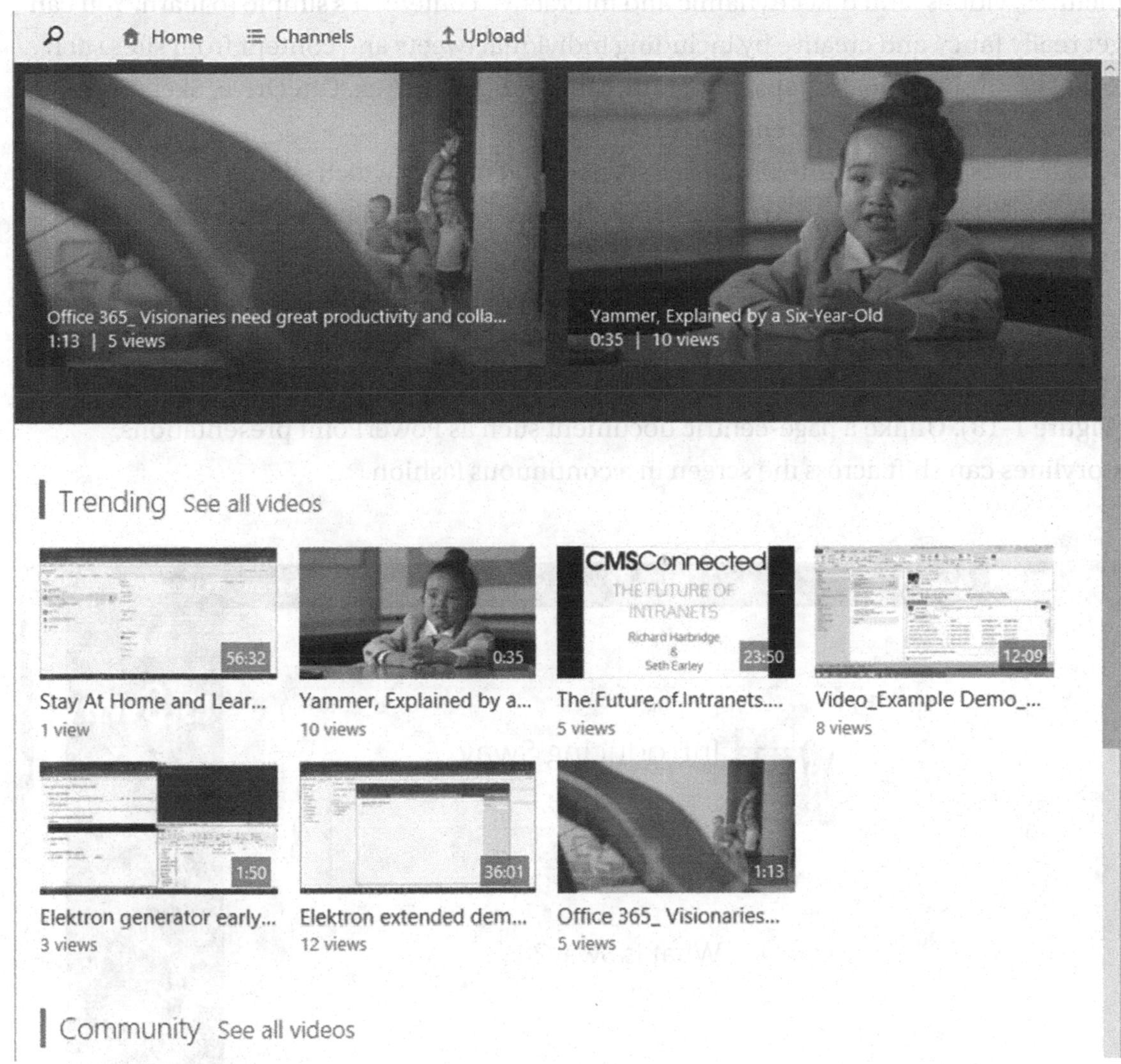

Figure 1-17. *Microsoft Stream is your corporate-wide hub for video content*

Through the use of Microsoft Graph, videos and the information associated with them can be shown in other applications.

Sway

Sway is a cloud-based canvas you can use to deliver captivating presentations using pictures, videos, and other dynamic and interactive content. It's simple to learn. You can get really fancy and creative by including individual tweets and content from sites such as Flickr, Giphy, Google Maps, Infogram, Mixcloud, Office Mix, OneDrive, Sketchfab, SoundCloud, Vimeo, Vine, and YouTube.

Since its launch in 2015, Sway has seen a rapid uptake, which should make you wonder whether it's better to use Sway or stick with PowerPoint based on your target audience and purpose.

A Sway (equivalent of a document or presentation) is composed of multiple cards that are combined into a storyline. Cards are containers that hold text, images, and videos. You can combine cards into groups. A collection of cards make up the storyline (Figure 1-18). Unlike a page-centric document such as PowerPoint presentations, storylines can shift across the screen in a continuous fashion.

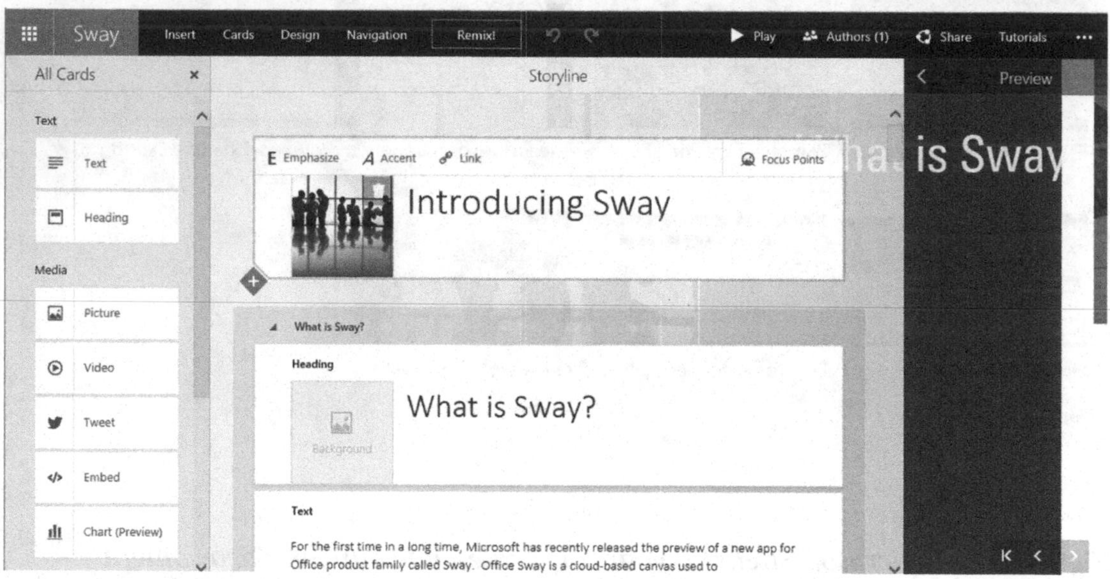

Figure 1-18. *Sway storylines are used to create interactive multimedia presentations*

One of the things that sets Sway apart from other presentation-focused applications is its ability to include live content from numerous sources that you can interact with, including Google maps and numerous other audio, video and picture sharing sites.[2] It lets you focus on the content without worrying too much about the formatting. You can choose from numerous canned designs, fonts, navigation patterns, and even control the level of emphasis on the card's transition animations. Not enough? You can try the Remix! option, which will randomly select from the designs, fonts, and layouts to give you a unique experience. Remix! is like a big gumball machine: you can see what's available but you never know what you're going to get.

Sway is great when you want to share your ideas online and you have some creative freedom. However, if you need to create document-based presentations that leverage strict branding guidelines, then this app will not meet your needs today.

Summary

Today's workforce is different than what it was a decade ago and will not be representative of what it will be a decade from now. In order to deal with these changes, Microsoft continues to innovate in the area of cloud computing to redefine the digital workspace. Since its birth almost ten years ago, Office 365 has and will continue to grow in the number of apps offering the functionality included in them.

If you haven't been exposed to Office 365 before and had a chance to read this chapter, then you should have a high-level understanding of what the various apps are and their purpose. Before I dive a little deeper on the various Office 365 apps and how they best fit in your organization, I will briefly deviate from the topic to introduce agile project management.

[2]Visit `https://support.office.com/en-us/article/embed-content-in-your-sway-1e1ab12a-f961-4a26-8afc-77a15f892b1d?ui=en-us&rs=en-us&ad=us` to get a full listing of the content that you can embed into Sways

CHAPTER 2

Agile Project Management

By now, you should have a general understanding of what Office 365 is and the many apps that make up this ecosystem. You should also realize at this point that leading projects in Office 365 requires a good understanding of agile techniques due to the rapid evolving nature of the platform. This chapter is dedicated to give you the necessary background on what agile project management is, how it differs from the traditional waterfall methods, and important points you need to consider. The next chapter will finish off the first part of the book by providing you with a framework that should work for any Office 365 project you will be leading.

What Is Agile Project Management?

If you've been working in the software industry or involved in IT initiatives recently, you've probably heard about concepts such as *agile project management* and *Scrum*. Whether you're involved in Office 365 or other projects it is a good idea to understand what these methodologies mean and how they get used.

In the late 1990s several new software development frameworks started to emerge. Although they grew out of different areas, they all emphasized the importance of close collaboration between the project team and business users, frequent face-to-face communication, short and regular development cycles for assessment of outcomes, and openness to change. These frameworks, collectively known as agile project management form a methodology that is used to deliver projects with inherent uncertainty and dynamism by adopting change. By embracing rather than avoiding change, projects are delivered with a high value to the customer. There are numerous popular agile frameworks used today in software development projects such as Scrum, Lean, XP, Kanban, and others.

H. Croitoru, *Agile Office 365*, https://doi.org/10.1007/978-1-4842-4081-6_2

The *Agile Manifesto* shown in Table 2-1 was first created in 2001 by several thought leaders who have spent much of their careers in project management and process optimization. The Agile Manifesto[1] puts the focus on activities and deliverables that vary from traditional waterfall processes.

Table 2-1. *The Agile Manifesto*

Agile		Waterfall
Individuals and interactions	*over*	Processes and tools
Working software	*over*	Comprehensive documentation
Customer collaboration	*over*	Contract negotiation
Responding to change	*over*	Following a plan

You may value the items on the right because they've helped your projects successfully in the past. But if you want to do things the agile way, then you will need to learn to place a higher value on the left-hand items. There are 12 *guiding principles* that supplement the Agile Manifesto and form the basis of any agile project, regardless of the specific framework used:

- **Product value early**: The highest priority is to satisfy the customer through the delivery of valuable software as perceived by the customer.
- **Welcome change**: Changes should be channeled throughout an agile project to optimize the competitive advantage the customer stands to gain.
- **Iterative delivery**: Software should be delivered to the client in frequent, short iterations lasting only a few weeks.
- **Daily business collaboration**: Business and technical team members must communicate and collaborate daily during the project.
- **Trust motivated team**: Entrust your team to delivery great software by motivating them and giving them a supportive environment to work in.

[1]Developed by Kent Beck et al., `https://www.agilealliance.org/agile101/the-agile-manifesto/`

- **Face to face**: Although not always feasible, every effort should be made to have the business and technical team members co-located so that face-to-face communication can take pace.
- **Working software**: Successful progress can be measured through properly functioning software.
- **Sustainable pace**: Expectations should be realistic of the project team. The agile process should promote sustainable development supported by all stakeholders.
- **Technical excellence**: Well designed, developed, and tested software enhances overall agility.
- **Simplicity**: Work done to achieve the customer value should be minimized. No additional work should be required.
- **Self-organize**: The power of the agile team lies in its ability to self-organize and produce the best architectures, requirements, and designs.
- **Reflect and adjust**: The team should review and assess its effectiveness on a periodic basis to find ways of optimizing it.

Throughout my career, I have used a number of project management frameworks but found that the *Scrum* agile methodology is best suited to Office 365. This is why I discuss mostly Scrum in this book, although many of the principles discussed throughout the chapters will apply to other frameworks.

Scrum

The name Scrum comes from the English Rugby game, though there's little that agile project management and the sport share. The term is used to refer to the way in which agile team members work closely together on a regular basis to solve problems. It was first introduced by Ikujiro Nonaka and Hirotaka Takeushi in 1987 to describe a hyper-productive development environment with a flexible, holistic product development strategy where a development team works as a unit to reach a common goal compared with the traditional sequential approach.[2]

---

[2]"New New Product Development Game," *Harvard Business Review*, 86116:137–146, 1986. January 1, 1986. Retrieved March 12, 2013

Scrum Overview

Before I describe the Scrum process, I will introduce some terms that are frequently used in the agile world. It's important that you familiarize yourself with these terms, particularly if you are going to become part of a team that is already familiar with Scrum. But first, Figure 2-1 provides a graphical representation of the Scrum process.

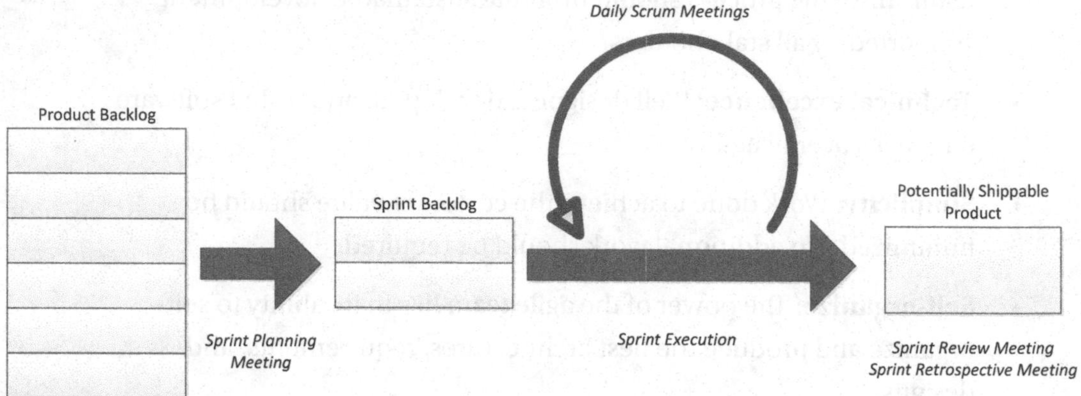

Figure 2-1. *Scrum overview*

The various items will be discussed in the remainder of this section.

Roles

There are three main team roles used in agile projects. These roles should typically be committed to the project to increase the chance of success. Depending on your background and interests, you may choose to take on any of these roles.

Product Owner

As the product owner, it is your responsibility to have the overall vision and authority to represent the customer's interest. In this role, you are a key project stakeholder who manages and prioritizes the user requirements into a product backlog throughout the project to maximize the value of the product. When not analyzing information or prioritizing the product backlog items, you will spend much of the remaining time supporting your Scrum team by answering questions and ensuring that the work is being done to meet the customer's needs.

In this role, you need to be highly involved and available to the team to deliver the best product. Product owners need to be business savvy and have a strong understanding of the customers, market, and business because they will drive many key decisions regarding features and functionality. Other important areas of knowledge include marketing, product development, and business analysis plus strong communication skills.

Another key responsibility for you is to communicate to the various stakeholders across the organization on the status of the project and the benefits and outcome of iterations. This task can be challenging since the demands of communication often vary amongst stakeholder groups.

Scrum Master

The Scrum master is often compared to the role of a traditional project manager or team lead, although there are many differences between the two. If you assume the role of Scrum master, you will need to ensure that your team adheres to the agile values and follows the processes defined by the team and organization. In this role, however, you'll find yourself spending more time on the soft skills, such as coaching, communicating with the various stakeholders, and resolving road blocks to ensure that your team can perform at the highest level. You are there to coach your team on the use of Scrum and motivate each member to achieve a common goal, while breaking down barriers that can have a negative impact on the team and process.

At first, this dichotomy in responsibility can pose some challenges because you'll need to exhibit authority over the Scrum process while being a servant leader to the team. Your team will look to you to shield them from external forces, such as stakeholders diverting their attention away from their focus, or other projects trying to use some of the Scrum team members for their own needs.

As Scrum master, you'll work closely with the product owner to make sure that the team is delivering what has been agreed upon during the sprint planning session and that the product backlog has been reviewed and prioritized for the next sprint.

By owning the Scrum process, you continuously monitor how well your team is performing and look for ways to optimize it. Due to the limitation of authority, any recommendations you make are limited to that of the process being used and can't have a direct impact on the Scrum team members.

Scrum Team

Another key different between agile and waterfall projects is in the composition and responsibilities of the team. In a waterfall project, the roles are clearly defined and responsibilities are assigned based on the role, but agile teams are *self-organizing*. Rather than assigning work to individuals based on their role, it is your team's responsibility to review and commit to delivering a potentially shippable product at the end of each sprint (sprints and shippable products will be discussed shortly). Dividing the work is the sole responsibility of the team. Scrum team members sometimes perform tasks that they would normally not undertake in a waterfall project and follow the motto of *Succeed or fail as a whole*.

When you assemble your Scrum team, make sure to include individuals who have skills such as architecture, design, programming, and testing due to the delineation between the roles and responsibilities of your team members. This will aid in increasing the output of the team.

A typical Scrum team is comprised of five to nine individuals. When there is a need to perform greater amount of work, the general preference is to use the concept of having Scrum teams of Scrum teams. In this case, each Scrum team acts as a black box but still assumes the responsibility for the delivery of the task it commits to.

Product Backlog, User Stories, and Requirements

In the Scrum world, requirements are represented from a user's perspective rather than a system's functional perspective. The user-centric requirements are called *user stories*. User stories are a way to represent requirements in the form of a user action and capture who the actor is, their goal, and the reason for this action. Although the product owner is responsible for managing the product backlog, user stories can be written by anyone and typically are of a simple structure such as:

> As a <type of user>, I want to <action or goal> so that <reason for action>.

User stories are the items that get captured and prioritized in the *product backlog* and are typically not too detailed when you first document them. In some cases, you may encounter user stories that represent large amounts of functionality. Such stories are known as *epics*, and you need to break them down into more detailed user stories as the project progresses.

A properly written user story also needs to include conditions of acceptance to make it testable.

Note Since user stories are first written in short form, it is important to remember that they are incomplete until discussions take place about them to elaborate on the necessary details. In some cases, it is good to refer to workflow diagrams and other business rule documentation to flesh out the details of the user story.

Minimal Shippable Product (MSP)

In addition to defining the user stories in the backlog and prioritizing them, the product owner needs to establish early in the project the minimal set of user stories or features that will provide enough value to make it a viable product. As user stories are added, deleted, and reprioritized, the minimal shippable product set will change. It is imperative for the product owner to consistently evaluate this set of user stories and work with the Scrum master and Scrum team to ensure that there are enough sprints left to deliver the minimal shippable product.

One strategy that can help in managing a changing set of user stories is to introduce a set of *contingency* user stories into the minimal shippable product. This slack will depend on factors such as how long the project is, how reliable the organization is in delivering projects on schedule, the type of project, and others. The contingency user stories are features that provide business value but are not critical for the release. Figure 2-2 shows a product backlog and how the contingency is used with a changing scope.

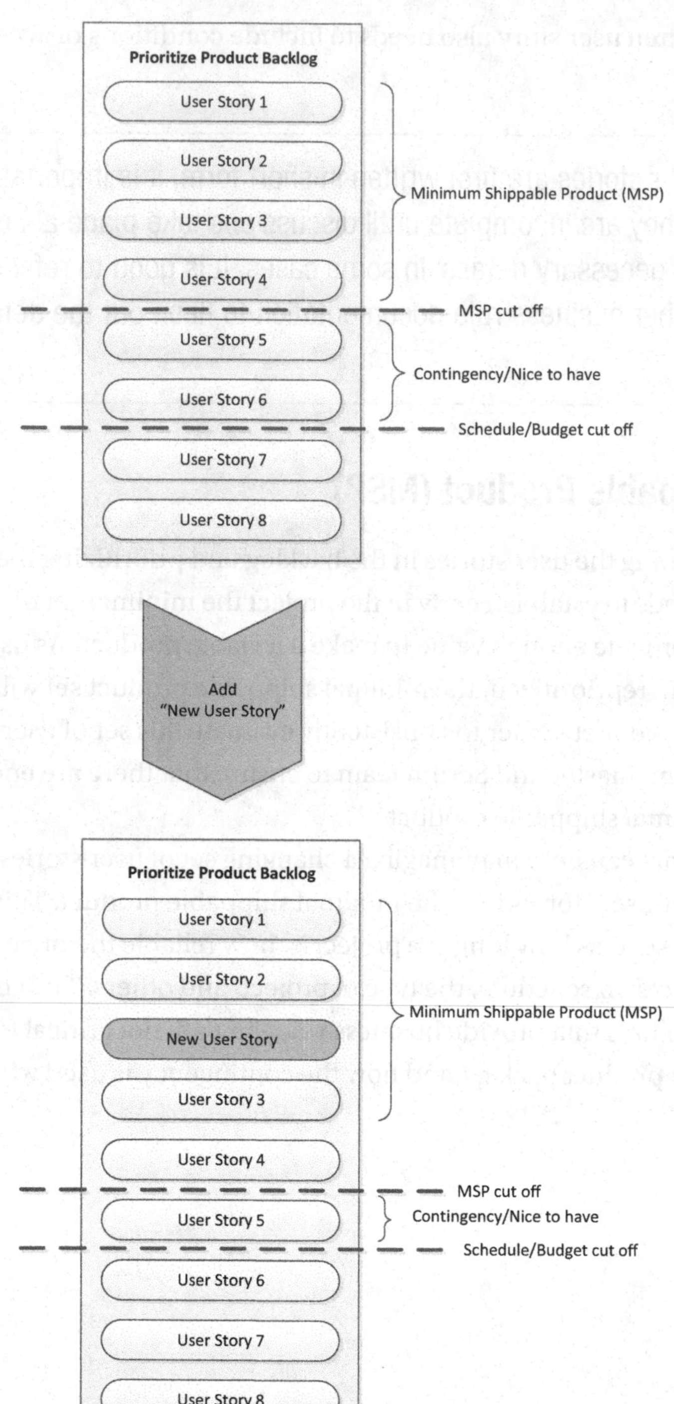

***Figure 2-2.** Minimal shippable product flow*

Sprints

The development phase in an agile project is divided into a series of two to four week "timeboxed" sequential iterations called *sprints*. Executing the development phase in equal-length sprints helps create a periodic rhythm within your team, which helps maintain a sense of routine and reduces the amount of change in how the team functions. Figure 2-3 depicts the four distinct sprint phases: sprint planning, sprint execution, sprint review, and sprint retrospective.

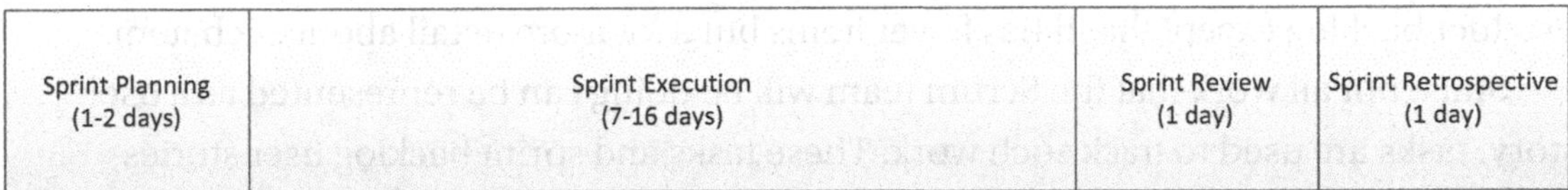

Figure 2-3. *Sprint phases*

Sprint Planning Meeting

Sprints start with a planning meeting. During this meeting, the product owner reviews the product backlog with the team and determines which are the highest priority user stories that need to be tackled in the next sprint. Your Scrum team, in turn, has a chance to solicit more information regarding these user stories to get a better understanding of what it needs to deliver. In each sprint planning meeting, the product owner and Scrum team discuss approximately two sprints' worth of user stories to ensure that the team has sufficient work laid out for it without over-committing itself. Estimations are performed for each user story to determine how much effort it would take to deliver. There are several common methods used, such as Planning Poker[3], to accomplish this but any method can be used. Planning Poker looks at the effort holistically in terms of complexity and risk and compares one user story to others to determine how many can be delivered. In my experience, this method works but takes some getting used to for teams that are new to agile and are accustomed to estimating work in actual hours. It's important to use a method where the outcome between sprints can be compared.

[3] "Planning Poker or How to avoid analysis paralysis while release planning," James Greening, `https://sewiki.iai.uni-bonn.de/_media/teaching/labs/xp/2005a/doc.planningpoker-v1.pdf`

Each of your sprint planning meetings need to produce two tangibles at the conclusion. First, each sprint should have a goal. This goal is represented by a short description of what the Scrum team will aim to achieve, such as:

- Develop a People Search experience with a custom display template.
- Develop a ticket purchasing form and workflow.

Sprint goals are a good way to provide your stakeholders with a high-level overview of what the team will be working on in the upcoming sprint. The second tangible that is produced in the sprint planning meeting is the sprint backlog. Think of it as a mini-product backlog except that it has fewer items but a lot more detail about each item.

Since not all work that the Scrum team will be doing can be represented as a user story, tasks are used to track such work. These tasks and sprint backlog user stories together represent the work that the Scrum team is committing to delivering during the iteration.

Sprint Execution

During sprint execution, your Scrum team designs, develops, and tests the sprint backlog items it committed to. Ideally, each day should begin with a mandatory 15-minute Scrum meeting to find out what each team member did the previous day, is planning to do on that day, and whether there are any impediments in their way. Other stakeholders are welcome to attend your Scrum meeting, but only to listen.

The goal of these Scrum meetings is to ensure that everyone in your Scrum team is aware of the work that has been completed and what work remains for the iteration. Issues that are raised during the daily Scrum meeting can vary from minor requests for information to major issues that can derail the project. It is the responsibility of the Scrum master to take ownership of resolving these roadblocks either directly or with the help of others inside or outside the Scrum team.

Sprint Review

Towards the end of each sprint, the team delivers a potentially shippable product that was designed, coded, and tested. During the sprint review meeting the attendees (typically product owner, Scrum master, Scrum team, and anybody else who has a vested interest in the project) have an opportunity to review the work delivered during the iteration and provide comments on it.

The sprint review meeting is kept to no more than two hours and you should not be creating any documentation for this meeting. Its purpose is to provide a demo of the product being developed.

Sprint Retrospective

After the review meeting, the Scrum team members gather and review how well they performed as a team. Sprint retrospective meetings are "working sessions" to enable the team members to speak out and share their thoughts on the team's collaboration and cohesiveness and inner workings. These meetings are not intended to review the actual outcome of the sprints themselves.

It is a great way to reset the team's expectation of each other based on the information gathered during the meeting and focus on ways to improve how everyone works together.

There are many ways to conduct retrospective meetings but a common method I used is *Start-Stop-Continue*. In this approach, each team member is asked to discuss in their eyes what the team did well and what wasn't done well. In addition, team members can recommend new things that the team should start doing to help optimize their collaboration and performance.

As the facilitator of this meeting, the Scrum master should ensure that the team stays focused on discussing matters that the team can control and avoid blaming individuals, which can lead to a divided team.

At the beginning of the meeting the Scrum master reviews the items discussed in the last retrospective meeting and specifically focuses on items of improvements that the team committed to achieving. Next, the team discusses everyone's input at a high level. If patterns of problems or issues are apparent, a deep dive should be performed on these items to better understand them. Finally, the team collectively agrees on items of improvement it can commit to achieving in the next iteration.

A key benefit of running these retrospective meetings after each sprint is that the Scrum team members have a chance to improve how they work together early on and iterate over the entire length of the project. One of the shortcomings in traditional post mortem project review meetings is that the team gets to share what didn't worked well but don't really get a chance to improve. Often, the lessons learned are forgotten and can't be applied effectively as project teams are dismantled after a project ends and new teams are created.

Agile vs. Waterfall

Traditional project management as a distinct discipline has been around since the 1950s. This approach has been adopted by many software development firms in the form of a "waterfall model" in which series of tasks are executed in a linear fashion. Figure 2-4 depicts the typical steps in a waterfall project.

Envision	Planning	Design	Development	Stabilization	Deployment

***Figure 2-4.** Waterfall overview*

The waterfall model is still used today and has been adopted as the basis for organizations such as the Project Management Institute (PMI) and Projects IN Controlled Environments (PRINCE2). With such a long and proven history of success you may ask yourself why a new approach should be used. There are situations that lend themselves to an agile approach while others still favor the traditional waterfall.

One of the first questions you need to ask yourself is how open your organization is to change. The answer to this question has little to do with project management methodologies or Office 365 per se, but how individuals will deal with a significant departure from the way projects are run today. Recognizing the need for change management is very important, and you may find yourself spending time educating your stakeholders on what agile is and the benefits of embracing it over the traditional method. You may want to consider leveraging an external expert who will provide credibility and help the organization in its adaptation of agile. With some coaching and a bit of luck, your organization will be open to trying this new methodology if they haven't done so before.

The next question to ask is whether the project you're about to embark on is suited for a traditional or agile approach. Although I am a strong proponent of the agile method, I try to remain neutral and realize that there are times when a traditional approach is better suited. So far, I have discussed the advantages of agile. Let's discuss some disadvantages you may face.

Disadvantages of the Agile Methodology

Implementing a purely agile methodology requires an increased level of participation by key stakeholders to answer questions, provide feedback, and assist in resolving roadblocks. An even heavier demand will be carried by the customer if they are assuming the product owner role. If your stakeholders fail to provide this level of engagement, they can slow down the process and even derail the entire project.

You may face a similar challenge when your Scrum team is not dedicated to your project. There are assumptions being made during planning and estimations that hinge on the fact that your team will be dedicated to you. In cases where this is not true, you will find yourself spending a significant amount of time securing resources and convincing sponsors and stakeholders on the importance of having the team dedicated and prioritizing them against other projects. This scenario is more prevalent in smaller companies where, due to resource shortages, each team member has a specific skill set and is allocated just enough time to complete their piece before getting reassigned to another project.

Even in large organizations that are largely waterfall-based resources are often shared amongst numerous projects. Thus, estimates of velocity are often too high and the work delivered at the end of a sprint has less completed user stories than initially planned.

A third reason that can make an agile approach less desirable for you is when your team is geographically dispersed. Scrum teams work best when the members are co-located. In today's global economy this may not be feasible. I have been able to successfully run agile teams using various Office 365 communication and collaboration tools that make it easier to make sure that every team member gets to be part of the virtual conversations. Still, no tool provides the same level of involvement as being co-located and staying informed by osmosis.

Educating the clients on the process and ensuring they follow it is very important in agile. When it comes to sprint planning, your clients must understand and respect the time-boxed nature of the project. You need to shield your team from mid-sprint adjustments to the sprint backlog. Of course, if the team has completed all the work they committed to early, it is acceptable to have your product owner prioritize new items if they can be delivered on time.

Due to the iterative nature of the agile approach and the ongoing changes in the vision of the end product, the Scrum team may be challenged in getting a grasp of the final system. This can result in a system that is limited in its ability to be enhanced. This problem is more prominent in larger-scale implementations or with systems that include a high level of integration.

Advantages of the Waterfall Methodology

Waterfall projects typically start out by defining in detail the goals, objectives, and requirements. This allows the customer and development team to agree early in the project on what will be delivered and provides the customer with a sense of certainty on what the outcome of the project will look like. Having the requirement signed off early in the project also simplifies the planning and design phases because it allows for an inclusive design to cover the full scope. Since the full scope of the project is known at the start of development, progress can be measured more easily. The customer's involvement can thus be limited to key milestone reviews, approvals, and status meetings.

Through careful estimation and planning it is possible to schedule work for the project resources in a manner that would minimize idle time on the project and allow them to focus on other tasks when not focusing on project-related activities.

Another benefit of the early planning is that the order in which the software is built can be scheduled based not only on human resource constraints but also on integration dependencies, key dates, and other factors.

Disadvantages of the Waterfall Methodology

One of the prominent areas where the waterfall methodology falls short is in the way requirements and changes are managed. A significant amount of effort is invested in documenting detailed requirements as they are understood early in the project by the customer. This daunting task often leads to extensive documentation that can be hard to visualize by the reader. Even when the project team can deliver the product as it has been documented, the customer often realizes that what they asked for is not really what they envisioned or need. The impacts of introducing scope changes in a waterfall project increase significantly as the project progresses. As shown in Figure 2-5, introducing scope changes during the revision or planning phases are often less expensive and risky because the changes are usually limited to updating the requirements documents. However, the same change would increase risk and cost significantly if introduced during design, development, or testing because not only do the requirements documents need to change but some of the work that was completed based on these documents needs to be revised.

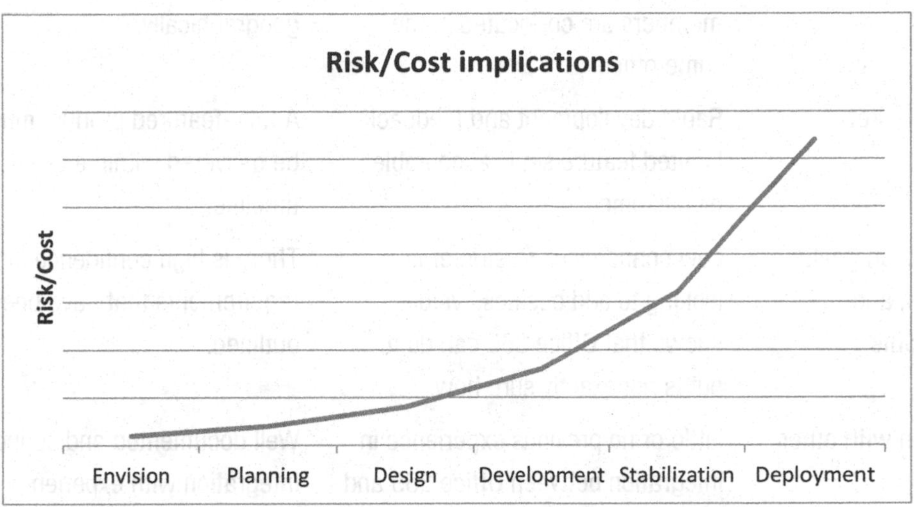

***Figure 2-5.** Risk and cost implications using the waterfall methodology as the project progresses through its phases*

Choosing the Correct Methodology

If you're not sure whether your organization or project are well suited for an agile process, consider using Table 2-2 as a guideline when planning your Office 365 project. This is only a high-level guideline as there are other factors that may influence your decision.

***Table 2-2.** Choosing Between Methodologies*

Factor	Agile	Waterfall
Customer availability	Available frequently throughout project and quick to respond	Limited availability, latency in providing responses
Scrum team allocation	Dedicated to a project with some exceptions of resources not required for all sprints	Partial allocation based on scheduled tasks

(continued)

Table 2-2. *(continued)*

Factor	Agile	Waterfall
Scrum team co-location	Majority of the Scrum team members are co-located in the same office	The project team is dispersed geographically.
Time to market	Rapid development and feedback. Limited feature set is acceptable by customer.	A fully-featured product must be delivered within a given timeline.
Confidence in goals, objectives, and requirements	Low confidence. Customer is looking to add business value, knows that Office 365 can do it, but is not exactly sure how.	There is high confidence in the requirements that have been outlined.
Integration with other systems	Little or no previous experience in integration between Office 365 and other, external systems. Poor documentation and support on how to integrate the systems.	Well documented and supported integration with experience to build on
Customer tolerance for scope, schedule, and cost changes	Flexibility in schedule and cost change is high to deliver more scope.	Schedule, cost, and scope are fixed and cannot be easily altered.

Summary

Agile project management methodologies have gained momentum over the past 30 years and are popular in the software industry. Agile offers many benefits over traditional waterfall methodologies. Still there are instances that warrant using the waterfall method. It is important to understand the nature of the organization that is undertaking the Office 365 project, how well it would adapt to such a paradigm shift, and whether there is sufficient commitment from both the customer and Scrum team to achieve a successful implementation. The next chapter will show you how Office 365 and Agile project management fit together.

CHAPTER 3

Office 365 Project Overview

If you have been reading this book from the beginning, then by now you should be familiar with the Office 365 family of apps and have a high-level understanding of what agile project management is all about. In this final chapter of Part 1 of the book, I will lay out the process I have been using successfully for delivering Office 365 projects. This process can be used for other types of projects, may need to be altered based on the technology, organization, and other factors.

Now that you know about Office 365 and agile project management, let's see how these two fit together. The process described in this chapter should not be taken as gospel, but rather should serve as a general starting point from which you will evolve your own successful project delivery process.

Process, Process, Process

When trying to learn a new process one can easily get lost in it. For processes that are waterfall-based a lot of documents and plans are created, particularly at the planning phase, as depicted in the sample process in Figure 3-1. By the time the planning phase is finished the project manager ideally has a good idea of what it will take to deliver the project to the stakeholders. In no way am I implying that such processes are bad. On the contrary. Organizations using these processes are continuously evolving and challenging themselves to provide the best chance of successful project delivery.

H. Croitoru, *Agile Office 365*, https://doi.org/10.1007/978-1-4842-4081-6_3

Knowledge Areas	Process Groups				
	Initiating	Planning	Executing	Monitoring & Controlling	Closing
Project Integration Management	Develop Project Charter	Develop Project Management Plan	Direct and Manage Project Work	Monitor and Control Project Work Perform Integrated Change Control	Close Project or Phase
Project Scope Management		Plan Scope Management Collect Requirements Define Scope Create WBS		Validate Scope Control Scope	
Project Time Management		Plan Schedule Management Define Activities Sequence Activities Estimate Activity Resources Estimate Activity Durations Develop Schedule		Control Schedule	
Project Cost Management		Plan Cost Management Estiamte Costs Determine Budget		Control Costs	
Project Quality Management		Plan Quality Management	Perform Quality Assurance	Control Quality	
Project Human Resources Management		Plan Human Resources Management	Acquire Project Team Develop Project Team Manage Project Team		
Project Communications Management		Plan Communications Management	Manage Communications	Control Communications	
Project Risk Management		Plan Risk Management Identify Risks Perform Qualitative Risk Analysis Perform Quantitative Risk Analysis Plan Risk Responses		Control Risks	
Project Procurement Management		Plan Procurement Management	Conduct Procurements	Control Procurements	Close Procurements
Project Stakeholder Management	Identify Stakeholders	Plan Stakeholder Management	Manage Stakeholder Engagement	Control Stakeholder Engagement	

***Figure 3-1.** Sample project management process*

When it comes to developing an agile framework, however, you still need to incorporate the overarching process that connects the sponsors and key stakeholders with the state of the project. Reporting on the progress, finances, and timelines of the project as well as keeping risk and issue logs are only some examples of what should be included in the agile process. So, what's the difference between waterfall and agile projects? Read on.

The Office 365 Agile Process

At this point, I would like to put the examples I mentioned aside and give you something more concrete. By the time you're done reading this book you should have Figure 3-2 appear in your mind whenever you think about running an agile Office 365 project.

***Figure 3-2.** Pictorial representation of the agile Office 365 process*

This simplified overview of the parts that make up a shock reveals three key components: end mounts, a coil, and a piston. In order for the shock to properly function, all components must fulfill their tasks and work together as a unit. Office 365 agile projects can be represented by the same three components. Let's have a look at the agile components and how they fit together.

The End Mounts

There are end mounts on each end of the shock. If you think of the long axis of the shock as a time scale, then one of the end mounts is the start and the other one the completion of the project. Regardless of the size or type of shock you have, you will always need end mounts on opposite ends. In the Office 365 world, each project starts and ends with a number of predefined activities.

Most of the activities that happen at the start and end of your agile project are repeatable to some degree, though the content may change significantly.

Starting Activities

At project initiation, you will work with key stakeholders to gain an understanding of the goal the project is trying to achieve or problem to solve. With a clear goal in mind, you will be ready to solicit requirements, which you will use to build the initial product backlog and identify the minimal shippable product (MSP). Throughout the project, you will continue to refer to the product backlog to determine what work lies ahead and in what order. Allocate sufficient time for the initial creation and prioritization of the activities.

Once you have a good understanding of the pending work, you should assemble your core team and set the initial ground rules for how the team will operate. As mentioned in Chapter 2, team members can change throughout the project, but you should try to limit these changes because they can be disruptive to the overall rhythm of the entire team.

Closing Activities

At the other end of the project are your closing activities, which will ensure that you are not only successful in the delivery of the project but also its success and uptake. Closing activities typically include training, knowledge transfer, user acceptance testing, and adoption.

I highly recommend involving your stakeholders early in the development process to give them a chance to see, review, and set their expectations. In reality, being a part of a project equates to added workload for many stakeholders and they may have only a limited amount of time available for review. Therefore, it is imperative that you plan to have formal user acceptance testing (UAT) to gather feedback from your key stakeholders once the key functionality has been implemented. The UAT could be managed as a sprint on its own if you wish, but no new functionality should be developed after this testing has completed to ensure that the tests cover the full scope of what is being rolled out.

Whether you are introducing Office 365 into an organization for the first time or making some updates to existing services, it's important to plan for sufficient knowledge transfer at various levels. Start by identifying and training the support staff, who will be taking ownership of the solution once it is deployed. Other key groups to train include any content authors and key stakeholders who will contribute or own content in Office 365. Finally, if your project will introduce any custom features, such as a new SharePoint Online intranet, then your end users should also be trained on where to find information and how to interact with the solution.

The Coil

The coil in the shock represents your sprints. This is typically where the majority of the project work takes place. Depending on the type of project you're leading, the sprints can be short or long, few or many. It is important to remember that they should be uniform in length to create a rhythm for the team.

As I discussed in Chapter 2, each sprint should start with a sprint planning meeting, where the work (sprint backlog) is identified and estimated based on current priorities. The remainder of the sprint should focus around delivering the work that was committed to by the team. On the final days of the sprint, the output should be reviewed with the product owner and other stakeholders. This will also provide an opportunity for you to seek feedback from your project team on how well the team performed through the sprint retrospective.

The Piston

All of the activities discussed thus far happen at a specific time within the project, either at the start, end, or throughout the sprints. There are, however, some overarching activities that should start early in the project and finish together with the closing activities. These activities, which are often overlooked or addressed too late in the project, can mean the difference between success and failure. Try removing the piston out of a shock. You're left with a slinky—not how you want your project to be executing.

Early and ongoing communication in agile projects is important due to the frequency of changes. Some organizations prefer to keep things under wrap until the near end of the project. This works if you have long projects with big impacts. However, with agile projects, there will be times when releases will be happening quite frequently, anywhere from a few weeks to a few months. It is a good idea to keep your organization informed of what's coming.

Not all projects involve migration of content. However, if your project does, then I cannot stress enough the importance of early and thorough planning! Unlike the development work, content migration will often require significant involvement and commitment of your stakeholders and content owners to review the content that is destined for migration. Reviewing a large number of documents is no simple task. It is time-consuming and mundane. If not properly performed, poor migration planning can result in project failure. Often, the actual migration of content will occur near the end of the project, when the solution is ready to store and manage the content. You should leverage all the time you have to plan, review, and prepare for the migration. Trust me when I tell you that you'll need it!

Unfortunately, I have seen too many projects end once training has been completed. With training completed, the ownership is transferred completely out of the hands of the project team and into the hands of a group who will support it going forward. A common gap I see is in ongoing change management and adoption.

Whenever you introduce any type of change into an organization, you need to be prepared for some level of friction amongst your users. Human nature and the resistance to change will sometimes trump common sense and advancements when it comes to technology. Copying and pasting a document into an email is easier and faster than getting a link and sharing it.

Adoption activities take time and energy and thus need to be planned carefully. Your sponsor's goal may be to have everyone at the organization using Office 365, but you may discover that only a small percentage leverage its functionality, while the rest resort to inferior, old practices to complete their tasks.

Use the time you have throughout the project to work with your sponsors to develop a change management and adoption strategy for the largest impact on the organization.

The last set of activities revolves around governance. Make sure that you work with your stakeholders to define the rules of engagement for the solution. You should be creating a governance plan that will describe how the various services should be used plus any restrictions and technical constraints that can be imposed. Review and update the governance plan regularly to make sure it addresses the current state of the environment.

Office 365 Project Overview, Revisited

To put things into perspective, have a look at Figure 3-3, which summarizes the various activities listed above into specific sections: start activities, sprints, supporting activities, and closing activities.

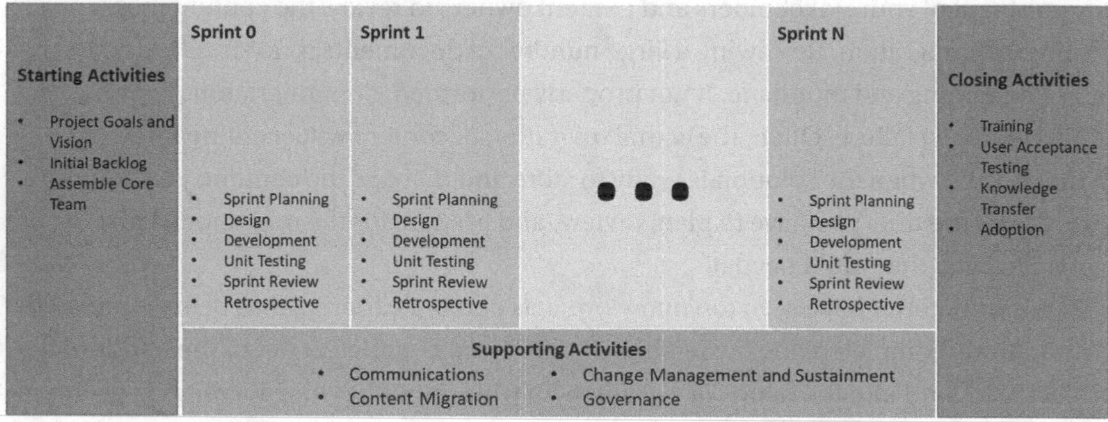

Figure 3-3. *Summary of the activities performed in an Office 365 project*

Except for migration, you should plan for all of these activities in your project. Failing to do so could result in a solution that doesn't meet the needs or is not accepted and adopted by the users.

So this is it, my Office 365 Agile project management process simplified. You should use it as a reference for how you will be managing your own agile projects in Office 365. In the remainder of the book, I'll provide some more details around these activities.

Welcome to Happy People

Congratulations! You've just been selected to lead an important project for Happy People, a multi-national agency dedicated to putting smiles on people's faces. As an organization, it is technically stuck in the 80s and is in dire need of a serious update. The CIO has decided to introduce Office 365 because it offers a lot of the functionality needed to manage all the company's communication, content, and collaboration. With offices in Seychelles, Maldives, Bora Bora, Hawaii, and Fraser Island, and travelling staff scattered just about anywhere on the globe, having 24/7 access to content is vital.

Your name has been mentioned to the CIO with high praises, who is eager to meet you and get this project off the ground. With six months to launch date, the company is looking to build a communication intranet portal on SharePoint Online and leverage other key apps, such as Yammer, Delve, OneDrive for Business, Video Portal, Sway, and the regular Office productivity apps.

Today, Happy People's content is scattered on some old file shares that it is eager to organize and add improved searching abilities. If you can make this project a success, then there will be many happier people on this planet. Are you up for the challenge?

Summary

Waterfall and agile projects are managed quite differently. Their deliverables and activities also provide little resemblance. Based on the shock metaphor, I presented activities, which represent the core work you should plan to perform when taking on an Office 365 project using an agile project management approach. Performing these activities by themselves will not guarantee success, but they will definitely increase your chances.

This chapter completes the overview on Office 365, agile project management, and how to combine the two. In the next few chapters, we'll dig deeper to better understand how these approaches can be successfully used to meet your business needs in an ever-evolving technological ecosystem.

PART II

Project Conception

CHAPTER 4

Business Outcomes

Leading a project without clear business direction is like chartering a boat blindfolded in the middle of the ocean. You could spend time and money, while the chance of success will be low. Therefore, budget sufficient time to get to know your users and their needs.

The activities discussed in this chapter may take place before your project even started or during the start of the project. By the time you're done with these activities you should have a long-term roadmap that will help your stakeholders achieve success as well as short-term goals with tangible results.

Working with the Right Information

Imagine you are Sherlock Holmes or your favorite investigator. With only a few clues at hand, you are asked to solve a mystery. This is how you should consider approaching your new engagement. Your users will share information with you, sometimes even great details on what they need. But, in reality, you will find that when you dig deep, some of the information may be slightly skewed or altogether incorrect. Furthermore, although your users may think they know exactly how the solution should work, there are often better ways to solve their business problems that they may not be aware of. This is where your expertise in Office 365 comes in.

Before getting into the weeds, it's important to understand the organization's strategy and to be able to map it to business outcomes. For example, based on the strategy that Happy People's CIO shared with you, if the IT manager was to ask for a server hardware upgrade, it would not align with the business goals and would distract from more long-term activities.

As I mentioned in the last chapter, your sponsor, the CIO of Happy People, has asked you to help implement a new solution to help with their communication, content, and collaboration needs. Being a tech whiz who just invested a significant amount of money

H. Croitoru, *Agile Office 365*, https://doi.org/10.1007/978-1-4842-4081-6_4

in Office 365, she's convinced that they should roll out as many apps as possible to reach their goal. Rather than acting on this information alone, you will provide the most value to your stakeholders by taking the information they provided you, expanding on some of the areas they mentioned, and even touching on areas that have not been mentioned at all to get a broad understanding of the long-term vision for them. Once you have this information captured, you can start digging deep, as deep as you can on the short-term needs. You need to work with your stakeholders and even challenge them on some of the information they provided you because their point of view may be biased or based on limited information. I've worked with many clients who thought they knew what they wanted and instead ended up with something that looked, functioned, and was technically differently from what they originally envisioned. When comparing it to their original expectations, the response has always been one of appreciation for not simply acting on the information they provided.

Diverging Approach: User Needs

Your first few meetings with your clients should be mostly focused on active listening and collecting information. This is not to say that you shouldn't gather additional knowledge for other parts of the project. But it is most vital at the beginning, when there is often the least amount of understanding of the end goal. Because of this lack of clarity, you will have stakeholders discuss anything that comes to mind, whether it is directly related to Office 365 or not.

Imagine your initial conversations with your key stakeholders from Happy People. The topic of improving communications will likely come up, as will better methods for collaborating on content. But before you know it, you may hear someone bring up the topic of mobile access for all remote users, dashboards for management to track overall company performance, the ability for clients to track their progress towards ultimate joy, or other topics, as depicted in Figure 4-1.

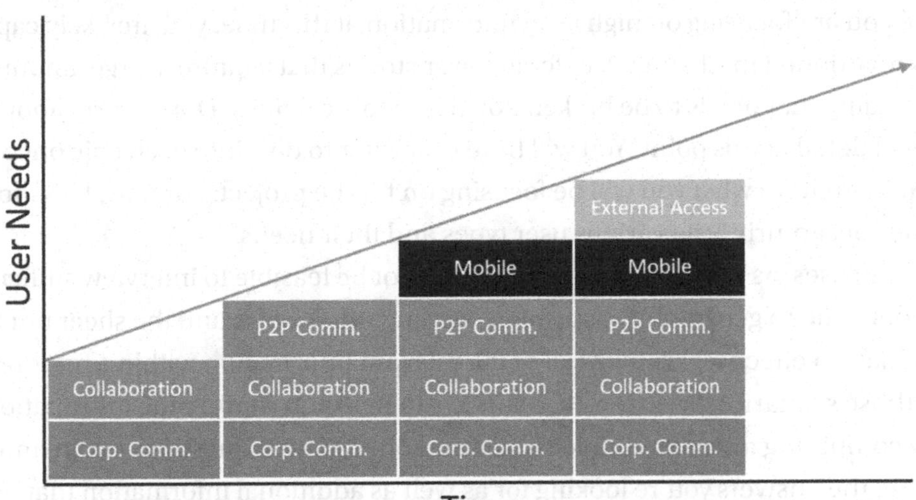

***Figure 4-1.** Diverging user needs*

Early on in this gathering process, start to categorize the information into logical domain areas and map them to strategic goals. This will help you get clarity on which areas to focus on based on the strategic needs. Table 4-1 provides an example of how some of the user needs can map to domain areas and strategic goals.

***Table 4-1.** Sample Mapping of User Needs to Domain Areas and Strategic Goals*

User Need	Domain Area	Strategic Goal	Priority
View corporate news	Mobile	Access Anywhere	1
Allow all staff members to submit praise for their peers	Corp. Comm.	United Workforce	1
Submit travel expenses via mobile device	Mobile	Access Anywhere	2
Eliminate the need for VPN to access documents	Collaboration	Operational Efficiency	3

Take in all of this information. If possible, even record the meetings (using Skype for Business or Microsoft Teams) so you have a chance to replay them and ensure that you haven't missed anything that was discussed because any statement, suggestion, or frustration can be translated into work needed to satisfy your stakeholders.

Since you are focusing on high level information at this time, you are likely capturing *epics*. As mentioned in Chapter 2, epics are user stories that capture a large amount of functionality that needs to be broken down into more details. Don't worry about this level of detail at this point. You will have time later to dive into each epic once it's clear that it is part of what you will be focusing on for the project. For now, let's look at techniques of capturing the various user types and their needs.

In some cases, as with Happy People, it may not be feasible to interview sufficient stakeholders due to geographic dispersion, varying time zones, and the sheer number of individuals to effectively capture all of the relevant information within a reasonable time. In those scenarios, try to leverage surveys to help you capture the information. By carefully combining a set of multiple choice and open-ended questions you're more likely to get the answers you're looking for as well as additional information that you weren't anticipating. Try to make it concise, but make sure it covers all the necessary areas. I'm a strong believer of letting users learn new technology by using it, which is why I create my surveys for anonymous submissions using Microsoft Forms (part of the Office 365 family of apps). The results can later be easily captured in Excel or other formats for analysis.

Gaps and Pain Points

Bad news travels much faster than good news (which is the reason we need a company like Happy People to improve our overall state of mind!) Though it's not necessarily a good thing to focus on the negative, there are times when that can lead to better productivity. After all, we have seen great industrial advances during and following wars.

Too often I have met with clients to discuss their needs and only a very small number of people were willing to speak out. Of course, there are differences in personality, level of knowledge about technology, the goal of the engagement, or other drivers that contribute to this effect. One approach I found that works well in most cases is to focus on gaps and pain points that users are experiencing. When I switched into this mode, the conversation got personal and more individuals opened up and participated. If you want to take this approach, just be cautious, as your conversations may turn into ranting sessions with diminishing value. Make sure to find a balance between engaging your users and getting valuable information out of them that you can later act on. Consider each gap or pain point as a user need or epic in itself that needs to be addressed at some point.

Persona

The information you're collecting is often based on the experience of the users who are providing it to you. Like the users who share with you their experience, there may be others in the organization that share similar stories or pain points but their opinion may not get heard because they are not part of the group of users you are meeting with. In order to provide a solution that is as inclusive as possible to all users, it's best to adopt the use of a *persona* with your user needs.

A persona is a fictional character who is or will be a user of your system (Office 365). Rather than representing specific individual and their needs, you should create personas that represent the typical user based on your knowledge of their needs. Unlike specific roles, you should build out a complete persona profile for each persona to help bring them to life. Personas should help you empathize with your users. Therefore, it's important that the personas you're developing are a true representation of your users. Typically, you can gather this knowledge through direct observation, interviews, or other types of research.

Table 4-2 lists the type of information to capture for each persona profile.

Table 4-2. *Persona Information*

Information	Purpose
Name and picture	Throughout your documentation, you want to refer to your persona by a name and associate a picture with them. Although they are fake, these pieces of information help create more of an emotional connection. Avoid using real names and pictures of individuals within the organization or other well-known people, such as actors or politicians. They could bias the overall effect of your persona.
Age	The age helps by giving a general understanding of the overall life experience of the persona. A 70-year old female likely has a different level of experience in technology than a 20-year-old male.
Behavioral traits	Tell us a bit about the persona. Do they bike to work or take the train? What do they enjoy doing on their spare time? You'd be surprised, but these fictional behavioral traits may be true for some users and can help shape the system in a way that you may not have considered otherwise.

(continued)

Table 4-2. *(continued)*

Information	Purpose
Common tasks	What are common tasks that this persona performs as it relates to their work day? Does the persona spend most of their day in the office entering data using a desktop computer? Or is most of their time spent outside of the office dealing with clients and filling out rudimentary paper forms?
Goals	Imagine what could make your persona's day more efficient and increase their morale. For the person working on data entry, maybe this could mean having a way to get the data entered automatically. For the person in the field, a mobile form could make their data entry faster and less error-prone.
Frustrations	Where goals are forward-looking into a future state, frustrations deal with the current experience that the persona is facing. Not being able to save or edit changes during data entry can be very time-consuming if the person needs to redo their work. Likewise, having to work extra time in entering the paper forms into a computer amounts to extra hours that could be used more efficiently growing the customer base.
Technical comfort level	How comfortable is the user with technology? Have they grown up with it and are they using it daily, or is it something that they use only when required?

You can visualize your persona in any way to bring out the key information. Figures 4-2 and 4-3 are examples of Katie Willard, a fictional persona working at Happy People.

KATIE WILLARD

BACKGROUND

- 38 years old
- Married with 3 children
- Loves spending time with her children, cooking, and reading books

Katie is part of the Human Resources team. With her go-getter personality and permanent smile, everyone likes working with her. Katie is driven by the ability to influence the overall work-life balance and well-being of her peers.

COMMON TASKS

- Responsible for addressing employee questions and concerns in a timely manner.
- Continuously seeks to improve the work environment and benefits.

GOALS

- Enable her peers across all Happy People locations to feel more connected and access information they need more readily.

FRUSTRATIONS

- Onboarding new employees is very time-consuming and the process is inconsistent.

TECHNICAL COMFORT

- Katie is very active on social media and uses her mobile phone and laptop throughout the day.

Figure 4-2. *Sample persona of a Happy People employee*

KATIE WILLARD

Life is too short to worry about the little things

COMMON TASKS
- Responsible for addressing employee questions and concerns in a timely manner.
- Continuously seeks to improve the work environment and benefits.

FRUSTRATIONS
- Onboarding new employees is very time-consuming and the process is inconsistent.

GOALS
- Enable her peers across all Happy People locations to feel more connected and access information they need more readily.

TECHNICAL COMFORT
- Katie is very active on social media and uses her mobile phone and laptop throughout the day.

BACKGROUND
- 38 years old
- Married with 3 children
- Loves spending time with her children, cooking, and reading books

Katie is part of the Human Resources team. With her go-getter personality and permanent smile, everyone likes working with her. Katie is driven by the ability to influence the overall work-life balance and well-being of her peers.

***Figure 4-3.** Alternate visualization of the same persona*

You can have a lot of fun building these personas and seeing them come to life. Just keep in mind that they should be realistic and believable, so that anyone reading them can empathize with them.

By understanding who your users are and their high-level needs, you have effectively answered the what, why, and who about your project. Your next step is to define a long-term strategy that will allow Happy People to achieve its goal. To identify the order in which these epics will be tackled, you need to devise a product roadmap.

Building a Roadmap

When you start to build a roadmap, you are, in essence, taking all the information that you've captured during the last part of the project and breaking it down into a grid. This exercise requires careful consideration because there are several factors that play into it:

> **Strategic Goals and Business Priority**: Always keep an eye on the goals to ensure that whatever you are delivering will address the needs of the business.
>
> **Technological Dependencies**: It is not enough to simply look at the business goals. You need to determine what, if any, technical

or other dependencies exist that may require you to accelerate or delay some of the work. For example, many of the apps in Office 365 depend on having the user's accounts and emails synced in the cloud.

Early successes: Introducing change is usually not easy and adds its own challenges. The larger the change, the bigger the impact and challenge. Rolling out Office 365 requires a great amount of planning and support because any hiccup can be seen as a failure and may deter users from giving it another try. Therefore, it makes sense to include some activities throughout the project that may not be high priority but have a high chance of success and adoption. In the case of the Happy People employees, if they have a need to eliminate their file shares so users don't need to use VPN anymore, then moving the users to OneDrive for Business would be a good choice early in the project. Typically, migrations to OneDrive for Business are not very complex and the learning curve is usually not too big because users can still work in a familiar environment by using their familiar folders.

Office 365 Readiness: As mentioned, Office 365 is an evolving technology platform that continues to get new features and apps over time. When assessing the user needs and trying to determine where in your roadmap to place it, make sure you consider the Office 365 roadmap as well so that you can leverage new features when you need them and avoid any custom development when it's not needed.

Cost Estimates and Duration: You won't likely have figured out all the details, costs, and timelines for each of the projects while building out the roadmap. But a high-level estimate may help in determining which initiative should be undertaken at what time.

Business Ownership: Each initiative within the roadmap should have a clear sponsor, identifying who will have full authority over the initiative's direction and success. Before you begin work on an initiative, it is not only important to know who your sponsor is, but you should also ensure that they or their delegates are readily available to ensure the initiative continues to move along.

The roadmap you are creating will help communicate to senior leadership what work is planned and in which sequence. Supporting the roadmap should be justification for each initiative on why it is needed, what type of resources may be required, and what overall impact it may have on the organization. Figure 4-4 depicts a roadmap for Happy People.

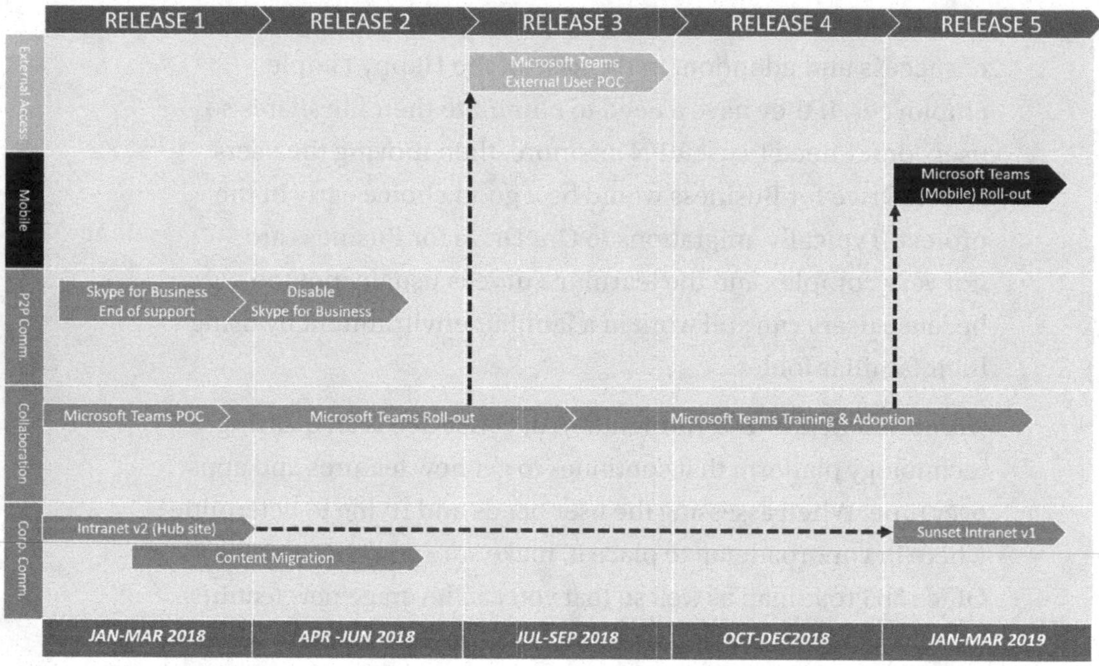

***Figure 4-4.** Sample IT roadmap depicting the various initiatives divided into their corresponding domain areas charted against a timeline*

Developing the roadmap is an activity that will be led by the product owner and will include full participation by senior strategic decision makers (e.g. CXO level), key stakeholders, and business representatives outside of IT. Don't skip this step. Even if your sponsors are not asking for it, you should be pushing the executives to support the development of such an IT roadmap to help you determine how best to invest the company's resources in full transparency.

As business and IT priorities change, so will the roadmap. Review it periodically with your stakeholders to ensure that it is still valid. At a minimum, such a review should take place near the completion of projects to ensure that there is continuation for the work. Once the high priority roadmap activities that you should undertake as part of the next project have been approved by the sponsors, then it's time to build out and prioritize the backlog.

Converging Approach: The Backlog

Earlier in this chapter, I discussed the user needs and how they tend to diverge from the initial goals to something that is often much greater and falls outside of the scope of this discussion. These discussions are important because they paint a clearer picture of what your users are experiencing and feeling. Once you've collected this information and mapped it out to your stakeholders, it's time to tackle the first release from that roadmap.

Note There are many agile tools available for managing your backlog. However, you can also leverage Office 365 apps for this purpose. Excel is a good candidate due to its simplicity and popularity for managing list-type data. As well, if your organization is already using SharePoint, then you can easily leverage this tool to capture and prioritize you backlog. You can also allow your stakeholders to directly enter additional backlog items, making them feel closer to the overall process.

User Stories, Epics, and Themes

From this point on, I will be referring to the information you've captured in the backlog as *themes, epics,* and *user stories.* To build on the brief introduction from Chapter 2, let's have another look at the definitions.

In the simplest form, *user stories* represent something that users want. User stories are often written in a first-person tense represented by a persona using a user/goal/reason structure:

"As a..." "I want to ..." "so that..."

This format not only helps the reader identify with that persona, but also helps you organize and prioritize the user stories more easily in the backlog. Imagine you have a number of user stories to add to your backlog. Without any structure, it would be hard for you to make sense of what the feature is meant to do, who will benefit from it, and what value it will provide to the overall product, as in these examples:

- View latest departmental news
- Send a personal message
- Book time off
- Share a document with a colleague

When you add structure to the user story as shown in Table 4-3, it becomes much easier to review these user stories with other stakeholders and determine in what order to action them.

Initially, when you document the user stories you will not have all the details around it. This is normal. Once a user story has been prioritized and is chosen for a sprint, the details will be defined during the start of that sprint cycle.

Some of the user stories captured may be too broad or complex to be completed within a single sprint. These are called epics. Look at the first user story in Table 4-3. From a first look you may think you understand everything there is to know about it. But it could be broken down into smaller scoped user stories. As shown in Table 4-4, when you split up an epic into multiple smaller user stories, these user stories get more detailed. With that, it will be easier to identify what conditions are required to meet the goals.

Table 4-3. *User Stories Using the User, Goal, and Reason Structure*

As a...	I want to...	So that...
departmental employee	view the latest departmental news	I can keep up to date with any important activities.
employee	send an instant message to a colleague	we can stay connected even when we are not online at the same time.
employee	book time off	I can get approval for my days off before booking my vacation.
departmental employee	share a document with my team member	we can collaborate on the document more effectively.

Table 4-4. Breaking Down Epics into Smaller, More Detailed User Stories

Epic	As a…	I want to…	So that…
View departmental news	departmental employee	read the latest news when I open the departmental landing page	I can stay current on what's happening within my department.
View departmental news	departmental employee	have departmental news filtered	I can keep my news focused to my own interests.
View departmental news	departmental employee	access old news that don't show up on the departmental landing page anymore	I can read it if I needed for reference.
View departmental news	departmental employee	subscribe to a news feed so that articles I'm interested in are emailed to me as well	I can read the latest news without visiting the departmental landing page.

Themes are used to group related user stories and epics. Using themes becomes useful when you are discussing the overall value that a release will provide. Though not mandatory, it's common to find related user stories being released at the same time. To continue our example from earlier, let's say that during your discussions with your stakeholders, improving intra-departmental and corporate-wide communications have been flagged as key goals for the first release. By leveraging themes, you can easily pull out all the related user stories and epics and move them up within your backlog. You may find yourself writing very similar user stories for slightly different themes, as shown in Table 4-5. This is the case when similar functionality is needed in different parts of the release product.

Table 4-5. *Grouping User Stories and Epics Based on Common Themes*

Theme	Epic	As a...	I want to...	So that...
Intra-departmental communications	View departmental news	departmental employee	read the latest news when I open the departmental landing page	I can stay current on what's happening within my department.
Intra-departmental communications	View departmental news	departmental employee	have departmental news filtered	I can keep my news focused to my own interests.
Intra-departmental communications	View departmental news	departmental employee	access old news that don't show up on the departmental landing page anymore	I can read it if I needed for reference.
Intra-departmental communications	View departmental news	departmental employee	subscribe to a news feed so that articles I'm interested in are emailed to me as well	I can read the latest news without visiting the departmental landing page.
Intra-departmental communications	Submit departmental news	departmental site editor	publish a news article on a specific date	departmental members can read it starting on that date.
Intra-departmental communications	Submit departmental news	departmental site editor	promote news articles	they appear at the top of the news listing.
Corporate-wide communications	View corporate news	employee	read the latest news when I open the corporate homepage page	I can stay current on what's happening within my organization.
Corporate-wide communications	View corporate news	employee	access old news that don't show up on the corporate homepage anymore	I can read it if I needed for reference.

(*continued*)

Table 4-5. (*continued*)

Theme	Epic	As a...	I want to...	So that...
Corporate-wide communications	Submit corporate news	corporate site editor	publish a news article on a specific date	all employees can read it starting on that date.
Corporate-wide communications	Submit corporate news	corporate site editor	promote news articles	they appear at the top of the news listing.

From Roadmap to Release

There is a false belief that you can build things much faster with fewer resources when using agile methods. This is not necessarily true, although you can definitely start seeing results much earlier. During your release planning, where you prioritize your user stories with the team, remember the following:

First, clearly define the release goals (or themes) before looking at the backlog. By knowing what the goals are, you can start to filter out user stories and epics based on the themes. This filtering will result in a graph depicted in Figure 4-5, which looks like a variation of Figure 4-1. When you start to define the goals for a release, you should next break down epics into smaller, more focused user stories. Although it's not a hard-and-fast rule, you should structure your epics so they can be delivered in a release. Similarly, the user stories should be small enough to fit into a single sprint.

Seeing the same themes appear more than once alludes to the fact that you may be working on the same theme in more than one release and that there may be breaks between continuous works on a specific theme. What is important here is the completion of related user stories within a release. Also pay attention to how many releases focus on goals for specific themes. This can show you the importance of the functionality associated with those user stories.

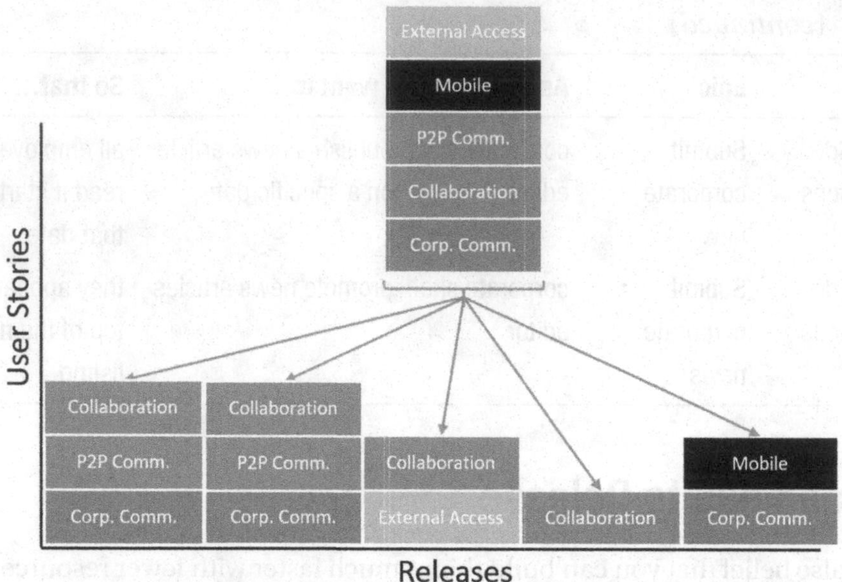

***Figure 4-5.** Creating releases based on user stories themes*

Take the corporate communications example mentioned earlier in the chapter. Based on Figure 4-5, user stories are delivered in release 1, 2, and 5 for this theme. The work may be broken down as shown in Table 4-6; it depicts how the longer-term goals can be broken down into multiple releases to provide an opportunity for early feedback on the solution as well as iteratively adding more functionality to further enhance the user experience.

Table 4-6. *Dividing Themes Across Multiple Releases*

Release Number	Goals	Notes
1	Fresh corporate news on the company homepage	Communication content owners can create new news articles and site visitors can view them on their desktop and mobile devices.
2	Region-based filtering	Communication content owners can tag news articles with specific regions. Site visitors will see news based on the region they belong to in their profile.
5	Anyone can submit corporate news stories	Provides a friendly way for users to submit new media-rich news articles to appear on the corporate home page. Communication content owners will get notified of submissions and have the ability to edit, approve, and schedule the publish date, or reject any submissions.

The second key point to remember during sprint planning is that for each release there are a number of activities that you should plan to undertake before, during, or after your development and implementation sprints, as discussed in Chapter 3. These activities will vary from one release to another but will typically include some sort of training, adoption, and change management. What this means to you is that the overall duration of your release will not equal the number of sprints to create functionality for your users. Depending on the complexity of the functionality being rolled out, some releases may include a few new features but a significant amount of hand-over support through training and adoption activities. These types of releases should not be undermined because they may provide a significantly higher business value than other releases that include many simpler features.

In essence, you have gone full circle by starting with some user stories, building out an elaborate roadmap and backlog, and then filtering the backlog to end up with a small, defined set of user stories. You could have skipped the first part and started looking directly at the epics and user stories for a single release. But what you would have lost in the process is important information about your users that may have led to further valuable-adding releases.

Throughout the releases, you need to make sure to validate whether the functionality being introduced will result in a viable product. You want to carefully select user stories that will collectively constitute your minimum shippable product (MSP). When released, your MSP product may not offer all the functionality your users requested. What it will do is provide insights into how your users are using the product. Their behavior will often differ from the original intents and help shape the future releases of the product. Make sure not to confuse the MSP with the minimum marketable product (MMP), which is more focused on earning rather than learning. The MMP is based on the first principle of the Agile Manifesto that states that

> *"Our highest priority is to satisfy the customer through early and continuous delivery of valuable software."*[1]

Summary

When introducing IT changes, it's not enough to simply look at the immediate needs of one stakeholder because there are often other factors that need to be considered. Obviously, the larger the change, the greater the impact to the organization. Therefore, such changes need to be socialized with a greater group of business stakeholders and their input needs to be considered during planning activities.

Capturing and presenting this information in the form of a roadmap allows you to easily share the plan with your team. This will not only give them an understanding of what changes are coming, but they'll also learn which activities they need to be involved in more deeply.

Start building your product backlog from your first meeting with your stakeholders and keep it updated with any additional information that is shared with you. This information will help ensure that your user's needs are being addressed as you move from one work activity to the next.

As you begin to plan out the next release, leverage user story themes to filter your backlog into the relevant epics and user stories. As you build functionality for each release, leverage the MSP to ensure that the solution will be used in the way intended and will provide the desired business value. Don't forget to also plan for change management, training, and adoption activates as part of each release.

With every introduction of new technology or changes to existing ones, the way in which your users interact with these systems and, more importantly, the content needs to be clearly stated and governed. This will be the focus of the next chapter.

---

[1]Principles behind the Agile Manifesto (`http://agilemanifesto.org/principles.html`)

CHAPTER 5

Governance

If you were to roll out Office 365 into your organization and let everyone start using it at will, I can guarantee that before long you would have chaos on your hands. In order to keep things under control, proper governance needs to be established. Governance can come in the form of technical controls such as permissions and prescribed rules, processes, and procedures. You can find commonalities in governance plans across organizations using Office 365. Yet there are unique business-driven differences to consider. This chapter will focus on establishing the key elements needed in an Office 365-centric governance plan.

Office 365 Governance

The governance you introduce to your organization around the usage and management of Office 365 will help ensure that the environment is well-kept and under control. Therefore, one of the most important documents you will need to create for your Office 365 environment is a governance plan. A complete Office 365 governance plan is composed of numerous guidelines, policies, and procedures that outline the administration, maintenance, support, and usage of your organizations' Office 365 environments.

The governance plan identifies lines of ownership for your business and technical teams, defining who is responsible for the back end (tenant configurations, licenses, and maintenance) and the front end (information architecture, taxonomy, user experience) areas of the system. Additionally, it establishes rules for appropriate usage of your Office 365 environments.

An effective Office 365 governance plan ensures you manage your system and use it for its designed intent to prevent it from becoming unmanageable. Such management involves both a strategic, business-minded team to craft objectives, rules, and procedures for the use of the system as well as a tactical, technically-competent set of

H. Croitoru, *Agile Office 365*, https://doi.org/10.1007/978-1-4842-4081-6_5

teams to manage the routine operational tasks that keep the system running. Users of the system will be empowered by support and developer teams/communities sponsored by the business leaders.

A governance plan alone will not guarantee the success of your solution. You still have to make sure that the governance plan is applied. However, not having a governance plan or having a plan that is either impractical or unrealistic will likely lead to failure.

The plan will focus on the business and technical aspects of your environment because a portal or collaboration solution is only as good as the value of its underlying content. A robust governance plan is essential to ensure that a solution delivers worthwhile content to its users in an effective way. Moreover, governance planning is especially important for Office 365 because its apps are designed to empower end users who are typically not information technology (IT) or content management experts and may not be aware of best practices that improve usability and can save them a lot of time and energy when creating and deploying new sites.

A solid governance plan establishes the processes and policies that you need to do the following:

- Avoid content proliferation (for example, unmanaged SharePoint sites and content that is not periodically reviewed for accuracy and relevance) by defining a content and site review process.
- Ensure that content quality is maintained for the life of the solution by implementing content quality management policies.
- Provide a consistently high-quality user experience by defining guidelines for site and content designers.
- Establish clear decision-making authority and escalation procedures so policy violations are managed and conflicts are resolved on a timely basis.
- Ensure that the solution strategy is aligned with business objectives so that it continuously delivers business value.
- Maintain a high-performing, current environment that will support the growth of the organization.

The governance plan is a strategic document. Its primary audiences are the business owners and the technical team that will collectively steward your Office 365 environment and the users who produce and consume the content.

A formal governance plan document includes several critical elements, each of which is discussed in more detail in the remainder of this starter governance plan:

- Vision statement
- Roles and responsibilities
- Guiding principles
- Policies and standards

Vision Statement

A vision statement describes, at a high level, how Office 365 delivers value to your organization and to each employee. A clear vision statement provides critical guidance to the inevitable decision trade-offs that you will need to make in thinking about your governance plan.

You normally work with your stakeholders at the start of the project to define the vision statement. As the project matures, you may find yourself refining the vision statement to better reflect your latest understanding of the goals. It is important for the organization to continue to share its vision.

With your knowledge about Happy People's goal, the vision statement may sound something like this:

> *"The portal enables the creation, management, and sharing of communication and assets in a business-driven environment for collaboration, classification, and access across the whole company. Through its capabilities, the portal will support the organization's information management needs and provide a business process framework for all business units."*

Roles and Responsibilities

The next step, following the creation of your vision statement, is the definition of the various roles and responsibilities that will help ensure that the governance plan is being followed to achieve the vision and update it to reflect changes within the organization.

To fully support Office 365 within the organization, the proper teams must be put into place. The roles and responsibilities define how the various employees mesh together to ensure success of the solution. Based on the size of the organization you're working in, several roles may be fulfilled by the same person. The individuals named in the governance plan will ultimately play an important part in Office 365 because they will help define the future direction and make overall policy decisions.

Based on your decisions, you can adapt the following examples of roles and responsibilities for your organization that have been used in other successful organizations. You will likely need to modify both the responsibilities and even the terms you use to describe each role for your organization, but these lists will give you a good place to start. Generally, a Governance Committee is made up of three groups, Strategy, Support, and Operations, as shown in Figure 5-1.

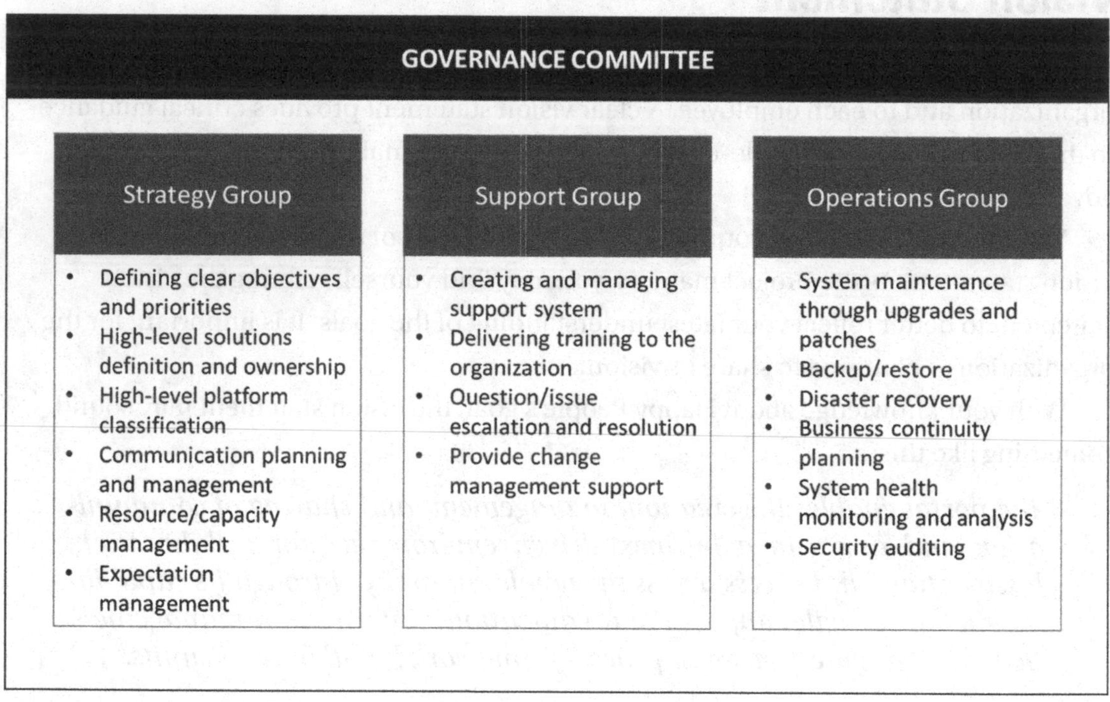

Figure 5-1. *Group responsibilities*

Strategy Group

The *Strategy Group* is responsible for setting the business objectives, technical insight, direction, and prioritization for Office 365. This group is the voice of the Governance Committee to the rest of the organization and it ensures that user input is taken into consideration when planning updates to the intranet.

Support Group

The *Support Group* helps identify other areas in the organization that could benefit from the use of Office 365 in their day-to-day activities. This group typically acts as the glue between the Operations Group and the users who are accessing the system for business needs. The group listens, understands, and analyses the needs of the organization and helps translate those specific needs into working solutions.

Operations Group

The *Operations Group* manages the more routine maintenance of the system by performing nightly backups, monitoring, and analysis, and keeping the environment current with security releases and upgrades.

Group Roles and Responsibilities

Each role within the organization is represented in the Governance Committee; however, some roles may be represented by the same individuals or teams. There are many inputs into the Governance Committee groups, but only a few people need to be given the responsibility for making the decisions around the management of Office 365. Table 5-1 shows the roles and responsibilities structure that can be put in place for Happy People to support the Governance Committee.

Table 5-1. Sample Office 365 Governance Group Roles and Responsibilities

Role	Responsibilities	Strategy Group	Support Group	Operations Group
Executive Sponsor	Sets the general vision of Office 365	•		
Business Owners	Manages and prioritizes the business needs to be addressed by Office 365	•		
Knowledge Manager	Manages the organizational taxonomy and knowledge management strategy	•	•	
Office 365 Owner	Responsible for the overall Office 365 environment Has ultimate responsibility to direct the implementation Office 365 in relation to the organization's goals and initiatives to ensure Office 365 alignment with other organization initiatives	•		
Office 365 Solution Architect	Liaison between IT support and the end users; responsible for Office 365 administration and user security	•	•	
Infrastructure Administrator	Monitors and manages the SharePoint online tenant and supports other systems that are part of the infrastructure, such as Active Directory, Exchange, and others			•
SharePoint Developer	Responsible for custom SharePoint development			•
SharePoint Designer	Responsible for SharePoint branding and solution layouts		•	
Help Desk	Supports end users through the function of the Help Desk and will likely handle the Tier 1 level user issues		•	
Application Team	Responsible for end user support at the Tier 2 level			•

Guiding Principles

Guiding principles are the foundational base on which the policies and standards are built. These principles help guide you towards the vision that you identified earlier. Every guiding principle is broken down into three parts:

- **Definition**: Short and concise description of the scope of the guiding principle
- **Implication**: Detailed overview of how this principle will affect the business users within your organization
- **Considerations**: Additional information to ensure that no important information about the principle is omitted

If you look at an example in Table 5-2 (one that should exist in all governance plans), you can see how the principles provide a foundation for use.

***Table 5-2.** Sample Guiding Principles*

Definition	Implication	Consideration
Owners must be defined for all content.	When a user interacts with content, it's important to determine who the owner of that content is in case there are questions relating to it or it needs to be updated.	Employees come and go. Make sure that the governance plan clearly states how content ownership changes are managed.

This is a simple principle, but the implications can be quite extensive in an organization. As mentioned in this basic example, ownership implies accountability for content and all content must be owned.

For Office 365, governance can typically be categorized into a number of common categories:

- General principles
- Content principles
- Publishing principles
- Collaboration principles
- Security principles

- Creative design principles
- Business process principles
- Business intelligence principles
- Training principles

These categories and sample principles are described in the remainder of this chapter.

Content Principles

Office 365 is to a large extent an enterprise management system for many organizations. It is therefore obvious that content principles make up a key component of any Office 365 governance plan. You will undoubtedly see examples of content principles like the ones shown in Table 5-3.

Table 5-3. *Content Principles*

Definition	Implication	Consideration
Single copy of documents	Each document should have one official version that is accessible to readers via a link that does not change when the document is updated.	One copy of a document
In-place document management	Documents should be edited in their original location so that any user linking to the old version will automatically see a later version when it's posted.	Someone may be linking to your documents. Update, don't delete!
Content management is a collaborative effort.	Although Office 365 may be governed by a small group of individuals, it is the responsibility of everyone in the organization to adhere to policies and ensure content quality.	We're all responsible for content management.
Avoid emails where possible.	Using links to documents instead of emails is preferred for many reasons.	No more email attachments.
Avoid copyright infringement.	Any copyright materials added to your Office 365 tenant must be accompanied by explicit permission in writing to avoid the risk of costly legal actions.	Don't publish what you don't own.

Publishing Principles

Publishing principles focus on who can see what content and when. Although publishing is often associated with communication portals, such as intranets or public websites, the same principles apply to other types of content that are shared internally. In short, someone is accountable to ensure that content is reviewed and scheduled to be available for consumption before others can see it, as described in Table 5-4.

***Table 5-4.** Publishing Principles*

Definition	Implication	Consideration
Content must be reviewed, approved, and scheduled before it is published.	Content approvers are ultimately accountable for the quality and timeliness of content appearing in your tenant.	Review before publishing. Once it's published, your users can see it.

Collaboration Principles

Collaboration principles help define how the various needs for multiple individuals to work together on content are addressed. These principles include identifying specific apps to be used for specific purposes and how they will be leveraged. Setting rules, such as the one described in Table 5-5, will help ensure that users can find the content more easily.

***Table 5-5.** Collaboration Principles*

Definition	Implication	Consideration
Ad-hoc teams leverage Microsoft Teams to discuss topics and share documents.	Content approvers are ultimately accountable for the quality and timeliness of content appearing in your tenant.	Review before publishing. Once it's published, your users can see it.

Security Principles

Security principles deal mainly with who has access to what and what type of access. When planning out security for your Office 365 tenant, questions around roles, permissions, and sharing of access and content internally and externally are commonly discussed, as in Table 5-6.

Table 5-6. *Security Principles*

Definition	Implication	Consideration
App-specific access is controlled via the Admin Center.	To limit what apps are available to specific users, the Office 365 Admin Center should be used to enable or disable access.	If they shouldn't be using it, don't let them.
Provide minimum level of required access.	General best practice is to provide users with the minimum amount of access they require to complete their work. This can generally help prevent mishaps.	It is generally easier to grant a user more access when they need it than fix a problem that was created as a result of too much access.

Creative Design Principles

Creative design principles typically apply to SharePoint Online because most other apps have very little, if any, way of customizing their look and feel. These principles typically deal with the branding and anything else that impacts the look and feel. Since the user experience can be impacted by the creative design, governing principles such as those shown in Table 5-7 are important so that users will not be negatively impacted.

Table 5-7. *Creative Design Principles*

Definition	Implication	Consideration
Leverage a consistent user experience.	The more familiar the user is with the solution, the more productive they will be. The Microsoft Office ribbon is a great example of this.	Keep it simple. Less learning equals less wasted time.
Mobile design is mandatory.	Many organizations have an increasing number of users who use mobile devices to access their corporate content. Therefore, it's imperative that the solutions provide a great mobile user experience.	A great desktop design is not enough anymore.

Business Process Principles

One of the goals of every organization is to cut out waste and optimize efficiency for its employees. What better way to do so than through the use of business process management and workflows. However, you need to ensure that the data is still properly handled by the system. Take the business process principals from Table 5-8 as an example.

Table 5-8. *Business Process Principles*

Definition	Implication	Consideration
Audit trail for workflows	Each workflow should be auditable to determine who initiated it and what steps it's going through in the event of a problem.	Running workflows blindly can result in situations where no one knows why things are happening.
Use lowest possible permissions.	When workflows are running, leverage the lowest possible level of permissions.	Avoid impersonating an administrator account when possible.

Business Intelligence Principles

Business intelligence is a great way to provide management with a high-level oversight through reports, dashboards, charts, etc. However, in the wrong hands, such information can have a negative effect on an organization. Table 5-9 provides an example of reducing the risk of data loss or leakage.

Table 5-9. Business Intelligence Principles

Definition	Implication	Consideration
Limit access to business intelligence information where possible.	Avoid situations where sensitive information is leaked beyond the intended audience.	Office 365 Business Intelligence reports can access almost all the information on content, users, and trends within the organization.

Training Principles

With an ever-changing offering that Office 365 provides, you need to consider that training is iterative and ongoing. Furthermore, because your users may not be in the same office, city, or continent, providing various options for training is important. Leveraging "just in time" and "just enough" training approaches typically prove useful in such an environment. Table 5-10 shows some great starting points for defining your training governance principles.

Table 5-10. Content Principles

Definition	Implication	Consideration
Deliver training to specific groups.	Based on the users' domain knowledge, needs, and availability for training, unique training programs should be developed.	General training has limited value. The training will miss some important parts or inundate the attendees with information they don't care about.
Deliver short, focused sessions instead of long ones.	Studies show that many users only retain a small percentage of what they learn. Keeping the sessions short will increase the change of users adapting these learnings into their everyday work life.	Typically, the length of video sessions should be no more than 3-5 minutes to showcase new concepts.

General Principles

Principles that are overarching in scope or don't fall into any of the other categories are grouped into the *general principles*. This also includes how other principles are generally applied, such as the samples provided in Table 5-11.

Table 5-11. *General Principles*

Definition	Implication	Consideration
All Office 365 content must adhere to corporate information technology-related policies, such as information privacy and confidentiality, records management, inappropriate content, etc.	Individuals within your organization that create, own, or manage content (that's pretty much everyone!) need to be aware the policies and procedures set out for IT resources.	Existing rules still apply. Should your mother, boss, or client be able to see this content?

Summary

A solid governance plan may not prevent every possible situation where users are not following the processes set forth, but it provides a framework to help keep your environment under control. It's important to realize that you and your governance committee must review the governance plan regularly to ensure that it's still aligned with the organization's vision for Office 365.

This chapter gave you an understanding on what it means to keep your Office 365 environment under control. In the next chapter, you'll look at what legal implications you need to consider when rolling out Office 365 within an organization.

CHAPTER 6

Legal Considerations

Despite the clear benefits that the cloud offers, some organizations are reluctant to relinquish control of their data and infrastructure. Such organizations typically manage their own environment or have a third-party service manage it on their behalf with very strict access control. In order for these organizations to even consider adapting Office 365 as part of their environment, it is important to understand some of the legal implications surrounding this technology. This chapter introduces some of these key considerations.

Data Security

The first question that is normally raised revolves around the data security within the data centers. Until recently, there was a notion that SaaS-based services such as Office 365 are less secure than corporate data centers. Due to this belief, cloud-centric companies such as Microsoft have invested heavily in cloud security. The reality is that these cloud services are now considered to be safer for your data than your own servers. Beyond the regular means of data encryption and monitoring for malicious software, Office 365 enhances your data security access through a number of means.

Multi-Factor Authentication

In *multi-factor authentication*, when a user attempts to log into Office 365 and the computer they are accessing Office 365 from is not recognized or has not been used to access Office 365 in a while, the service will request a second level of authentication to confirm the user's identity. Such authentication levels often include entering a numeric code that has been provided via SMS, email, or voice message.

H. Croitoru, *Agile Office 365*, https://doi.org/10.1007/978-1-4842-4081-6_6

Data Loss Prevention

Office 365 employs *data loss prevention (DLP)* that can limit what data can be shared inside or outside the organization. Through DLP, your organization can reduce the risk of sensitive information leakage.

Mobile Device Management

When a user in your organization wishes to connect to your Office 365 tenant, *mobile device management (MDM)* can be applied to that device to ensure that the employee does not breach corporate data policies. In addition to the automatic installation and configuration of applications, MDM solutions can also be used to wipe devices of any applications and content if an employee leaves the organizations or engages in activities that are detrimental to your organization.

Data Location

Today, Microsoft hosts a number of data centers across the globe, with new ones being added on a regular basis. See Figure 6-1.

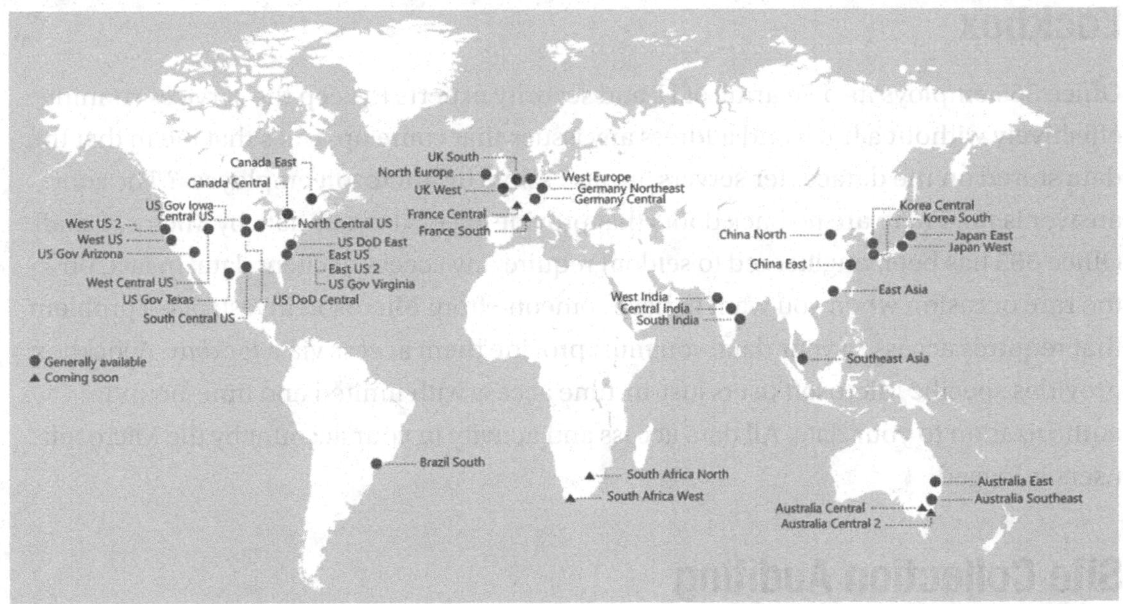

Figure 6-1. *Global Microsoft Azure datacenter map (Source: Microsoft,* `https://azure.microsoft.com/en-us/regions/`*)*

Choosing the right location for your data center is important to ensure that you are protected by your local data sovereignty laws. Being an Australian company, Happy People hosts most of its IT infrastructure in Fraser Island and plans on leveraging the Australia East data center. This means that the data is subject to Australian laws. However, Microsoft, being a US-based company, is also governed by the USA Patriot Act, which gives US national security and law enforcement the right to survey any data in any of their datacenters if there is any suspicion of terrorist activity.

Data Access

Now that you're comfortable with the idea that your data is securely stored and can't be accessed by just anyone from the Internet, there still the question around who accesses your data and when.

Lockbox

Office 365 employs its own army of IT and security experts to keep the services running effectively without a hitch and address any issues that come up. Does that mean that the data stored on the datacenter servers are accessible by Microsoft employees? The short answer is no. There are no back doors that provide access to your data by Microsoft staff. Office 365 has been engineered to seldom require any access to client data. In fact, on the rare occasion when you want to have someone from Microsoft investigate a problem that requires access to your data, you must provide them access via a *lockbox*. A lockbox provides specific Microsoft users just-in-time access with limited and time-bound authorization to your data. All data access and activity in your account by the Microsoft users is logged.

Site Collection Auditing

Within SharePoint Online, you can audit the activity and generate customized reports about an individual document, item, column, content type, search, or permission level through the SharePoint *Site Collection Auditing* settings. These Excel reports can be configured to capture file open, edit, check in/out, move, copy, delete, and restore events.

Data Transparency

Microsoft takes a serious stance to ensure that you have full visibility into what is happening or planned to happen with your services and data. Over the past few years, Microsoft has maintained a 99.9% uptime through the use of a Development Operations (DevOps) team and phone support staff that are available 24/7. To minimize any loss of data, your data may be copied across multiple data centers for redundancy. Typically, the redundancy occurs within your selected region. However, in the event that Microsoft needs to move your data into another region, you will be provided with a one-month notice.

The Data Governance tab in the Security & Compliance app provides an overview of the data that is being managed in Office 365 for your organization. See Figure 6-2.

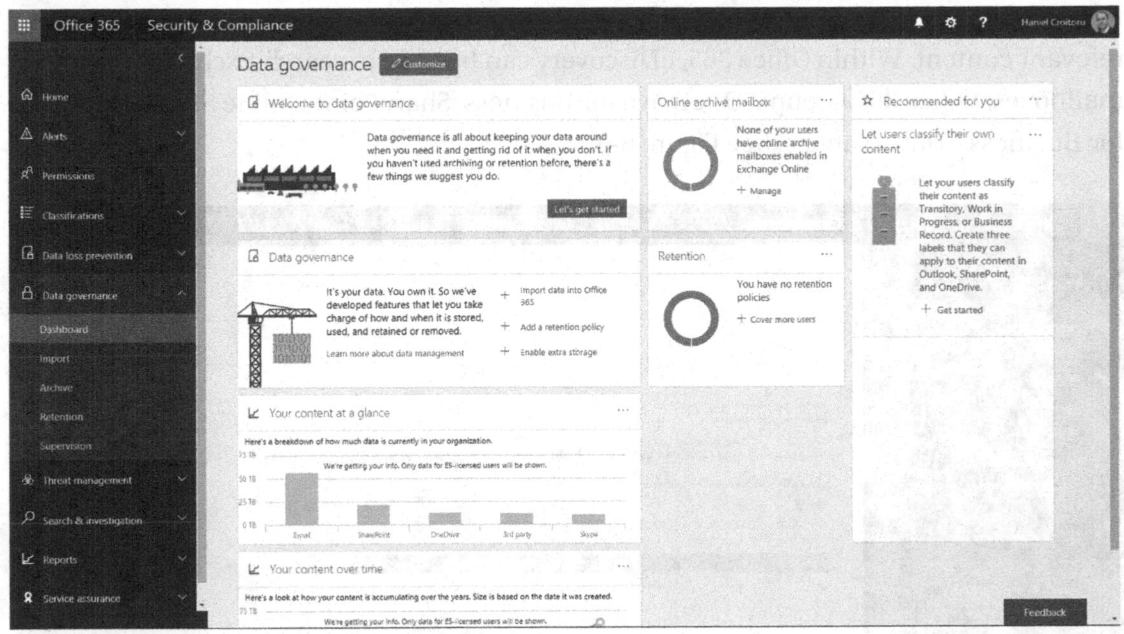

Figure 6-2. *Data governance dashboard*

Data Compliance

A number of common standards, such as ISO 27001, FDA 21 CFR Part 11, HIPAA/HITECH, FedRAMP/FISMA, and SOC-1 and SOC-2, are met with Office 365 without the need for any customizations. To ensure continuous compliance, Microsoft takes a proactive approach to continuous improvement through a specialist compliance team that tracks standards and regulations and then recommends enhancements to the products and services.

Most organizations are also bound by a number of company or federal regulations, which require retention of the data for a predefined amount of time.

eDiscovery

In the case of external actions, such as litigation, investigation, or audit, organizations need to be able to produce content that is relevant to the matter. *eDiscovery* provides records managers within your organization with the tools to discovery any documents and all metadata associated with these documents and place a "hold" on them. The hold essentially copies the content to another location that is locked down and cannot be deleted until the matter is closed. Content for eDiscovery is found using the search index that lets you preview the results and choose the sites you would like to search for the relevant content. Within Office 365, eDiscovery can be used to search Exchange online mailboxes, Office 365 Groups, OneDrive for Business, SharePoint Online Sites, and Skype for Business Conversations. See Figure 6-3.

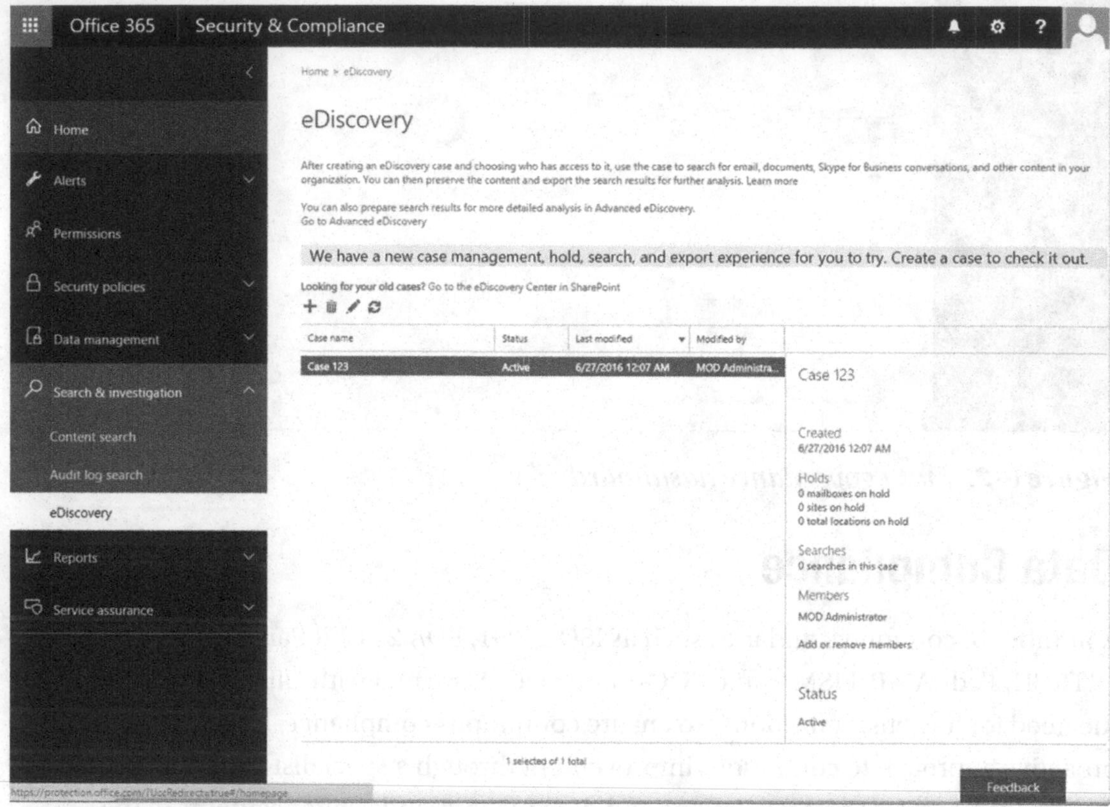

Figure 6-3. *eDiscovery is used to find content from various sources within Office 365*

Summary

Recently, organizations have become more comfortable with the idea of moving their content into the cloud as companies such as Microsoft continue to innovate and produce services and products that increase the level of security and limit the access of the content to any unauthorized users.

In the next chapter, you'll start building up the team that will help you deliver a successful Office 365 implementation.

CHAPTER 7

Building a Winning Team

So far, I've talked mostly about defining the solution you are trying to build. A clear understanding is important to achieve your goals. However, what is just as important is having a team that will help you achieve these goals. After all, the largest investment your sponsors are making will likely be in your team. In agile projects, teams often run leaner than traditional project teams. This increases the importance for you to select team members who have the right business and technical skills and are able to work well together. As in a chain link, any one member of your team can cause the entire project to fail. In this chapter, I'll discuss what you need to consider when assembling your team.

Roles, Responsibilities, and Capabilities

One of the first things project managers do when they bring together their team is identify the various roles they will require and what the responsibilities for each role will be. The relationship between role and responsibility often varies between organizations or even between departments or project teams. This is a result of roles maturing and adjusting to meet the organizational needs.

Although roles and responsibilities are often good indicators for you to identify your team, sometimes you need to look further to find the best match. Over the years, I have found that there are times when you may not have access to individuals who hold the role or are assigned the responsibility of doing a task. Yet they may be very capable and even enthusiastic about getting involved. This scenario is particularly true for agile teams, as the members of such teams are typically self-managing and are expected to determine who is responsible for what piece of work. The internal division of labor within the team may even change between sprints, allowing different individuals to get involved in various parts of the project.

H. Croitoru, *Agile Office 365*, https://doi.org/10.1007/978-1-4842-4081-6_7

Your Agile Team

With all that said, let's have a look at the type of roles and capabilities you should be planning for in your project. In Chapter 2, I briefly introduced the roles of the product owner, Scrum master, and Scrum team. The Scrum team can be made up of many different roles and, depending on the type of project you are implementing, the mix of people needed can change drastically.

For instance, Microsoft Stream is a YouTube-like corporate video streaming service that was released last year and is available to most Office 365 tenants today. Stream does not offer any customization at this time; all you can do is configure a few settings on it. In this case, your team will likely include a business analyst or architect to configure the settings and someone from the business to test out the configurations and access for the users. You will also need someone to handle the training, communications, and adoption needs.

If your project involves more elaborate customizations, such as building a SharePoint Online site or developing custom connectors or bots for your Microsoft Teams or other services, you will need to have a full technical team to manage the architecture, design, development, and testing of such a solution. Let's dive a little deeper into each of the roles you will likely need for Office 365 projects.

Project Sponsors and Key Stakeholders

Project sponsors and key stakeholders are not part of the project team you're assembling per se. Yet, they play a crucial role in the overall lifecycle of your project because they provide you with the means (in the form of a budget) to allocate your team to the project. Depending on the nature of your project and individual interest, their day-to-day involvement will vary.

Imagine a project that is rolling out a small upgrade to a system that is used by few users and has little impact on the way they work. In this scenario, you may find your sponsors or stakeholders to be fairly disconnected from the project.

However, the project you've taken on for Happy People is very different. It will require buy-in from many users and will impact the working habits of everyone at the organization. Your key stakeholders will require representation from most departments and even some ambitious power users who are interested in learning the latest technology and sharing their knowledge with others. This scenario will require more communication with the stakeholders as well as meetings where decisions need to be agreed on.

Project sponsors and key stakeholders have a lot of power over the project. Yet, as Uncle Ben mentioned to his nephew, Peter Parker, in the movie *Spiderman*, "with great power comes great responsibility." It's important that your stakeholders recognize their power and use it wisely.

- Communication is the key contribution they will offer on the project and the team. When dealing with risks or issues, it's important that they recognize that they are part of the same team, a team that is doing its best to achieve success on the project. Singling them out or sharing negative feedback improperly will likely demotivate the team and have a spiraling effect on the overall performance of the team.

Product Owner

The product owner represents the users or audience who are impacted by the project. In many cases, product owners are one of the key stakeholders mentioned above. However, there are times where someone else, even you, will need to play this role.

As product owner, the individual assuming this role needs to have a deep understanding of the way the business is functioning. It's good for these individuals to meet with business users on a regular basis to gather feedback around pain points, wish lists, and opportunities to improve the way the business is functioning. All this information needs to be synthesized and managed by the product owner in the backlog. Having strong communication skills is important to ensure that all the information is clearly articulated and shared with the team in such a way that they understand what they need to deliver.

Product owners need to invest a significant amount of time in the project and be available daily to support the team and answer any business-related questions the team may have. On a regular basis, they will review and reprioritize the remaining work in the backlog to ensure that the team is always working on what matters the most to the users. The product owner will need to gain an understanding about the complexity/cost and impact to help prioritize the items in the backlog.

Your best choice of a product owner includes the following traits:

- Able to collaborate and act as a real team player. Rather than dictating to the team what to do, the product owner should support the other team members (developers, testers, architects) and be respectful of their time. The product owner should try to remove noise from the team by answering requests for information. The product owner needs to be a champion of the solution and take on the responsibility of demoing it to others.
- Be a visionary and clearly articulate to the team how they will be able to measure success quantitatively. Being transparent with the team will lead to a more cohesive environment where the team members will be more willing to do what it takes to get the required work done.
- Set high but realistic expectations with the team. Aiming for aggressive but achievable goals is something many developers thrive on. The product owner should review the outcome of the developments regularly with key stakeholders to ensure that the solution is still meeting their original goals and determine if the product needs to pivot in any way.
- Provide frequent support and recognition to the project team. Motivate them on an ongoing basis because they will help the product owner be successful.

Business Analyst

In some cases, availability of product owners can be quite limited due to other responsibilities. If that is the case for your project, try to get one or more business analysts who will work closely with product owners to gather all the information about the product and organize it. While some of the work that a typical product owner would do falls on the business analysts, the product owner is ultimately accountable for prioritizing the work and providing approvals on the overall direction of the project.

If your project will leverage business analysts, get them into the project early on so they can understand the vision and direction and can help guide the team by providing all the detailed information they require.

- A business analyst needs to be a strong written and spoken communicator and be detail oriented to eliminate any guessing by the technical team regarding the solution they are building.
- As the team is working on the solution, there will likely be some back-and-forth sharing of information. A business analyst with strong collaboration skills will help address these gaps.

Scrum Master

Every project team needs someone to help the team stay organized and focused on achieving its goals. For agile teams, this role is fulfilled by the Scrum master. To be a good Scrum master, you need to be (or choose a team member) with very specific traits.

First, the management style is very important. Agile teams, by definition, are autonomous when it comes to solving problems and assigning the work to be completed. Therefore, your Scrum master should not use a micro-management approach with the team. Rather than checking up on the team and requesting updates on progress, a good Scrum master should offer to help the team by shielding them from external distractions.

With autonomy of the team comes the responsibility of continual improvement. It is not sufficient to have the team improve and reach a point of complacency. Team members should always seek ways to further improve the way in which they work together. Therefore, a good Scrum master should be able to balance shielding the team from external forces that will push their limits and internally pushing the team to increase their throughput and quality.

In a perfect world, you would have a Scrum master dedicated 100% of the time to a project. However, this is economically unjustified in many cases. In reality, there may not be a need or enough work for a Scrum master to be allocated full time to a project, unless things are going really badly (which has its own issues). As a mentor and coach, your Scrum master should be there to provide support and guidance but should still be able to do it in a structured way that frees up some of their time for other activities in the organization.

When picking a Scrum master, you should look for someone who has the following traits:

- Responsible for the team's adoption of the process without assuming the power needed to ensure successful delivery of the project.
- Humble in their approach and celebrating what they helped accomplish rather than what they accomplished.
- Able to embrace and nurture a collaborative team environment where team members feel able to raise issues openly and feel supported discussing them.
- Although the role may not require full-time allocation, the Scrum master should be fully committed for the duration of the project.
- One way to avoid disruptions to the team is by being able to influence others external or within the team. Depending on the visibility and impact of the project, influencing some high-profile stakeholders can prove challenging at times.
- In theory, a Scrum master does not need to have specific knowledge about the technical solution or business needs. However, it goes without saying that the more knowledge your Scrum master has in the domain they are working in, the better they are equipped to support their team.

Solution Architect

If any type of development or extensive customization is required, then you need to have a solution architect on your team. The solution architect's role is to understand the overall technical landscape or the organization and define how the future solution will fit into it.

For Office 365-based solutions, the solution architect must be aware of the solutions, how they work together, what the roadmap is for future improvements, and also what options are available for extending the existing capabilities. Some common focus areas for solution architects are

- **Security implications for users**: Who will be able to access the solution and what will the various permission levels allow users to do?

- **Integration with other systems**: How can content from third-party services be brought into Office 365 or vice versa? How will such systems authenticate with each other? What type of protocols will they use to communicate with each other?
- **Capacity and limits of the services**: There are many types of limits to consider when building solutions in Office 365, such as the amount of storage available, number of concurrent connections permitted to a service, and amount of data that can be transferred within a given time.
- Understanding and knowing how to use the Microsoft Graph application programming interface (API) to securely connect multiple Office 365 services and devices.

Besides technical expertise, solution architects should possess several traits to help them lead the technical team and answer questions for the team:

- Be able to clearly and succinctly articulate information to the team and external stakeholders. Solution architects need to be able to listen, explain, influence, advise, empathize, and negotiate, while navigating complex project environments.
- Recognize risks in the proposed solution and find ways to mitigate them.
- Provide pragmatic approaches to building solutions that will help the team achieve the goals without over-engineering the solution. When challenged, solution architects should be able to look at various options and provide the best approach moving forward without any bias over who provided the approach.
- Lifelong learners who will keep up with the latest industry trends to ensure that the solution will align with best practices of today and in the near future. This also means that solutions should be architected in such a way that they don't become too dependent on currently approaches and can be upgraded at a later date.

Developer

The role of the developer has changed significantly over the last few years. In the days of SharePoint 2010 and SharePoint 2013, much of the development happened using a specific development framework, namely the SharePoint Server-Side Object Model. With this framework, developers were able to easily access, manipulate, and share any content within SharePoint and even integrate other solutions into it. However, there was a downside to this flexibility. Many solutions were built for organizations, which did not conform to best practices as recommended by Microsoft or the industry.

Fast forward a few years and move SharePoint to the cloud. Here, the playing field is vastly different. For starters, most users use SharePoint in a shared tenant. This means that any solutions that could possibly affect a SharePoint farm on-premises could cause all users on a shared tenant to be affected. For that reason (and others), Microsoft modified the customization approach of SharePoint and other apps, where changes are made on the front end or outside of SharePoint to limit the potential impact these customizations have and reduce the access to the overall content. A developer looking to customize SharePoint today needs to have a good understanding of the following technologies in order to efficiently create new solutions:

- **JavaScript (JS)**: A scripting language that can be embedded in web pages and other applications. Alongside HTML and CSS, JavaScript is one of the core technologies that enable SharePoint customizations today as they introduce the changes from the client/browser side, not the server backend.
- **TypeScript (TS)**: A superset of JavaScript that generates clean JavaScript output. TypeScript is designed for the development of large applications and may be used to develop JavaScript applications for both client-side and server-side execution.
- **React**: A JavaScript library for building interactive user interfaces. React can be used as a base in the development of single page or mobile applications. Complex React applications usually require the use of additional libraries for state management, routing, and interaction with an API.
- **Node Package Manager (npm)**: Manages the JavaScript for a project. It is used to install, share, and distribute code and manage the dependencies in a solution.

- **Node.js**: An environment that allows JavaScript to be run outside of a browser. Node.js can be used by developers to generate server-side scripts, where dynamic web pages are produced before they are loaded by the user's web browser. This consequently results in Node.js producing JavaScript code that is managed in a single place but available for server-side and client-side scripts.
- **Gulp**: A toolkit used for streamlining the build process for front-end web development. Built on Node.js and npm, Gulp automates time-consuming and repetitive tasks, such as code minification, concatenation, cache busting, unit testing, linting, and optimization.
- **Webpack**: Generates dependency graphs for JavaScript modules to that allow developers to use a modular approach in their developments.
- **Yeoman**: A scaffolding tool used to generate a JavaScript starter template, manage code dependencies, execute unit tests, optimize code for deployment, and provide a local development server.
- **Git**: A source code version control system for tracking changes and coordinating work among several team members.
- **Visual Studio Code**: From the Visual Studio family of products, Visual Studio Code is a source code editor that focuses on developing and debugging modern web and cloud applications.
- **SharePoint Modern Framework (SPFx)**: A page and web part model that provides full support for client-side SharePoint Online development, easy integration with SharePoint data, and support for open source tooling. The SharePoint Modern Framework leverages a number of the technologies listed above (namely JavaScript and React) to build reusable web parts and customize the user experience.
- **Representational State Transfer (REST)**: A protocol used by various services to access and manipulate textual representations of resources and share information. Developers use the REST API to access information from various apps within Office 365 or outside and manage this information as needed.

- **Microsoft Graph API**: A Microsoft developer platform that connects multiple services and devices. Initially released 2015, the Microsoft Graph builds on Office 365 APIs and allows developers to integrate their services with Microsoft products, including Windows, Office 365, and Azure. Microsoft Graph also brings new functionality and connectivity between Windows and other OS platforms, including Android and iOS.
- **Microsoft Patterns and Practices (PnP)**: An open source initiative coordinated by SharePoint engineering to share documentation, guidance, samples, and reusable components for the community. PnP is often used to manage and automate deployments, which are an important part of the development lifecycle.

The extensive list provided above contains tools your developers need in order to efficiently build custom solutions in SharePoint Online. There are other useful tools, such as Fiddler and Postman, that will help your developers debug any problems or build the solutions faster.

Besides all the technical domain knowledge, you want your developers to have the right personality to help the team be successful:

- Be open communicators. Rightfully, you should not expect your developers to stand on a podium and give keynote speeches. But, having developers who are afraid to stand up and share what is on their mind can hinder the team's ability to work as a cohesive unit. Moreover, if there is something that is bothering them, they could slow down overall progress.
- Attention to detail is important. Better attention to details throughout a sprint will inevitably result in a lower number of bugs being reported.

Citizen Developer

The role of citizen developer is a fairly new one, where general users who are a bit IT savvy are able to create business applications for consumption by others within their team, company, or even the general public. The main benefit of these citizen developers is that they can leverage fourth-generation language-style development platforms and cloud computing services to provide working solutions to others.

Building a survey using Microsoft Forms, a sophisticated travel expense form using PowerApps or the workflow behind them using Microsoft Flow are a few examples of the type of solutions that citizen developers can provide. If there is a need for those types of solutions and developers aren't readily available or are too costly for the project's budget, you can consider adding some citizen developers to your team. Still, it's a good idea to pair them up with someone technical, such as your solution architect, who can guide them on using best practices, as well as testers to verify the solution.

Your citizen developers will form part of your core team. Therefore, it's important that they understand and conform to the processes set forth by the Scrum master and work and communicate well with other team members.

UX/Creative Designer

User experience (UX) and corporate branding are important factors in the adoption of new technology. There must be a balance on the amount of functionality and content provided and the way it is presented to the user. Whenever a custom solution provides information to a user or solicits input, a creative designer should be involved to help design a user experience that follows best industry practices for both desktop and mobile applications.

In Office 365, most of the creative design and user experience customizations are available for SharePoint-based solutions, including SharePoint Online and Office 365 Groups, as well as PowerApps.

Since the user interface is the part that users will see most of the time and interact with, the creative designer can greatly influence how well a solution is perceived. Positive feedback of the solution will have a positive impact on the team. On the other hand, if the solution is not well received because of the user experience, then the capabilities will not matter as much because users may be less inclined to use the system.

A creative designer on your team needs to possess the following:

- Solid understanding of user experience and design best practices to ensure that the solution will be easy to use for various user types across the organization.
- Understand and comply with Microsoft-recommended best practices for branding SharePoint sites.
- Skills to generate creative designs that will work in Office 365 without negatively affecting other apps besides the intended ones.

Content Authors

Some projects involve rolling out solutions that contain curated content. For example, you may introduce a new SharePoint-based intranet or leverage Microsoft Stream to share corporate videos for your organization. In these cases, you need to plan for your content to be created by the team in time for the launch of these services. Typically, content authors may need some training to know how to use the new tools and be given clear guidelines on how to create the content. Their work often happens in the latter part of a project.

When the content created is less structured and more social in nature, such as Yammer or Microsoft Team conversations, there is no need for content authors to create such content.

- Most of the time spent by content authors is in the creation of content. Thus, strong communication and overall written skills are imperative.
- Content authors also need to have a level of technical comfort in order to use the new tools to create content.

Quality Tester

Whenever any custom development takes place, you should have someone on the team test it before it's shared with the users. In a perfect world, developers would produce solutions that are flawless. In those scenarios, there would be no need for testing (if you happen to have such developers, please refer them to me). In reality, bugs are inevitable in code. However, they are not always a result of bad coding practices. On the contrary, bugs often arise from incomplete or vague specifications.

Suppose you've asked the team to build the weather widget depicted in Figure 7-1. If the specs simply indicated that the widget should display the current weather in the city they are in and a weather icon, then this would suffice.

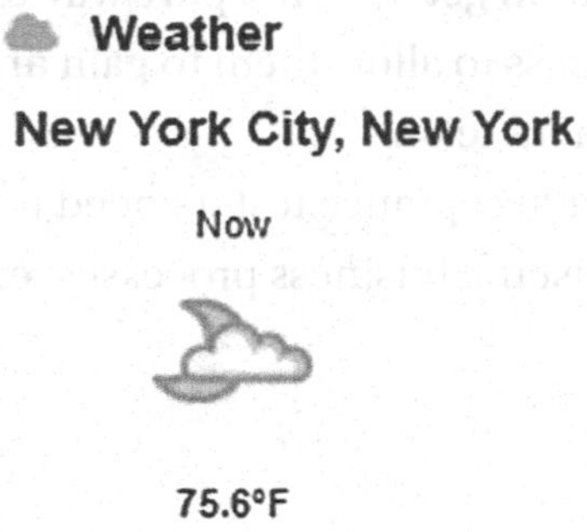

New York City, New York

Now

75.6°F

Figure 7-1. *Custom weather widget*

But what if the business user expected to see the results in Celsius rather than Fahrenheit? Those types of details need to be provided to the developers before they begin working on the widget.

Choose your quality testers wisely and make sure that they have the following qualities:

- Very detailed oriented to review the solution according to the specifications and identify specific scenarios that are not meeting expectations.
- Extrapolate the requirements to test out scenarios that may not have been called out in the specifications. If a widget needs to take an input of a whole number 1 to 10, the quality tester should also test numbers that fall outside that range, decimals, and non-digit entries.
- Clearly communicate their findings back to the team so it can investigate and resolve issues.

User Acceptance Tester

If you have ever rolled out a solution without having the business review it, then you can appreciate the need for user acceptance testing. Often, project deliverables are defined and the solution is built exactly to those specs, just to find out at launch time that the business users were expecting something totally different.

The point of user acceptance testing is to validate that the solution works in specific user scenarios. Ideally, your user acceptance testers are business users who will be regular users of the system and have had some hands-on introduction to the new solution.

User acceptance testers should get involved part-way through the solution development/deployment process to allow them to gain an understanding and provide early feedback to the development team.

Like the quality testers, user acceptance testers need to be detailed oriented when testing the solution against the business processes, extrapolate scenarios, and communicate their findings.

Summary

A cohesive and well-functioning team is critical to your project's success. There are many roles that you may need to include in your agile project team depending on the scope. Their responsibilities and capabilities may differ, but most of the roles share some important traits, including good communication and collaboration skills. These traits are the building blocks for a cohesive agile team.

In the next chapter, you'll look at the process of designing solutions and identifying possible alternatives based on various criteria.

PART III

Execution

CHAPTER 8

Designing the Solution

Deploying a solution in Office 365 requires planning. This is no different than any other technology being rolled out. Whether you are using a traditional waterfall or agile approach, your team still needs to think about the end goal and determine the best approach to get there.

If you've been reading this book from the beginning, then by now you know that many project activities and outputs differ depending on whether you're running your project as agile or not. The design aspects of your solution are no different. In this chapter, you will look at how to approach the design for your Office 365 solution using an agile methodology. Most customizations in Office 365 are in SharePoint-based apps, so I'll focus on them.

Just-in-Time Design

As you may recall from Chapter 2, most of the work in agile projects happens in a cyclical, iterative fashion. Each iteration, or sprint, begins with the selection of the work (sprint backlog) and then proceeds with the design, development, and testing of the items created. The design process therefore is an integral part of each sprint and starts just in time (JIT) before development starts, as shown in Figure 8-1.

H. Croitoru, *Agile Office 365*, https://doi.org/10.1007/978-1-4842-4081-6_8

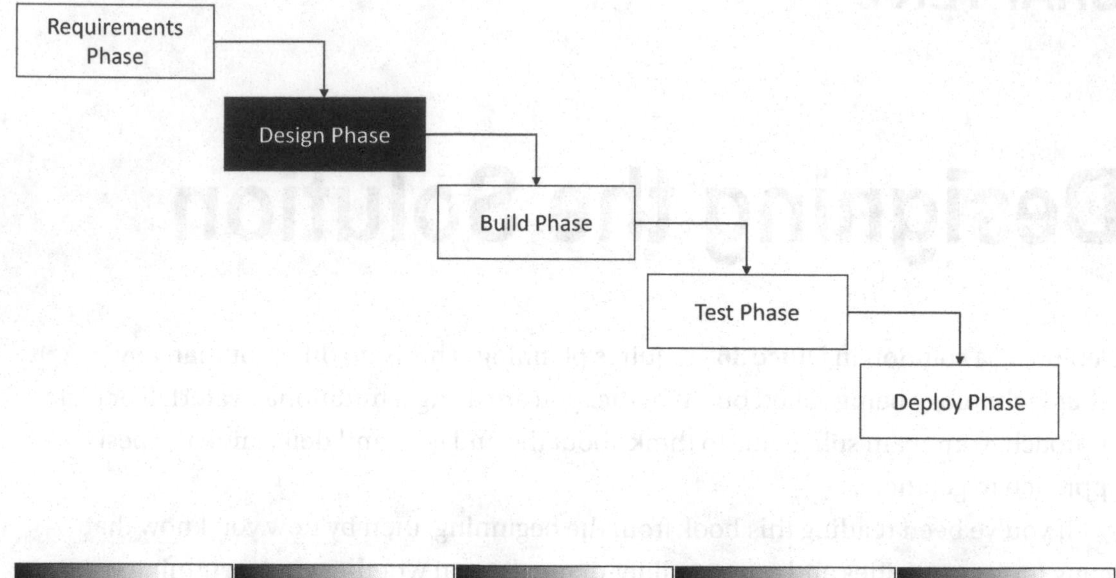

***Figure 8-1.** Design phases in traditional waterfall projects (top) and agile projects (bottom)*

The idea is that a developer should know what design to follow. However, the design can continue in parallel with development as long as the developers have their direction.

Due to the short duration allotted for sprint design work, the designs are never perfect or complete. In fact, they should be evolving and improving over time and provide the team with just enough detail to develop the items they are working on. Having the development team participate or even lead the design activities will allow them to proceed with the development with less detail. On the contrary, if someone else creates the designs, such as the solution architect, then more detail is required to let the developers know how to build the items and avoid having the developers do their own design in parallel.

Designing Ahead

At times, it may be beneficial to spend some of your team's time on work that is planned in future sprints. Of course, there is a risk that some of this work could be deprioritized, thus resulting in some wasted time. However, if you're confident that the work being designed will, in fact, remain in scope, then you stand to benefit from designing ahead.

You can think of designing ahead as a form of risk mitigation for your project. If there are elements of the solution that are technically complex or risky to develop, it would be good to give your architects and developers a chance to think through the solution a bit more and ensure they understand it thoroughly before building it. Happy People provides travel recommendations to their clients based on emotions, vibes, positive energy flow, and least agonizing travel schedules, requiring complex heuristics to come up with such results. The travel staff has gone through extensive training to understand and "sense" their clients. Unfortunately, the technical team has not been exposed to the same level of training and would greatly benefit from the extra design time, working with the experts on identifying rules on how such a solution could provide viable recommendations.

Another common scenario for designing ahead is when there's a need to integrate with legacy systems that may be poorly documented or technically limited. Without the proper support and understanding (imagine a legacy expense management system that Happy People uses daily), your team would spend a lot of time in understanding the functionality and how to extract or send data into such a system.

In Chapter 7, I mentioned the importance of having easy access to your stakeholders. If that is not the case, then you run the risk that your team may be slowed down while waiting for information from others. One way to mitigate this risk is by designing ahead and getting as much of the information needed early on.

Documenting Your Design

When it comes to documenting your agile solution, it's expected and accepted to be lighter than that of a traditional project. This, however, does not mean that you should abandon all documentation. The documentation you create still plays an important role in describing what was built, how it functions, and how your users interact with it.

Before jumping into the various types of documentation that may be applicable, let's remember that the work defined for a sprint are user stories that come from the product backlog. Within a sprint, the goal should be to create entire features, which will make it easier to package, test, and document them. With that in mind, let's see what types of documentation you can expect to produce in Office 365 solutions.

From a recent survey done at Happy People, one of the most desired functionality was to have a widget that would recommend to clients the best possible location to visit for weather and a choice of activities based on budget and dates. Table 8-1 lists the user stories that were selected for this widget.

Table 8-1. Vacation Planning Widget User Stories

As a...	... I want to...	... so that...
Happiness client	share information about my desired trip	My happiness advisor can make some recommendations where to go on my next vacation.
Happiness advisor	provide budget range and date range	I can provide my clients with multiple options where to take vacations.

Information Architecture

Information architecture defines the overall structure of the content being managed by a system. In the case of Office 365, the information architecture includes the overall taxonomy, sites, lists, document libraries, and security for SharePoint Online and general data structures for some of the other apps.

In the example listed in Table 8-1, you can break down the solution into two parts. The first user story needs to allow the user to capture the following pieces of information:

- Lowest budget (numeric)
- Highest budget (numeric)
- Start date (date format)
- End date (date format)

The second user story leverages the first four pieces of information to look up vacation locations that match the budget and date ranges.

If the happiness client is sending the information on a form, such as Microsoft Form, some additional pieces of information would be good to capture so that the client can be reached:

- Name (alphanumeric)
- Email address (alphanumeric)
- Phone number(alphanumeric)

Of course, you could capture many more details regarding the client, payment methods, etc. However, those additional pieces of information are not relevant or necessary to build the vacation recommendation widget in a sprint.

Functional Specifications

During the sprint planning meeting, the team gets a chance to ask questions regarding the feature to help estimate the efforts and, later, design it. Some of the questions should revolve not only around how the user interacts with a feature under normal circumstances, but also what the system should do if any erroneous information is provided.

There's no need to create an exhaustive list of all edge conditions or validations, but if the team is aware of any specific scenarios, why not capture them for the development team?

Note Consider the scale to which the solution needs to be deployed. SharePoint Online[1] and other Office 365 apps are constrained by certain limits that need to be respected when designing and building solutions. I have witnessed several large-scale Office 365 implementations where solutions were inadequately designed for a smaller scale. Tests cases passed under these circumstances, but once the solution was rolled out into production, issues were reported almost immediately.

Functional specifications can also be used for test executions to validate the behavior of the system. I'll discuss test case creation and execution in the next chapter.

Wireframes

Wireframes are low-fidelity blueprints for visual components based on the user stories and information architecture that are used to determine what type of content will appear on a screen and in what hierarchy. They can also be used to convey functionality. If done properly, you should be able to create wireframes for components very quickly. It's important to note that any level of detail around the look-and-feel would be wasted here because those elements are typically covered in a high-fidelity creative design. Figure 8-2 provides an example of just enough details for the vacation recommendation widget (left) and too much detail (right).

[1]SharePoint Online Limits, `https://support.office.com/en-us/article/sharepoint-online-limits-8f34ff47-b749-408b-abc0-b605e1f6d498`

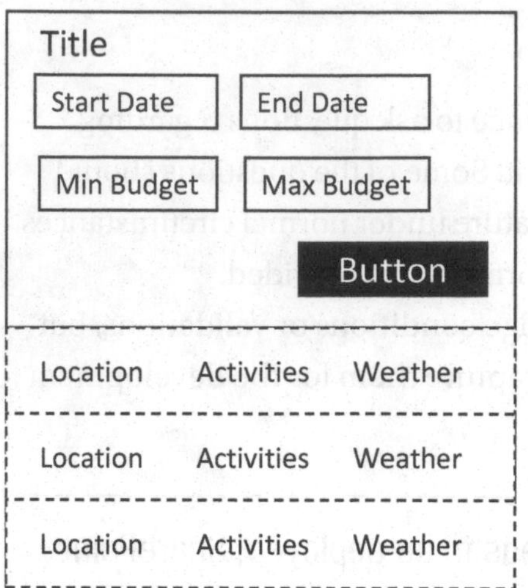

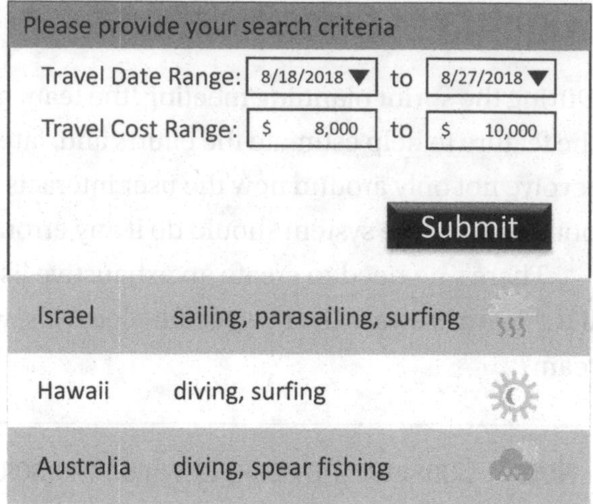

***Figure 8-2.** Examples of wireframes with just enough detail (left) and too much detail (right)*

If you were to only look at the user stories in Table 8-1, you might not have any idea of how it should work. All that the user stories tell you is what input the user provides and what results are provided back. Would you know where to display the results based on the criteria provided? The wireframes help you understand the visual and spatial requirements otherwise not captured.

Some will argue that wireframes are a bit of overkill for agile development. However, I have seen the benefits of wireframes where they clearly communicate ideas in a visual form to the Scrum teams.

Creative Designs

Creative design, as I discuss here, is the culmination of user experience and branding of a solution. In many cases, the user experience is what is often measured for ease of use and adoption by the user community, while the branding makes the solution unique to an organization and helps increase employee engagement.

At the core, creative design and agile methodologies form a type of dichotomy due to their distinctive philosophical differences. When you talk to a creative designer, they like to see the big picture of the solution by thinking about planning, strategy, and working out all the details of their design and user experience. Your agile team, on the other hand, is much more focused on the minimum amount of detail they require to complete their tasks, and they understand that they will iterate over time. While your developers may get frustrated when too much time is spent on overthinking the solution design, creative designers could get discouraged from the lack of attention to detail by the developers.

Both groups have their reasons for why they think the way they do. To the developer, meeting the functionality needs is important to say it's DONE. The creative designer, on the other hand, wants to ensure that the user can not only functionally complete their work but can do it easily. In my experience, if you want to integrate creative design into an agile framework, your designers will need to think about the big picture but provide the details piecemeal to the team on an as-needed basis. Over time, as you progress through the sprints, your solution's functionality will evolve as will its overall user experience.

One approach you can take during the sprint design phase is for the creative designer to call out areas where they foresee changes needing to be made without actually applying them. The developers can then use this information to build the solution with an anticipation of those changes. Looking back at Figure 8-2, the creative designer could provide some simple guidelines or recommendations to the developers to consider, such as

- The dates should be selectable from a date widget rather than text.
- Location and activities listed in the results will be free-form text.
- The weather will be represented by an image.

This level of detail is very low but sufficient at the early sprints. If your team is building a different component for your solution, once your first component has been built, you can reference some of these design considerations in later sprints. This is a slight departure from the purist agile that only looks at the work for the current sprint. However, if you are already spending time doing some design work and it's faster to take the design that already exists, then why not?

Note It goes without saying that both the creative designer and the developers need to be aware of the branding guidelines[2] and recommendations set forth for SharePoint by Microsoft to ensure that the creative design is achievable.

---

[2]SharePoint site branding and page customization solutions, `https://docs.microsoft.com/en-us/sharepoint/dev/solution-guidance/sharepoint-site-branding-and-page-customization-solutions`

In the later sprints, the creative designer should follow up and fill all the design gaps by providing the developers with details around exact position and size down to the pixel, font families, and colors. If the developers have leveraged parts of the design mentioned above, there's a better chance of minimizing the amount of changes that need to be made.

Summary

Designs are used to provide the team with additional details beyond the user stories and help the team collaborate on how they will implement the features. Depending on the scope of a sprint, the amount of design needed to provide the developers with sufficient details will vary. Although generally lighter than in traditional projects, agile-run projects still need to include their own design activities to ensure that the team is aware of what is being delivered and how. Information architecture and functional specifications are likely to be needed for most sprints, while wireframes and creative designs are only applicable when visual components that users will interact with are being built.

Now that you have an understanding on what goes into planning Office 365 solutions using an agile methodology, I'll discuss in the next chapter how to select, build, and test the solutions.

CHAPTER 9

Developing and Testing Solutions

Customizing Office 365 for an organization is sometimes required in order to address specific business needs. As with most other enterprise-level solutions, it is important that the correct decisions are made around what needs to be customized and how to develop and test these customizations.

As mentioned in a previous chapter, the main app that lends itself to customization in Office 365 today is SharePoint Online. This chapter will discuss numerous technical elements and approaches. Don't worry if you don't understand all the details. What is important is for you to get a general sense of how solutions are built and tested.

Choosing the Right Solution

Due to the consistent evolution of Office 365 and introduction of new features, Microsoft makes it easier to roll out a solution with little or no custom development. Developers love to build things. That's what they are paid to do, and they love to take on new challenges. However, before your development team assumes that they will be building new features in an upcoming sprint, your team should begin by reviewing the user stories and then determine what options are available. The team should ask three questions:

1. Is the feature really required?
2. Are there Office 365 or third-party options?
3. Has it been built before and do we just need to update the solution?

Let's have a look at the possible outcomes to these questions to see how your team should proceed.

H. Croitoru, *Agile Office 365*, https://doi.org/10.1007/978-1-4842-4081-6_9

Real Need

Business stakeholders are sometimes like children in a candy store. They want it all, and they want it now. In my experience, the real need sometimes changes when effort and/or money are introduced into the equation.

For example, a client I worked with really wanted to get information from their human resource (HR) system to appear inside a Delve page. In their eyes, this was easy. The data was available already, so how difficult would it be to simply display it in another page? However, when I discussed with them the reality of having to customize the SharePoint user profile to hold this content, relate the accounts between Office 365 and their HR system so the data can be related, and set up a mechanism to continuously poll for changes, they realized that this would be much more complex and not as critical after all. They ended up settling for easy access to the HR system via the Office 365 App Launcher with Azure Single Sign-on (SSO) enabled. In my opinion, this was a good choice. While it would have been nice to have each employee's data in their Delve profile, it was something that users would only access occasionally. The decision not to implement this feature freed up the developers to focus on other user stories from the backlog that impacted most users daily.

I could write an entire book on examples such as the one I listed above, where business priority was influenced by cost. So, my recommendation to you is to use your own judgement during prioritization and find out the *real need*.

Using Office 365 Features

Over the past few years, we have seen Office 365 mature at a rapid pace, with new features being introduced, existing features enhanced, and entire new apps being rolled out. While some of the apps are meant to serve a very specific purpose, such as Microsoft Forms, others are meant to be used as the core working apps, including SharePoint Online and Microsoft Teams. Still, there may be a need to customize the apps to your organization's specific needs.

SharePoint is typically the most common candidate for customizations. This is partially due to its popularity and the central place it occupies in IT landscapes as a corporate intranet in many organizations, as well as the way it has been positioned by Microsoft and perceived within the technical community over many years.

Generally, there are five types of customizations you may want (or need) to introduce to SharePoint to meet the user needs, as shown in Figure 9-1.

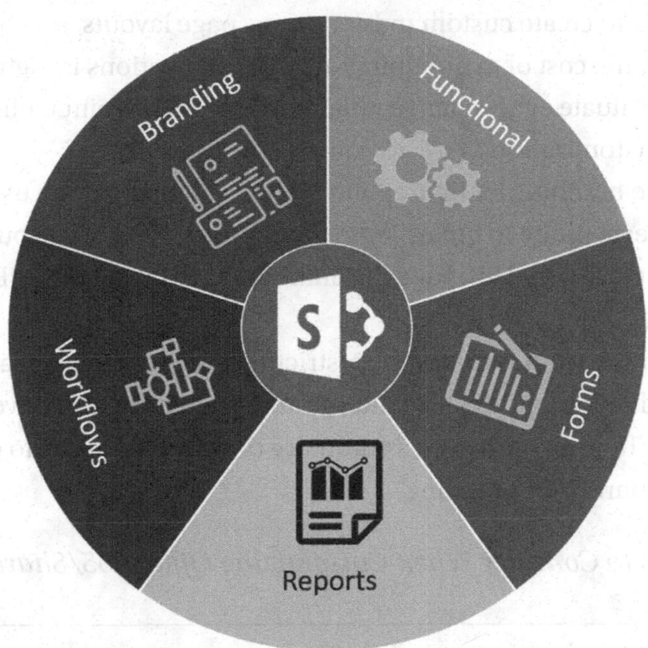

Figure 9-1. *Types of customizations typically applied to a SharePoint-based intranet*

By following Microsoft recommendations and best practices, your team can build solutions that will not be negatively impacted as new features or functionality is rolled out into Office 365 in the future.

Branding

Organizations that used SharePoint on-premises prior to Office 365 (such as SharePoint 2010 or 2013) are likely familiar with the flexibility these older versions offered when it came to branding. Mechanisms such as *master pages, page layouts,* and *JS injections* were very common in creating corporate intranets that didn't resemble the out-of-the-box SharePoint at all.

SharePoint Online is different. Rather than being a siloed application, it is part of Office 365. Therefore, any changes that are made need to consider other Office 365 apps that leverage SharePoint as building blocks, such as OneDrive, user profiles, and Delve. Conversely, when developing customizations, your team needs to remember that Office 365 continues to evolve. The team should avoid putting themselves in a position where they need to continuously update their customizations to keep current with the latest Office 365 enhancements.

It is still possible to create custom master pages, page layouts, and other branding elements. However, the cost of maintaining such customizations is high because the team will need to evaluate every change rolled out into SharePoint Online to determine if it impacts such customizations.

Customizing the branding for SharePoint Online should be done using *SharePoint themes*, which are least prone to break. If the themes do not provide you with the results you need, then the team could leverage the SharePoint Framework (SPFx) to customize the user experience.

Just be sure that the team respects the restrictions set by Microsoft around branding customizations and follows Office 365 Patterns and Practices (PnP) development recommendations. Table 9-1 provides a summary of Dos and Don'ts to consider when customizing your SharePoint branding.

Table 9-1. *Things to Consider When Customizing Office 365/SharePoint Branding*

Do	Don't
Implement custom branding using SharePoint Themes	Customize master pages
Add logos	Override the Office 365 Suite Bar
Customize the Office 365 login page	Customize branding for SharePoint personal sites
Change the layout of SharePoint pages using web parts and web part zones	
Build responsive SharePoint sites	
Include a custom header and footer in modern SharePoint sites	

Functional

Functional customizations act on processing data and present results in a certain way without the need of a trigger to invoke these customizations. In SharePoint, you can think of *webparts* as being functional customizations.

Recall in Chapter 8, I discussed designing a widget that would recommend to clients the best possible location to visit for weather and choices of activities based on budget and dates. Such a widget is highly customized for Happy People, and it would likely require the team to build it. However, if you are looking for some more common features, you may find that they are available as part of Office 365 or offered by various independent software vendors.

Take, for instance, a common weather widget that displays the current weather based on a person's location. The use cases for such a feature are simple and reused across many industries and organizations. As shown in Figure 9-2, Office 365 offers such a feature in the form of a SharePoint web part available to you in SharePoint Online.

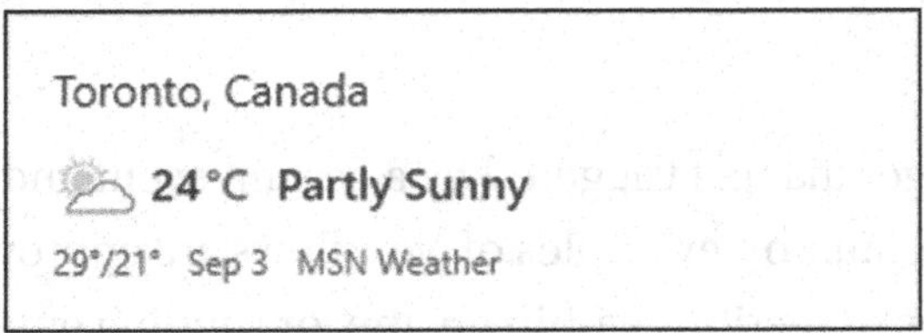

***Figure 9-2.** SharePoint Online modern weather web part*

If you were to search the Web for "SharePoint modern weather web part," you would find numerous free and paid options available, as shown in Figure 9-3.

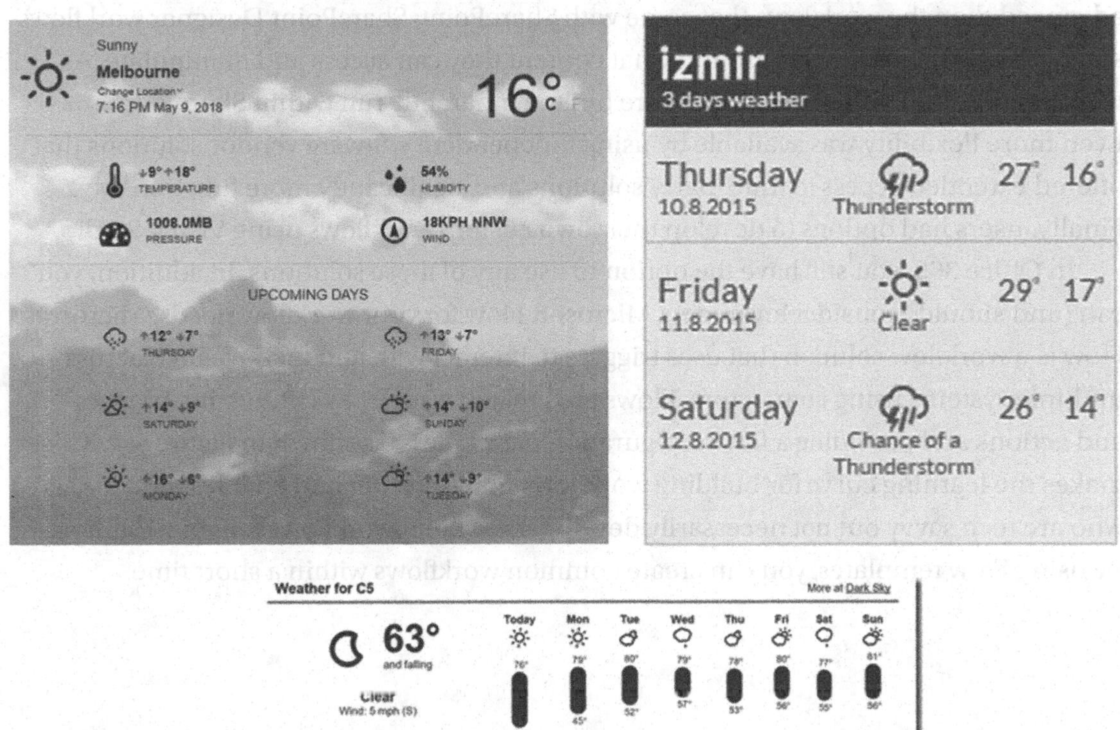

***Figure 9-3.** SharePoint Online modern weather web parts available by third-party software vendors*

Again, before your team rushes into development, do your due diligence to find out what is already available. Sometimes you will find solutions that only meet a part of the user stories. Using your persuasive personality, try to get agreement from the business to accept that solution. In some cases, you may even be lucky and find solutions that lend themselves to be modified, so that your team can still achieve full functionality but without the cost of building the solution from the beginning.

Workflow

Workflows are packages that get triggered by a certain event and perform specific actions on some data. Some common examples of workflows are approvals of content, moving content between apps or sections within an app, or sending emails.

Workflows for SharePoint on-premises have been around for some time. A few basic workflows, such as simple approvals, were shipped with SharePoint and had to be turned on for users to leverage them. If there was a need for more customized workflows, users traditionally turned to SharePoint Designer as a low-cost solution. Although more advanced than the workflows that came with SharePoint, SharePoint Designer workflows still have several limitations around what content they can access and manipulate. As well, SharePoint Designer workflows are built to inherently run within SharePoint. Even more flexibility was available by using independent software vendor solutions that offered extended access to third-party solutions and significantly more functionality. Finally, users had options to develop their own custom workflows using Visual Studio.

In Office 365, you still have the option to use any of these solutions. In addition, you can (and should) consider leveraging Microsoft Flow for your workflow needs. Microsoft Flow is a workflow solution that uses triggers to interact with and manage data across multiple systems using connectors. Flows are created visually by connecting triggers and actions and providing a few configuration parameters, as shown in Figure 9-4. This makes the learning curve for building workflows much shorter and enables individuals who are tech savvy but not necessarily developers to build workflows for your solution. By using Flow templates, you can create common workflows within a short time.

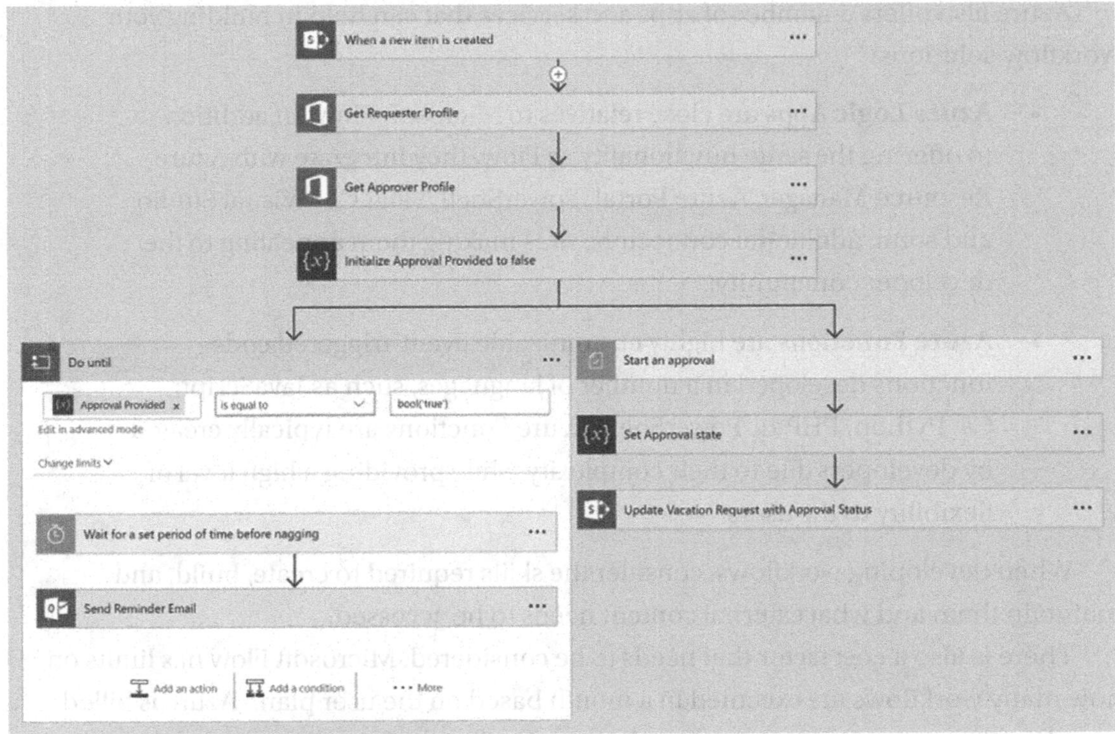

Figure 9-4. *Microsoft Flow uses a visual canvas to create workflows*

Today, there are over 230 connectors, allowing you to connect to most Office 365 apps as well as many other popular systems such as Salesforce or Google. Flows can be triggered from within or outside SharePoint Online, including a mobile Flow app.

To make it even easier to integrate with SharePoint, Microsoft includes access to Flow directly from SharePoint lists and libraries, as shown in Figure 9-5.

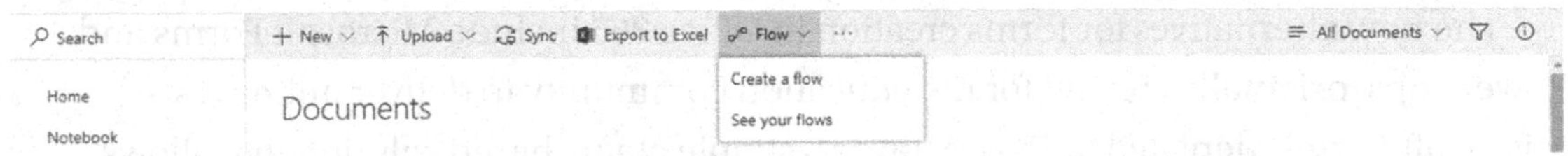

Figure 9-5. *Flow is integrated directly in the modern SharePoint lists and libraries*

This way, whenever items are added or modified, a Flow will be triggered.

Sometimes you may have to connect with systems that are stored on-premises. To create these connections, Microsoft Flow leverages gateways to extend its functionality and interact with data in SharePoint on-premises, SQL Server, Oracle, Informix, Filesystems, and DB2.

Azure also offers a number of apps and services that can help in building your workflow solutions:

- **Azure Logic Apps** are close relatives to Microsoft Flow. In addition to offering the same functionality as Flow, they integrate with Azure Resource Manager, Azure Portal, PowerShell, xPlat CLI, Visual Studio, and some additional connectors, thus making them appealing to the developer community.
- **Azure Functions** are highly customizable event-triggered code functions developed in a number of languages, such as JavaScript, C#, Python, PHP, or PowerShell. Azure Functions are typically created by developers due to their complexity while providing a high level of flexibility to the users.

When developing workflows, consider the skills required to create, build, and maintain them and what external content needs to be accessed.

There is also a cost factor that needs to be considered. Microsoft Flow has limits on how many workflows are executed in a month based on the user plan.[1] Azure is billed based on the resources consumed[2] or the App Service plan[3] used.

Forms

Forms are used to capture user input. In some cases, the information captured is used as input for workflows. SharePoint uses forms to capture item information to be stored in lists. This is still the default option for SharePoint Online today. Other methods used in the past included InfoPath, SharePoint Designer, third-party solutions, or custom development using Visual Studio.

The new alternatives for forms creation in Office 365 include Microsoft Forms and PowerApps, originally created for the education community to deliver online tests. Microsoft Forms, depicted in Figure 9-6, is a simple cloud-based solution that allows users to create forms of up to 100 questions using a combination of seven different field types: text, choice, date, ranking, rating, Likert, and Net Promoter Score. Forms

[1]Microsoft Flow Plans, `https://flow.microsoft.com/en-us/pricing`

[2]Azure Consumption Calculator, `https://azure.microsoft.com/en-us/pricing/calculator/?service=functions`

[3]Azure App Service Plan, `https://azure.microsoft.com/en-us/pricing/details/app-service/plans`

are responsive by design and can be shared with users within your Office 365 tenant or anonymously outside your organization. Once a form has been completed, the results can be viewed online, exported to Excel, or used as input to a Microsoft Flow.

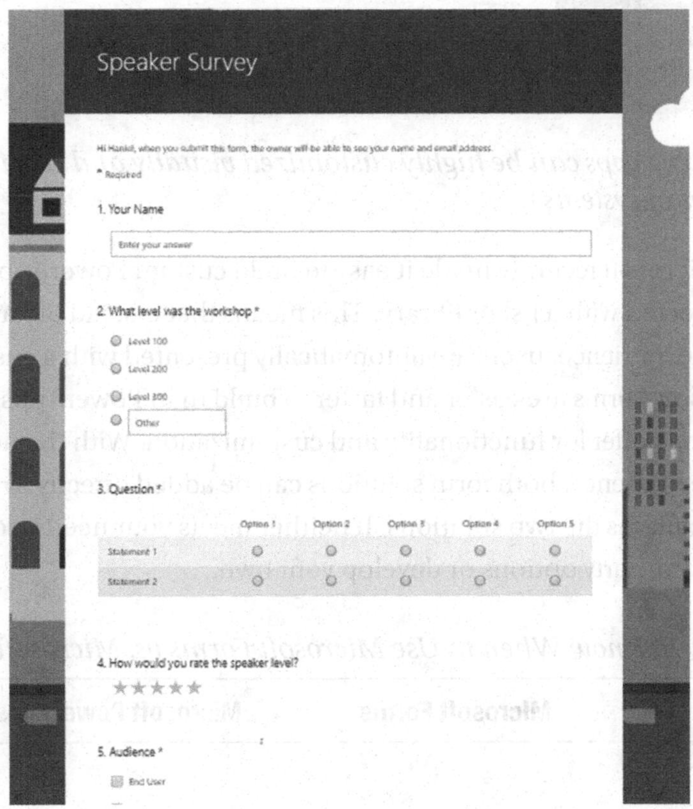

Figure 9-6. *Microsoft Forms used to capture basic information from a user*

If the needs for a form are more complex, then you should look at Microsoft PowerApps. With access to the same large array of connectors as Flow workflows, PowerApps can easily pull information and interact with content from a number of Microsoft and third-party applications. Unlike Forms, which gives you a limited number of field types and virtually no branding options, PowerApps lets you customize forms extensively, as shown in Figure 9-7.

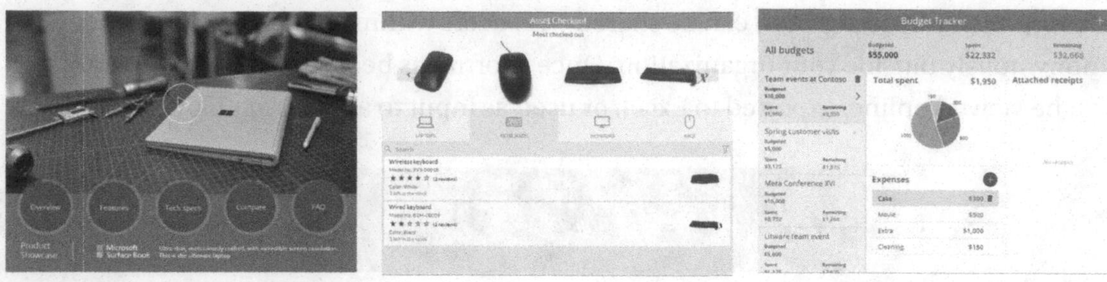

***Figure 9-7.** PowerApps can be highly customized visually and can include content from many types of systems*

Like Flow, Microsoft recently made it easy to build custom PowerApps forms that are directly connected with a list or library. This means that instead of having the default SharePoint form experience, users are automatically presented with a custom form.

While Microsoft Forms are easier and faster to build than PowerApps, they are limited in what they offer for functionality and customization. With the new SharePoint Online modern experience, both form solutions can be added directly to a SharePoint page. Table 9-2 explains the two solutions. If neither meets your needs, you can, of course, look at third-party options or develop your own.

***Table 9-2.** How to Know When to Use Microsoft Forms vs. Microsoft PowerApps*

	Microsoft Forms	**Microsoft PowerApps**
Structure		
Variety of question types	Yes	Yes
Logic (e.g. branching)	Yes	Yes
Default answers	No	Yes
Pre-load fields	No	Yes
User experience		
Usage	Native browser support	Detailed app when not integrated in SharePoint or Microsoft Teams
Responsive	Yes	Yes
Customize design	No	Yes
Anonymous access	Yes	No

(continued)

Table 9-2. (*continued*)

	Microsoft Forms	Microsoft PowerApps
Responses		
Export results	Yes	No
Integrate with Flow	Yes	Yes

Reports

Reports are often used to pull together and consolidate related data from various sources. Before the explosive increase in mobile device usage, reports were often formatted in a way to make them easy to print. This addressed the need for sharing reports with other users but provided reports that were typically fixed with the content they provided. Reports were commonly created using SQL Server Reporting Services (SSRS), Excel Services, or through a variety of third-party solutions.

The Microsoft Power BI, shown in Figure 9-8, is a suite of business analytics tools that deliver data insights from numerous Office 365 and hundreds of external data sources. Rather than providing static reports, Power BI allows you to create dashboards that let your users perform ad hoc analysis using natural language queries.

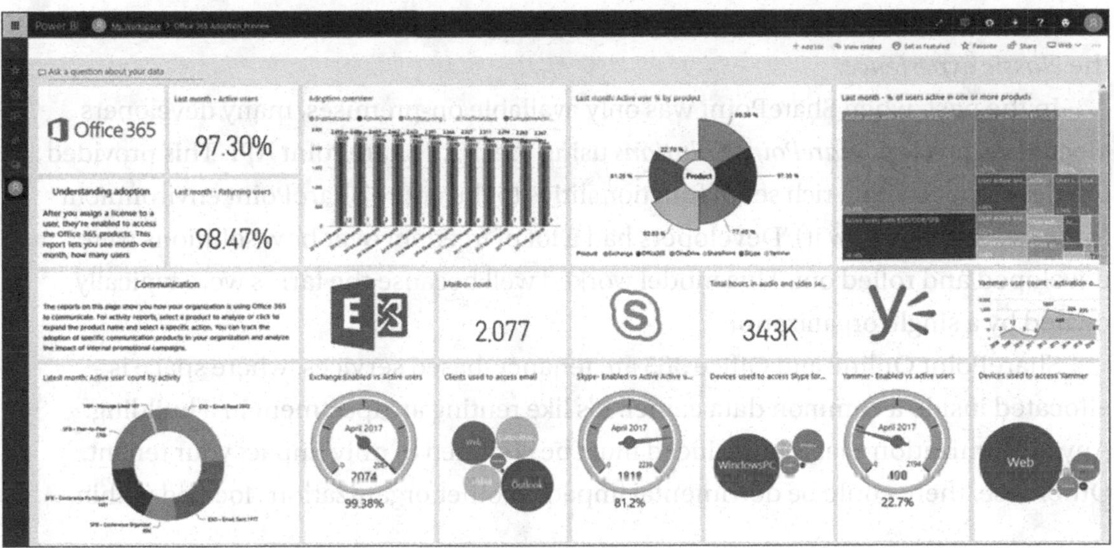

***Figure 9-8.** Microsoft Power BI is used to create real-time dashboards for ad hoc data analysis*

Recently, Microsoft announced the release of SSRS reports for Power Bi to allow existing investments be made into reporting solutions to be migrated in Office 365.

Though very flexible in its functionality, the premium version of Power BI comes with a price tag[4] that may be inhibitive to some organizations.

Development

If you've validated the *real need* and determined that neither Office 365 nor third-party vendors will provide you with the right solution or at a reasonable cost, then you need to look at the last alternative: custom development. Developing an Office 365 solution is different from developing a new solution from the ground up. Your development team will be leveraging a mature, feature-rich platform that can help cut development time. On the flip side, it's important that the team understand and respect the constraints and approach they need to take.

Many factors about the technical environment, target systems, framework, and business users need to be considered to ensure that the result will meet the needs of the users.

Developing SharePoint Solutions

SharePoint has gone through a lot of significant changes in the past two years. Most notable is the *modern experience*, which provides users with a fresh new site design and user interface that is easier to manage and includes many inherent improvements over the *classic experience*.

In the past, when SharePoint was only available on-premises, many developers elected to develop *SharePoint Solutions* using the .NET SharePoint API. This provided the developers with a rich set of functionalities to the entire SharePoint environment (or *farm*, as they know it). Developers had a lot of freedom over how solutions were developed and rolled out. This model worked well because the farms were typically owned by a single organization.

SharePoint Online and Office 365 are tenancy-based services, where space is allocated inside a common data center. It's like renting an apartment in a building. Any customization that is introduced must be confined to only impact your tenant. Otherwise, there could be detrimental impact to other organizations located within

[4] Power BI Premium calculator, `https://powerbi.microsoft.com/en-us/calculator`

the same data center. To address the needs of the developers in SharePoint Online, the following options are available.

SharePoint Add-Ins

SharePoint add-ins are apps that are installed and run within a SharePoint site. Add-ins come in two flavors. SharePoint-hosted add-ins are stored within SharePoint and are exclusively written using JavaScript (remember, no server code allowed). Provider-hosted add-ins are applications that are external to SharePoint and can reside in other environments. Provider-hosted add-ins can be written using any language of choice and use either *CSOM* or *REST* APIs to communicate with SharePoint.

JavaScript Injection

JavaScript injections allow developers to write JavaScript code and add it to any SharePoint page. The code is executed when a page is rendered. By leveraging the SharePoint client-side APIs, developers can access and manipulate the SharePoint content. Unlike the SharePoint add-ins, which require a more elaborate deployment process, JavaScript injections do not require any special development or deployment tools beside a text editor and SharePoint site to upload the scripts to.

SharePoint Framework

The SharePoint Framework is used to standardize how JavaScript customizations are developed. The JavaScript customizations can leverage the standard SharePoint APIs and access content using Microsoft Graph, Office Graph, and other APIs.

Though the code is client-side, SharePoint Framework customizations are deployed like SharePoint add-ins.

Continuous Integration and Deployment

The fast pace of development in an agile environment necessitates having integration builds and testing environments ready as soon as development has finished. To facilitate with and automate these activities, two development and operations (DevOps) processes are commonly used.

Continuous Integration

Continuous integration (CI) is used to merge all completed development work into a single, shared work stream, thereby allowing the project team to always access the latest completed body of work. The main goal is to avoid situations where integrations between multiple versions of code need to happen manually. One of the key premises of continuous integration is to integrate small changes often, thus reducing the rework and cost and time associated with it.

Continuous Deployment

Continuous deployment (CD) is used to ensure that the code produced can be deployed and released into an environment. Like continuous integration, continuous deployment aims at automating manual, repetitive tasks for the development team.

While continuous deployment can save you time by deploying code as it becomes available, there are times when you need to introduce controls (in the form of approvals). A good example of this is when deploying to non-testing environments. As you can see in Figure 9-9, deployment to the UAT and production environments requires manual approval before being deployed.

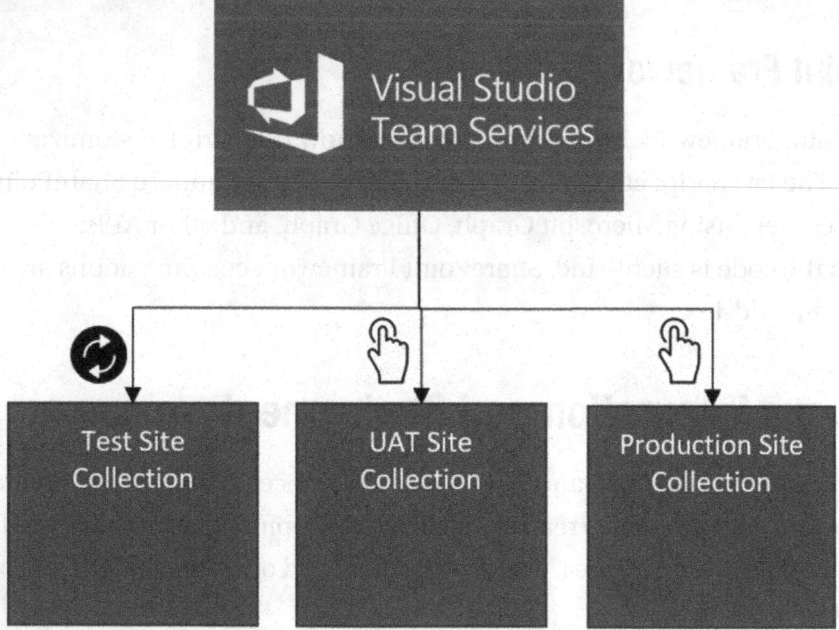

Figure 9-9. *Visual Studio Team Services is used to continuously deploy changes to the various environments*

Caution Some organizations are very particular about having each deployment go through a review and approval process before deploying to production. It is, therefore, imperative that you understand the governance around software deployments before setting up continuous deployment into any environments.

Testing

In Chapter 8, I introduced the concept of just-in-time design, where design is limited to the features or scope of work for a specific sprint. As depicted in Figure 8-1, testing follows a similar paradigm. During each sprint, the quality testers (described in Chapter 7) need to test the functionality that was developed to ensure it meets the user stories, known as *Quality Testing*. In other words, quality gets "baked in" to the process at every phase. In theory and the ideal world, the developers would have time to address the critical issues found. Anything that could not be fixed within the sprint is a change to the scope that would be added to the product backlog and prioritized against all remaining items.

One of the caveats of agile testing and limiting the testing activities to only the work being performed is that as features are being built or modified, they may impact work that was performed in previous sprints. Take, for instance, the weather web part that displays a single icon and temperature for a location. The time it takes to load may be 0.1 seconds, which is acceptable. In a later sprint, there may be a need to make the weather web part display up to 20 locations at a time, increasing the load time to 5 seconds. This performance may not be acceptable anymore and would result in additional rework to make the results load faster or provide an alternative to a blank web part, such as a spinning icon.

When testing the solutions being developed, it's important to strike a balance in the amount of testing being performed. You may not want to have the team test functionality that is inherent to Office 365 because it has been thoroughly tested by Microsoft before releasing these items. At the same time, it's important to understand how such features are interacted with or modified as part of any customizations. Depending on the user needs and functionality being introduced, there are several types of testing that you should consider for the team. Not all will apply in every case, but it's important to be aware of them:

- **Load testing** ensures that the system is still able to perform under expected load, such as simultaneous number of users or requests for information.
- **Performance testing** to determine the responsiveness of the system and stability under specific workloads. Performance testing typically produces quantitative results that can be compared to predefined goals.
- **Penetration testing** to evaluate the security of the system. Penetration testing is typically performed using simulated attacks on the system. The goal is to identify any vulnerabilities that may allow unauthorized access to features and data.
- **Accessibility testing** is used by organizations that must provide an accessible work environment for its employees. Accessibility testing ensures compliance to protocols, such as Web Content Accessibility Guidelines (WCAG) 2.0.[5]
- **Compatibility testing** to confirm that the solution functions as expected on various operating systems and browsers.

Due to the short development and testing cycles, where the entire Scrum team aims to deliver production-ready code at the end of each sprint, developers are encouraged to think more like testers, whereby they continuously check their code, while testers are encouraged to think like developers and go beyond the typical destructive testing tendencies.

There are times when there simply isn't enough time to correct all the defects raised by the testers. Therefore, it is prudent to plan to have at least one testing sprint that is solely devoted to issue remediation. If all goes well and the effort to fix all the issues doesn't fill up the sprint, then the team could elect to work on some items from the backlog. It would have to be agreed upon with the product owner that these backlog items would be stretch goals, assuming the team has the capacity to work on them to avoid any feature creep mid-sprint.

[5]Web Content Accessibility Guidelines (WCAG) 2.0, www.w3.org/tr/wcag20

Testing Environment

There are mixed opinions on where to test solutions that are being developed. Having a dedicated testing environment in a separate Office 365 tenant, as shown in Figure 9-10, provides the testers and developers with a common place where the latest changes can be deployed to without having to worry about any potential impact to the production environment.

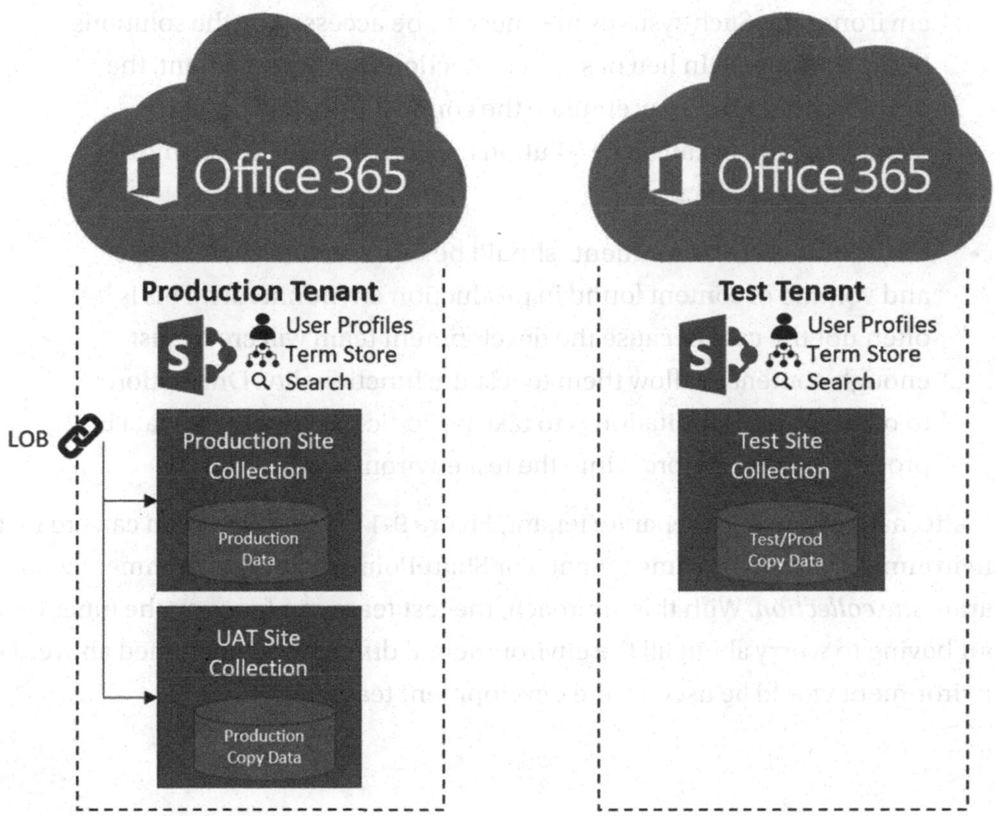

***Figure 9-10.** Separate Office 365 tenants being used for production and testing*

One of the main challenges of using a separate tenant is that the overall setup of the production environment is not the same. Some of the common gaps include

- **Licenses** cost money. Rather than assigning licenses to users in test environments, some organizations will try to avoid the extra cost. When registering for a new tenant, users get a 30-day trial before needing to spend any money, but that is rarely enough time for the development and testing to complete.

- **User accounts** may be handled using different mechanisms. For example, the corporate production tenant may leverage Azure Active Directory accounts, while the test tenant may use the basic Office 365 accounts. Both types of accounts are just as relevant when it comes to accessing the system. However, the way user profile properties are not the same, which could impact the solutions being built.
- **Line-of-business systems** may be connected to the production environment. Such systems may need to be accessed by the solutions being developed. In lieu of such connections in the test tenant, the development team may emulate the connections. This poses an element of risk because the solution may not be fully tested until deployed to production.
- **Content** in test environments should be representative of the type and volume of content found in production environments. This is often not the case because the development team will create just enough content to allow them to test the functionality. One option to overcome this limitation is to take periodic backups of the data in production and restore it into the test environment.

An alternative to using a separate tenant, Figure 9-11 depicts how you can create a test environment within the same tenant. For SharePoint, the test environment would be a separate *site collection*. With this approach, the test team can focus on the functionality without having to worry about all the environmental differences mentioned above. The test environment would be used by the development team only.

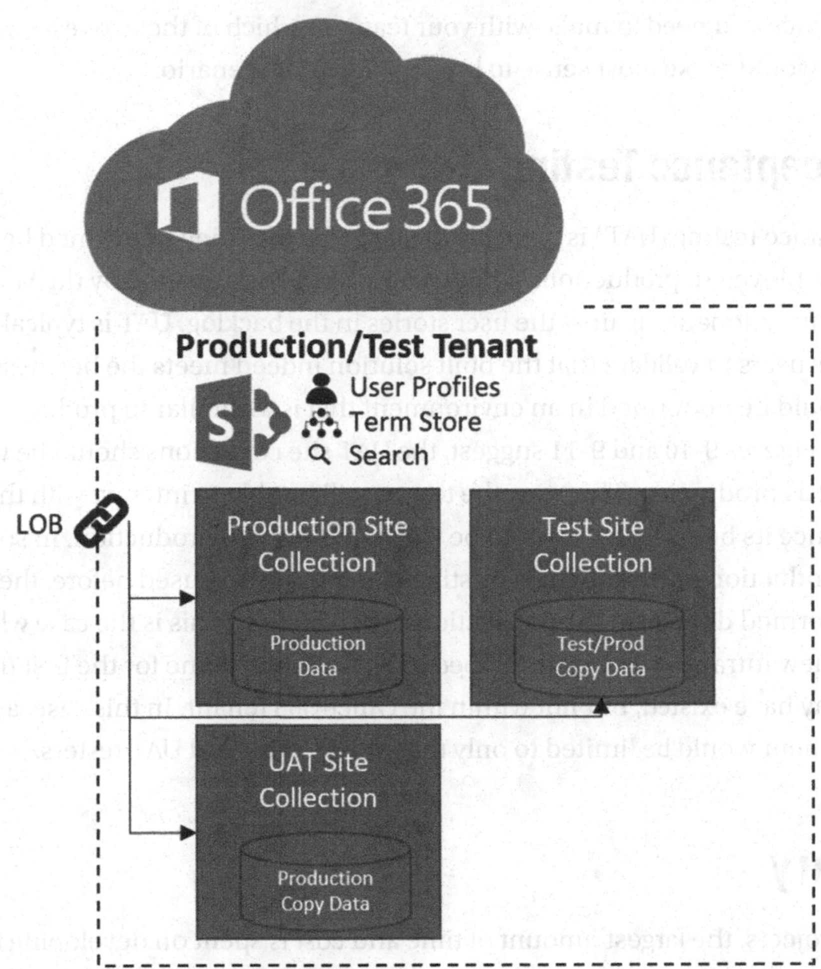

***Figure 9-11.** Single Office 365 tenants being used for production and testing*

Caution Some services in Office 365 and SharePoint Online are configured and managed at the tenant level, such as the User Profile Service, Term Store, and Search. If the solution will introduce changes to these services, then it's best to handle them as their own release and thoroughly test them out separately before deploying the full solution to the production environment.

There may be some initial effort required to connect all the different pieces to the test site collection (environment), but ideally that should only be required once for set up.

It is a choice you need to make with your team on which of the two test environment approaches would make most sense to leverage for your scenario.

User Acceptance Testing

User acceptance testing (UAT) is typically the last type of testing performed before a solution is deployed to production. While quality testing is executed by the Scrum team to verify the functionality against the user stories in the backlog, UAT is typically run by a few business users to validate that the built solution indeed meets the business needs.

UAT should be performed in an environment that is as similar to production as possible. As Figures 9-10 and 9-11 suggest, the UAT site collections should be within the same tenant as production. This way, the testers will be able to interact with the solution and experience its behavior as it would be when deployed to production. In some cases, when the production environment is pristine and hasn't been used before, then the UAT may be performed directly in the production site collection. This is the case when, for example, a new intranet is being developed in SharePoint Online for the first time. Other intranets may have existed, but not within the Office 365 tenant. In this case, access to the environment would be limited to only the project team and UAT testers.

Summary

For many projects, the largest amount of time and cost is spent on developing the solutions. As a project lead, you want to ensure that the team is on the right track and is making the right decisions around how the solutions are getting built, tested, and deployed.

In this chapter, we looked at the type of customizations often found in SharePoint sites, how they get developed, and important considerations around the various testing approaches. Rather than giving you a deep understanding of the various technologies, my goal was to skim the surface and help you understand some of the important considerations when planning an agile project in Office 365 that requires custom development.

This chapter concludes part 3 of the book around the execution of the sprint model. In the next chapter, we'll look at the activities that follow the sprints, which are required to properly deploy the solution to production and transition the project to the operations team.

PART IV

Deployment

CHAPTER 10

Training

The need for training of new products or releases is usually easy to explain. However, for some reason training often doesn't get the required level of funding and focus required.

Training, as a whole, is a broad topic that covers many areas from your Office 365 tenant administration to the end users. There are many ways to deliver training to your organization. Although there are no wrong approaches, there are likely ones that will work better from one project or organization to another. This chapter is dedicated to discussing how training fits into your overall Office 365 project.

The Need for Training

There are many studies over the years that highlight the value of providing proper systems training. Training will often mean the difference between success and failure with potential catastrophic results. Imagine you're boarding a new Boeing 787 Dreamliner to go to your favorite vacation destination. Now, imagine that the pilot is a young person who learned how to command a plane using their Xbox flight simulator. Would you feel safe taking that flight?

Training (or lack thereof) can have a significant impact when rolling out new technology into an organization. By providing your users with the required training on systems that will impact their day-to-day work tasks, you're enabling them to remain at least as efficient as they were before. Without such training, you will leave your users wondering how such changes will impact them and may result in increased frustration and lowered morale. It's therefore no surprise that rollouts of great technologies have failed in the past due to a lack of understanding by the users rather than the systems not achieving what they were set out to do.

H. Croitoru, *Agile Office 365*, https://doi.org/10.1007/978-1-4842-4081-6_10

It is not sufficient to put together some quick materials just for the sake of saying that training was delivered. Your training goals should be clearly defined prior to any time being invested in planning, developing, and delivering training to your organization. In order to measure training impact, you should ask yourself the following four questions:

1. How did the attendees feel about the training experience? Have their training needs been met, or were there gaps in expectations?
2. Has the attendees' general Office 365 or specific solution knowledge level increased between the start and end of the training sessions?
3. Have attendees adopted the new information taught to them in their day-to-day job? Are they doing anything different on their job?
4. Are there measurable business benefits as a result of the training? Do employees perform tasks faster or with higher accuracy as a result of the new system and accompanying training?

By capturing information about these questions, you will be able to direct iterative improvements to the training materials and facilitation.

Creating a Training Plan

I'm sure that by now you agree that providing the proper training to your users should be mandatory. Great! Part of your overall project plan should include a training plan. As you may recall from Chapter 3, training is one of the areas that does not follow the typical sprint model, as shown in Figure 10-1.

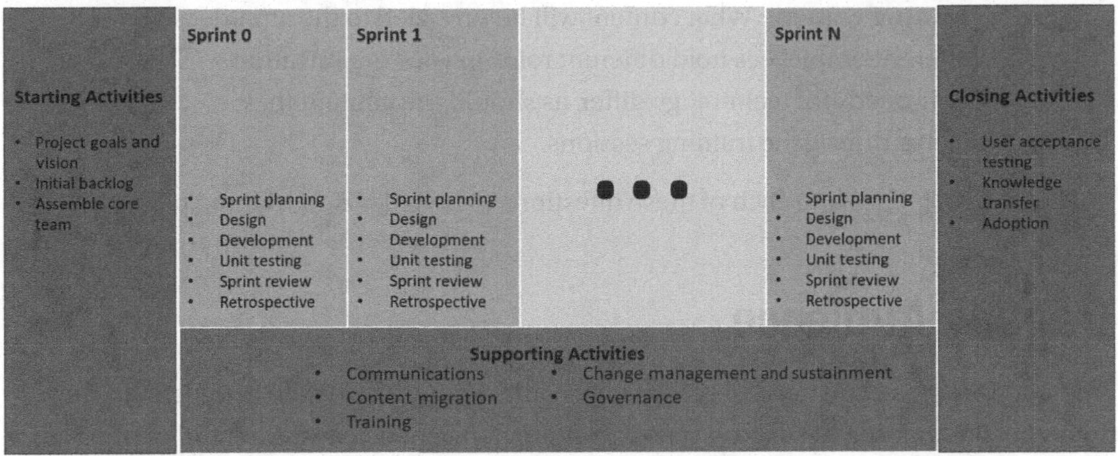

***Figure 10-1.** Office 365 agile project management process*

The reason for not having individual training session after each sprint is that it takes time to prepare training materials and, as you learned in Chapter 2, it's entirely possible that some features or functionality may change from sprint to sprint. In some cases, leveraging outdated training materials can actually be worse than not providing users with any materials because there is a level of trust by the user when you hand them official training documentation. In the absence of any materials, users may go explore and find solutions themselves.

When you prepare a training plan, you need to answer the following five questions to ensure that you're covering all the necessary bases:

1. **Training audience**: Who are you delivering the training to? Is there anything specific you need to know about their location, knowledge, or anything else?
2. **Training formats**: In what form will training be delivered to its audience? Will you be leveraging a single format for everyone or several formats based on the needs?
3. **Training locations**: Related to the training formats, you need to think about where training will be delivered. Will training take place in person, via virtual meetings, or independent learning? There are benefits and shortcomings to each of these methods.
4. **Training times**: When will training be delivered to your users? Will it be a one-time event for a release or do you envision having numerous training sessions that attendees can attend at their will?

5. **Training content**: What content will be provided to the attendees? Different employees hold different roles in your organization. Their needs for technology differ, as should the content they receive during the training sessions.

Let's dive deeper into each of these questions to help devise a training plan.

Training Audience

First and foremost, you need to get to know your training audience. By understanding their specific training needs, you stand a better change of delivering a training program that is most impactful to them. Here are a few things to consider about your audience.

Location

Where your users are located plays an important role in the training delivery. Many employees like to get the personal attention and instruction of a skilled trainer. While this can work well for an organization where most employees are co-located, it may not be feasible for a geographically dispersed organization.

Domain Knowledge

Try to understand the depth of knowledge your users have around the technology that is being implemented and its impacts on the business. With this information, you can help cater the training materials so they will provide your users with just the right amount of information to keep them engaged without overwhelming them with content they already know or is way too deep for what they need to know.

Role

Every user has a specific role within the organization. Delivering a generic set of training to all users provides less value than having role-specific training. On the flip side, it is not feasible to create a unique set of training materials for each individual role. It is up to you and your training team to identify some logical user groups to give them the training tools they require and benefit most from without inundating them with information that is irrelevant to them.

Table 10-1 provides an example of role-based training for an organization that is rolling out Microsoft Teams for internal projects.

Table 10-1. *Role-Based Training for Microsoft Teams*

Role	Activities	Focus areas
Team admin	Administer service, govern teams	Office 365 Admin Center, licensing, global settings
Team owner	Create teams, manage users, manage connectors and team permissions	Manage teams, members, channels, settings, apps, connectors, member permissions, guest permissions, @mentions, fun stuff, apps
Team member	Participate in conversations, view and collaborate on documents	Conversation and Files tab, introduction to other tabs

You should also consider a staggered training approach, where each trainee at a higher level should be familiar with everything that the lower level understands plus the content being introduced for their level. This means that for the scenario described in Table 10-1, team members should only attend team member training. Team owners, in turn, should attend the team member and team owner training, while the team admins should attend all the training sessions (assuming they haven't gone through this type of training previously).

Availability for Training

Wouldn't it be nice if each time a project is rolled out, the organization can take a few days to get trained on it? In reality, the amount of time available for training is often short and can vary based on the role of your users. Furthermore, the amount of dedicated, uninterrupted focus time may direct you towards non-real-time training where users can do as much as they are able to at a given point in time.

If your users are co-located, then bringing them together for a focused training session is often more effective because attendees can benefit from questions asked by others to learn about new changes.

Training Formats

You don't have to look hard to see that there is an entire industry built specifically around training for Office 365 and related products. The amount of content is mind-boggling and varies in form, length, depth, and content. To give you a rough idea of what is available for training, a simple search for *Office 365 training* in my favorite search engine returned over 38,300,000 results! Granted, not all of these materials are relevant and there's likely lots of duplication. However, there's a very good chance that you will find what you are looking for through a quick search.

There are several training formats available, each with their own advantages and disadvantages. Offering a mix of these training formats is best because different users have their own preferences for learning. Generally speaking, you can group these formats into three areas: live, self-directed, and social.

Live Training

With live training, there is a predefined time period and agenda provided for the training session. Attendees may have some materials provided to them as the training facilitator walks them through the session. If you're planning on having someone on the team deliver training to your team, then it's important to consider who the audience will be, where they will be, and how many will be in attendance. Delivering a training session to three people from the same department who are sitting next to you is very different from delivering the same material to a group of 30 that are distributed and have different needs and levels of understanding. One way to deal with a larger training crowd and varying needs is through the use of champions.

Champions are individuals within the organization who have a heightened level of understanding as well as a keen interest in helping their peers work more efficiently. Through the use of champions, the task for training a large organization can be broken down into several levels where each training group is small and focused on very specific content. Figure 10-2 provides a simple example where a single trainer trains three IT staff members. These three individuals then train a group of champions who, in turn, train members in their peer group.

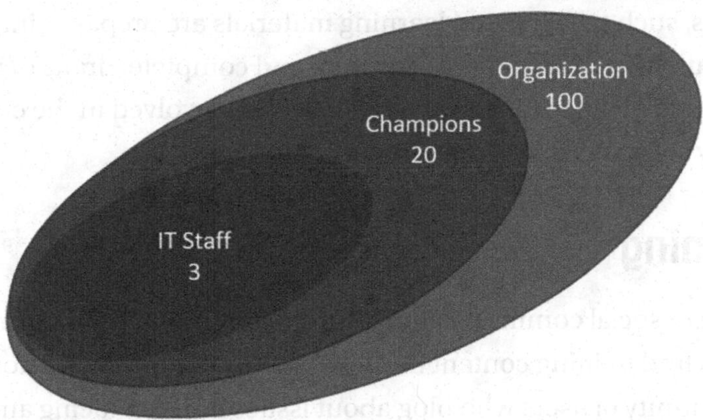

Figure 10-2. *Leveraging training champions to break down the size of training sessions*

Keep in mind that these champions are helping out of goodwill or some incentive. Training is often not their core skillset. Therefore, the individual(s) responsible for creating the training programs need to work closely with these champions in order to provide them with the materials they need to be successful.

Tip Always record live training sessions. They provide free reference materials to your users.

Self-Directed Learning

Self-directed learning enables participants to partake in training activities at their own pace and from whatever location they are in. The formats for self-directed learning are in written form or one or more prerecorded audio or video recordings.

- **Written training materials** usually come in the form of user manuals or slide shows. These materials are not difficult to create because the author has a chance to write the training package in pieces and make changes as the materials get created.

- **Prerecorded materials** are similar to the written materials but are provided in the form of audio or video recordings. With prerecorded materials, more work goes into the preparation because the author needs to ensure that the quality is good. It's not easy to modify a recording or make changes in the middle of a narration.

In many cases, such self-directed learning materials are prepared internally by staff members. To ensure that the content is accurate and complete, drafts of materials should be reviewed by some of the technical people who were involved in the creation and rollout of the new solutions to validate the content.

Social Learning

With the increase of social communication and collaboration, it's becoming more and more common to find training content in such non-traditional forms. Today, you will find a large community of users who blog about issues they are facing and ways to overcome them, how-tos, and best practices. These scenarios may not always match your users' specific needs but can provide some benefits.

Other forms of social learning include leveraging communication networks such as Yammer. In this case, organization-specific groups or channels are formed for the purpose of discussing how-tos or FAQ information or for users to ask questions. These networks are a great way to surface up questions or areas of concern that may not have been initially considered when the training program was put together.

Training Locations

Training today is delivered either in person or online. In in-person training sessions, the individual facilitating the sessions is physically in the same location where the training is taking place. In online training, the trainer and attendees are not co-located.

Those born in the 70s and before are most familiar with their learning taking place in person. In-person learning is one of the best forms of initial training because it provides attendees the opportunity to seek immediate feedback for their questions. It is also the method that is most personable. It may sound funny, but in my years of consulting, I have found that users are often reluctant to reach out and ask questions and would shy away from trying something because of their perceived risk of "breaking the system." Having an actual person in front of them enables them to get that level of attention they need to answer their questions.

Providing in-person training, however, is not always feasible for an organization. Imagine you're ready to roll out the intranet for Happy People, and your users are spread across the globe with offices in Seychelles, Maldives, Bora Bora, Hawaii, and Fraser Island. The time to travel to all the locations and the cost is extensive and expensive. In this scenario, you should consider leveraging online training methods.

Online training is delivered over the Web. When properly set up, they can help in making the virtual presence seem almost in person using audio and video equipment. With webinars, your users in each location could co-locate or work out of their own personal spaces. Trainers could be located in one specific corporate location or be remotely working out of their own offices.

Tip Make sure to consider the time zones your users are in when planning to deliver live online training sessions.

Training Times

I'm a lifelong learner. No matter how many courses I've taken, books I've read, and certifications I've received, there's always more knowledge to be acquired. This is particularly true when working in an environment such as Office 365, where new apps and updates to existing ones are regularly rolled out.

With the new Happy People Office 365 rollout planned later in the year, you may be wondering what training would be best for the team. Table 10-2 provides an example of the types of training activities you should consider.

Table 10-2. *Training Time Recommendation for an Office 365 Rollout*

Objectives	Scenario	Training time	Participation	Goals
Increase awareness of Office 365	New roll-out of Office 365 into an organization. At this point, Office 365 is in transition as users are being onboarded to the new platform.	Soon after the project has been announced	All employees should have access to a live presentation or prerecorded webinar.	There's always some level of angst when new technology is being rolled out as users may wonder how it will impact their day-to-day work. The goal of the initial training is to reduce some of that fear.

(*continued*)

Table 10-2. *(continued)*

Objectives	Scenario	Training time	Participation	Goals
Obtain familiarity in Office 365	Office 365 access has been provided to users; basic out-of-the-box functionality has been made available.	After users have been made aware that they now have access to Office 365	All employees should have access to a live presentation or prerecorded webinar.	Give users an opportunity to try out some simple tasks while being walked through the process. Combining this training session with some quizzes can help gauge the level of understanding and quality of the materials being provided.
Learn job-specific skills	Users are required to start using Office 365 for their daily tasks.	After the basic training session have been completed or before new custom solutions in Office 365 are being rolled out	Individuals from specific working areas or with needs for specific apps	Enable training attendees to gain the necessary skills in Office 365 to benefit their work
Boost productivity	Office 365 and custom solutions are now the official method for working within the organization.	Office 365 and custom solutions have been fully rolled out within the organization; users have a working knowledge of the tools.	Individuals from specific working areas or with needs for specific apps	Further advance user skills to leverage much of the functionality needed for them to complete their work more efficiently
Skills mastery	Office 365 and custom solutions have been adopted and there's a continued drive for improvements.	Office 365 and custom solutions are being used correctly; users are asking what else they can do with the platform.	Advanced users who wish to become champions in their domain	Create a Center of Excellence where champions can contribute to help the long-term training needs of the organization

Training is time consuming. Not everyone will find value in these sessions and many may try to shy away from it. At times, that may be fine. However, in some scenarios training should be mandatory as it can impact the quality of work with potentially terrible results.

Consider a simple scenario where Happy People needs to share a document with one of their happy clients. A training session has been provided that teaches your users how to send documents via secure links so only specific users can open them. But rather than sharing via a link, an employee has sent the document as an email attachment. To make things worse, you find out later that the email attachment contained personal information from another client, including name, credit card information, and more.

When mandatory training sessions are being created, you need to have a way to determine who completed the training and what they learned. One way to do this is by providing short quizzes at the end of a training session that cover the material.

Tip Consider using Microsoft Forms (`https://forms.office.com`) for quiz creation. They're quick to put together and can be automatically graded by the system.

These quizzes get stored together with the person completing them and a timestamp. You can even build entire workflows for tracking multi-step training programs to see where each attendee is in the process.

Training Content

So far, we've covered many aspects of the training program you need to think about when preparing an Office 365 training plan. In this final section, let's have a look at what you need to consider when preparing the content. Your users will differ in background, skills, and way in which they learn. Providing them with a menu of training options is best.

First Stop: Microsoft

Microsoft offers an extensive set of free training documentation and videos online for all its products. I'm not suggesting that this will provide you with the materials you you're looking for 100% of the time, but there's a good chance that you can use a lot of the base information on the Microsoft Support sites. Some of the more common ones are listed in Table 10-3.

Table 10-3. *Microsoft Official Training Resources for Office 365*

Site	Link	Description
Microsoft Support	`https://support.office.com`	The Support site includes information on how the various products work and instructions on performing tasks.
LinkedIn Learning	`https://learning.linkedin.com`	Provides video courses at all levels from beginner to advanced
Microsoft Virtual Academy	`https://mva.microsoft.com`	Course-based learning where you can create your own training program and even receive certifications
Microsoft Docs	`https://docs.microsoft.com`	The home for Microsoft technical documentation, API reference, code examples, quickstarts, and tutorials for developers and IT professionals
Microsoft Hands-on Labs	`www.microsoft.com/handsonlabs`	On this site, users can practice with the latest cloud products and services in a live environment and advance their cloud skills for free.
Microsoft Office 365 Training Center	`https://support.office.com/en-us/office-training-center`	Lets users create their own training programs for various Office 365 apps using Microsoft materials

In addition to the Microsoft official sites, there are some popular blog sites where many members from the community come together to discuss products, approaches, issues, and other topics. Some of the blogs that focus more on Microsoft technologies are listed in Table 10-4.

Table 10-4. *Popular Blog Sites Containing Office 365 Content*

Site	Link	Description
Microsoft Tech Community	`https://techcommunity.microsoft.com/`	This blog site is managed by Microsoft and includes content from many product evangelists, users, and other community members. The content is grouped into spaces for the various products as well as more general domain knowledge, including Azure, Developing Cloud, Diversity and Tech, Adoption, and many more.
Microsoft Power Users Community	`https://powerusers.microsoft.com`	This community blog focuses primarily on Power BI, PowerApps, Microsoft Flow, and Microsoft Stream. There are lots of great examples of how to perform certain tasks and improvements for these products.

Your users and project team members will likely gravitate to some of these sites more than others to fill their knowledge gaps, which is not uncommon. Just keep in mind that depending on the source, the information may not be completely accurate.

As mentioned, the number of hits I got when searching for Office 365 training was very large. There are many independent companies that provide great training solutions. Some organizations offer prepackaged training modules or engagements for the various Office 365 products and services. Others can customize the training to your organization's specific needs. As the need of every project and organization differs, I recommend you look into these companies based on your specific training needs.

Microsoft FastTrack

For organizations that have 50 or more active Office 365 Enterprise or Office 365 Business users, Microsoft offers FastTrack (`https://fasttrack.microsoft.com`), a service that provides personalized assistance to help IT professionals and partners get onto Office 365. When organizations engage in FastTrack, they typically go through three stages:

1. **Envison**: Initial discussions focus on defining the goals for Office 365 rollout and identify materials to assist in the process.
2. **Onboard**: Through the use of digital resources, users are able to engage with Microsoft engineers to receive remote assistance.
3. **Drive value**: Leverage best practices, tools, and guides geared towards the specific needs of your users in their various roles.

FastTrack is also available to government or non-profit organizations using Office 365.

Customizing Training Materials

Leveraging generic training materials is definitely a great way to get your training program off the ground. Much of the functionality that your users will need can be found in such references, such as an introduction to the various apps and how to perform simple tasks.

There are times when those materials will not suffice. Maybe your organization has created customizations, such as a sleek intranet, or is leveraging some of the apps in a unique way. In those scenarios, you need to look at creating custom training materials. As mentioned, the two common formats are written and audio/video.

Written training materials are usually simple to create because the author has a chance to write the training package in pieces and make changes as the materials gets created. Once the draft has been created, it's important to have it peer reviewed by some of the technical people who were involved in the creation and rollout of the new solutions to validate the content. Consider having different versions of the document for the various roles.

When creating recordings, you need to ensure that the content is not only accurate, but also captivating and easy to follow. In the past, having an expert talk through an entire video used to work. However, with technology, training needs have changed. You should consider the following tips when leading creation of training videos for your organization.

Content Should Be Easy to Follow

Remember that the person who is creating the training video is usually more knowledgeable than the person who is viewing the content. Avoid using industry jargon and too many technical terms. Keep the language easy and simple to follow. After the expert has finished writing the script, ask someone who is non-technical to review the script and highlight any areas that need clarification.

Choose Your Narrator Carefully

A person who is technically strong may not be great at presenting the content. Being recorded while reading a script can cause some people to feel stressed, awkward, or uncomfortable in front of the camera. If finding an expert who is good in front of the camera proves difficult for you, have the experts spend time to personally training someone who will be better for the recording.

Promote Self-Directed Learning

Imagine having a video that is an hour or more in length. Following it would be painful for the users and there's a good chance that most users would never see the end. Rather than creating one large video, consider breaking it down into shorter videos that are no more than 5 minutes in length. Each video should touch on a very specific topic with a clear start and finish that doesn't depend on other videos. At the end of the video, provide references to related materials your users may be interested in. Different users will likely go down a different path based on their specific needs.

Use a Clear Naming Convention

By carefully naming your videos, you're making it easy to look at a list of videos and have your users pinpoint the one they need. Furthermore, if your videos are stored in Office 365, then users will be able to search for them easily by name. Rather than calling a video *Training Video #35*, consider using a more meaningful name, such as *Office 365 How-To Video #35 - Sending email attachments via secure links.*

Organize Videos in a Logical Manner

Whether it's by app, department, or other grouping, it helps users to get to the materials they need to quickly.

Tip Consider using Microsoft Stream (`https://stream.microsoft.com/en-us/`) for storing your training videos.

Keep Introductions Short

It doesn't make sense to have a long introduction about Office 365 and the narrator's background at the start of each video. Although it may be great for self-promotion, think about the person who is viewing the videos. What they're looking for is targeted content, not fluff. Try keeping the intro to a single page/slide that lasts no more than 5 seconds. The only purpose of this slide is to let users know that they are watching the right video.

Get to the Point

There's no need to highlight how great Office 365 is or even the purpose of specific apps. Keep it short by only mentioning what the video itself will cover. For example, *This video will demonstrate how to get a secure link for a document stored in your intranet or OneDrive and share the link via email with recipients outside the organization.* Notice how in this example there is no mention of Office 365, how Outlook works, or even SharePoint as the intranet? Yet the viewer will still know what they're getting from this video.

Show the Content, not the Narrator

Sometimes there's a benefit to showing the narrator in the video. But what the audience is usually most interested in is the content itself. Rather than keeping the narrator on the screen for long periods of time, show the content they are discussing. This way, your users will benefit from hearing what the narrator is talking about while seeing it in front of them.

Use Close-Ups

At times, your screens may be busy with lots of content and widgets that can get distracting to the viewers, especially if they are moving or changing in any way. Therefore, focus the video on the specific part of the screen that is most relevant to the topic of discussion in the video. For example, when talking about the document link sharing functionality, there's no point showing the entire screen, as shown in Figure 10-3.

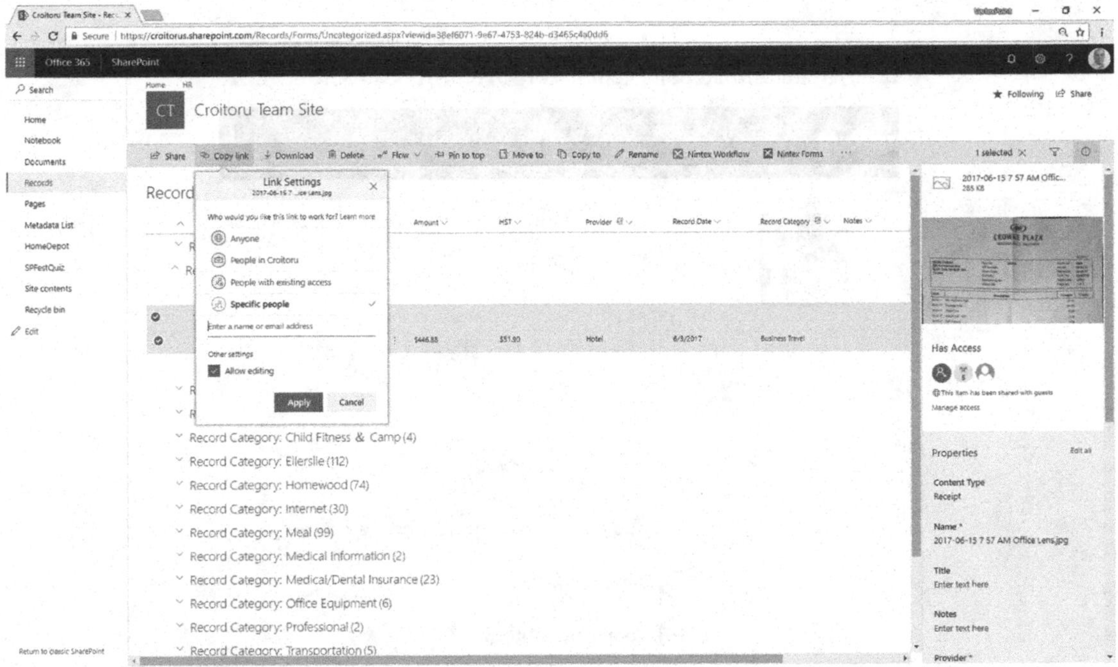

Figure 10-3. The focus area of the video is too wide for the topic being discussed

It's better to keep the video focused on the part that the user is concerned with, as demonstrated in Figure 10-4.

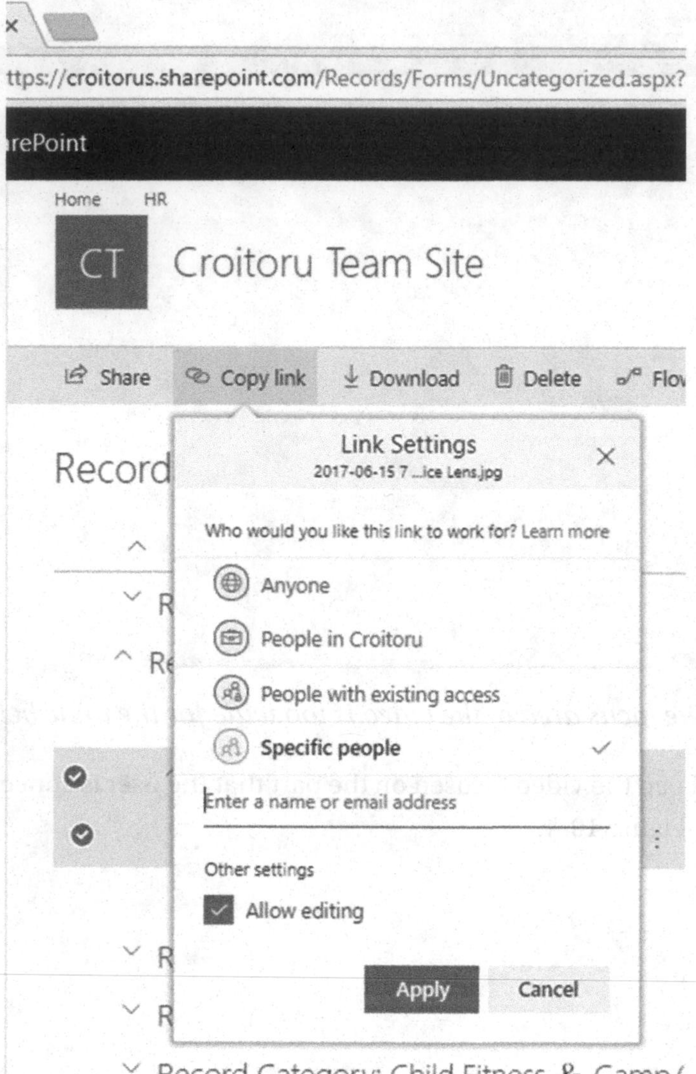

***Figure 10-4.** Close-up of the content most relevant for the topic of a video*

Leverage Additional Visual Clues

Some content can't always be explained easily in a video. In those cases, consider using additional visual representations to get the message across, such as slides, diagrams, or animations. For example, if you want to give users an understanding of how their new intranet portal is structured, you can leverage a mind map or organizational chart, as shown in Figure 10-5.

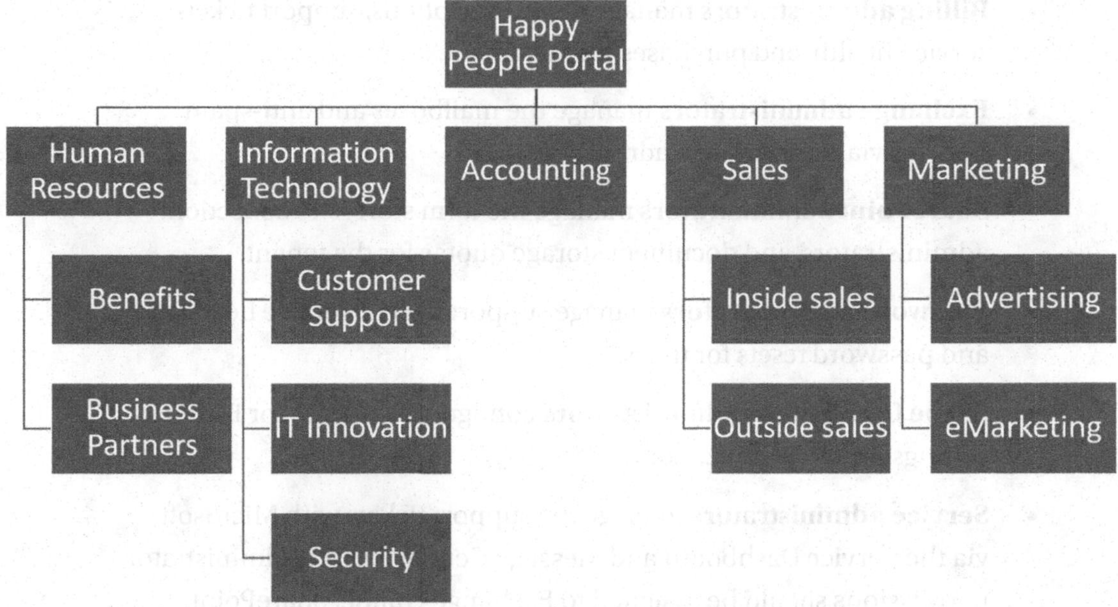

Figure 10-5. *Leveraging additional visual clues to convey information in training videos*

Role-Specific Training

Your organization is made up of employees that have different business roles. The skills required for these roles will overlap to some degree. In addition, several of the apps in Office 365 have a number of admin roles associated with them. So how do you devise a program that works best for your staff? To optimize the training experience for your users, training programs should be catered to specific business and admin roles. Below are some examples of Office 365 admin roles as well as business roles you should consider planning for in your Office 365 training.

Office 365 Admin Training

Office 365 tenant administrators are responsible for managing the technical and licensing elements of your tenant. There are ten administrator roles that can be assigned to users inside the organization. Each of these roles will provide users with specific abilities to manage specific elements of your tenant:

- **Global administrators** have full administrative control over the entire Office 365 tenant. They are the only ones who have the ability to grant admin roles to other users.

- **Billing administrators** manage the subscriptions, support tickets, service health, and purchases for the tenant.
- **Exchange administrators** manage the mailboxes and anti-spam policies via the Exchange admin center.
- **SharePoint administrators** manage the term store, site collection administrators, and document storage quotas for the tenant.
- **Password administrators** manage support tickets, service health, and password resets for users.
- **Skype for Business administrators** configure the Skype for Business settings for the organization.
- **Service administrators** manage the support tickets with Microsoft via the Service Dashboard and Message Center. Service administrator permissions should be assigned to Exchange Online, SharePoint Online, and Skype for Business. Admin roles should also be assigned to the service admin role so they can see the health of the service, and change and release notifications.
- **User management administrators** manage user accounts, Office 365 group memberships, and can reset passwords and monitor service health and support tickets.
- **Report readers** can view all activity reports in the Office 365 admin center.
- **Security and compliance center roles** are available in Office 365 E3 and E5 subscriptions. The roles defined under this category are compliance administrator, eDiscovery manager, organization management, reviewer, security administrator, security reader, service assurance user, and supervisory review. All of these roles play a role in configuring and monitoring of security and compliance in your tenant.

As you can see from the descriptions above, there is some overlap in the roles, but each role has unique tasks defined for it. To keep the training focused and relevant, it's therefore best to customize the training materials for each admin role.

IT Admin Training

Besides the Office 365 admin roles defined above, which cover some of the apps, there are additional app-level admin roles that are typically handled by IT, including

- **OneDrive admins** determine whom content can be shared with, how much storage each user has, and what devices can access the content. OneDrive admins can also set up notifications when links to content are shared externally.
- **Yammer admins** configure the design, usage policy, and network configurations.
- **PowerApps admins** can manage data policies users and view reports on PowerApps user licenses and quotas.
- **Flow admins** can manage data policies users and view reports on Flow user licenses and quotas.

Providing admin training for these apps is important if they are being rolled out and the groups supporting them need to gain more knowledge around them.

App Admin Training

At this level you're in the app itself. App admins may be responsible for managing a subset of the functionality with the app. Such tasks are often handled by power users or champions that are part of specific business groups. Some examples of app-specific admin training are

- **Office 365 Group owners** can perform all tasks in Office 365 Groups. Office 365 Group owners can assign other users to become owners as well.
- **Microsoft team owners** can perform all tasks on a team, including managing the users, connectors, channels, and other settings. Team owners can assign other users to become owners as well.
- **SharePoint site collection admins** have full control over the specific site collection they are assigned to.

This type of training can be reused between different business groups for the most part. However, at times, training materials may include some governance-related content. In those cases, you need to carefully assess what governing rules are applied and determine whether or not they apply to different groups within the organization.

End User Training

End user training is the area that needs the most attention because it includes the largest audience and variety of use. Let's take Yammer as an example. To administer the app is straightforward, with a predefined set of available options. However, different departments may use Yammer for different purposes and in different ways. While one department may use Yammer groups for their day-to-day communication purposes, other departments may rely on Yammer only for posting business-related how-to information.

Another common example is for intranets. In the case of Happy People, there is a specific group of users responsible for posting curated content, such as news, industry updates, and events to the home page. This group typically consists of communications or marketing users. In order to post the content, the users need to understand the content creation and publishing process and life cycle. The rest of the organization doesn't need to be concerned with these details and only needs to know how to consume the content.

The bottom line is that you need to map out all the types of training required based on what is being rolled out. While the Office 365 tenant admin, IT admin, and to some degree app admin training can be mostly fulfilled by existing Microsoft content, specific uses of the app admin role as well as end user training materials will contain the majority of custom training content.

Center of Excellence

Training is an activity that your users should and will engage in on an ongoing basis. As the use of Office 365 and the number of unique customizations and special uses increases, so will the amount of training materials. It's therefore a good idea to establish a Training Center of Excellence for your organization.

The Training Center of Excellence provides users with the resources, best practices, support, and research on various areas to help them improve their productivity. Your Training Center of Excellence should include a collection of all the training materials that have been created to date as well as links or reference libraries to external training materials. To make it easy to find content, group your content in a way that will be logical for your users, such as by organizational structure (e.g. department, functional group, division) or task (e.g. how-tos).

You want to ensure that your training materials will provide accurate guidance for your users. Therefore, it's best to establish a training governance board that will periodically review the training content and determine if any of the content needs a refresh.

Tip Consider setting up a Flow that will notify the training content owners once training materials have reached a certain age.

Summary

Training needs to be included as part of a rollout plan for Office 365. There are a number of factors that determine how training is delivered, such as the user's technical knowledge and location, preference for training formats, where the organization is in the Office 365 adoption, and more. To address the training needs for your organization, start by creating a training plan to help answer some of these questions and devise training materials and delivery that will aid in the success of your rollouts.

Once initial training has been delivered to the organization, you can then focus on the remaining activities for rolling out the solution into production. This is the topic of the next chapter.

CHAPTER 11

Release Planning

Congratulations for getting this far in leading the customization efforts of Office 365 for your client. At this point, you and your team will have built out and tested what is required for your users. The next step in the overall process is to put it into production. To make this process as smooth as possible, you need to carefully plan your release.

In this chapter, I'll introduce the concept of release planning and I'll touch on several important activities that you need to undertake as part of a release. By the end, you will be equipped with a high-level checklist that includes the various activities and also identifies key stakeholders involved in this process.

What Is Release Planning?

In Chapters 2 and 4, I introduced the concept of the backlog and sprint planning. At the start of the project, a backlog is created to determine the minimal amount of functionality required for a shippable product. During sprint planning, you establish goals for each sprint based on the backlog and work towards that initial goal. Based on the team's velocity, you are able to determine how much work they can complete within a sprint and plan for completing the work. This is one of the key drivers for when a release can take place. But there are other factors that can impact your release dates.

Releases can sometimes be influenced by events that are outside the project and are "fixed," such as fiscal year end for using up a budget, industry or corporate events, or other contractual obligations. Imagine a CTO has made a commitment to roll out the new Office 365 intranet and communication platform to a multi-national organization with close to 100,000 employees. Everyone is waiting with anticipation and high hopes of improving how they work. Now imagine yourself telling that CTO that you need another two sprints to complete the work because of the sprint's velocity. Those scenarios are never easy to deal with and as a strong project lead, you can help mitigate.

H. Croitoru, *Agile Office 365*, https://doi.org/10.1007/978-1-4842-4081-6_11

The reality is that your initial release plan rarely satisfies all stakeholders, where more functionality is expected in less time. As an agile project lead, you need to navigate around these obstacles and map out a release schedule that will be realistic and will satisfy most stakeholders. With an agile framework, your stakeholders can see parts of the product come to life early on rather than waiting for all the work to be completed.

Remember that the goal is not to create mega-releases of new solutions. When you are working in an agile project management framework, having shorter release cycles is recommended. This will help you provide your users with a working solution faster. The important part here is to communicate to your users continuous improvement over time.

For some key stakeholders, you can (and should) involve them at the end of each iteration so they can see the incremental progress. This will help increase their confidence that your release will happen as planned or provide support to communicate any potential gaps or "deviations from the course." Let's see what is involved in building a release plan.

When I ask some project leads what is required in releasing a solution, the answer I usually get is around the software itself. But, as you'll discover shortly, there is a lot more that needs to be considered to make a software rollout truly successful.

In agile projects, you should expect to plan early and adjust your plan often as needed. This also applies to release planning. One of the primary mechanisms for course correction is allowing the release plan to evolve in response to all kinds of feedback. It will take at least a couple of iterations for team velocity to normalize. Iterations will sometimes deliver less functionality than was planned, and sometimes more. Features, architectural choices, design choices, or framework and technology choices might prove to be too risky or simply unworkable. The user interface might require revision. Staff might be lost or added. Feature priorities could change. All of these factors will require you to revise and refine the release plan continuously. When each new iteration plan is published, you should also revise the release plan to reflect the new reality.

Deployment Document

The deployment document should serve as a recipe book that describes in sufficient detail how a technical solution is deployed into an Office 365 tenant. In this context, "sufficient" does not imply that you need to explain every configuration and customization option within Office 365. Below is a summary of several sections that any deployment document should include.

Prerequisites

What works well here is to identify all the prerequisites that a person needs to complete before starting a deployment. Depending on the type of solution you are creating, prerequisites typically fall into any of the following areas.

Domain Knowledge

There are many technologies that an Office 365 solution can touch. For an individual to perform a successful deployment, they must have the necessary domain knowledge to use key tools that are leveraged for a deployment. Such tools may include PowerShell, Azure, or Visual Studio Team Services (VSTS) (recently renamed to Azure DevOps). A deployment document should guide the user where such tools will be used, but should not educate the user on all the inner workings.

Tools

This one is fairly straightforward. When you leave on a trip, you make sure that you have enough gas, your GPS, and your favorite music for the road. The same holds true when you prepare for a deployment. All tools and the versions for each tool should be clearly documented. Stating prerequisites such as "PowerShell and .NET" is not specific enough because there are numerous versions of each and not all will work together.

Accounts

Since you are working in the cloud, you are working in an environment where most the actions are performed by authenticated users. For deployments, user accounts are always required for making any changes to the Office 365 configurations or apps. The deployment document should list what accounts you will be using and what permissions will be needed to complete the work

---

Caution Never store passwords in any document. This is particularly true in the deployment document due to the elevated permission levels for these accounts.

Office 365 Configurations

Before starting the deployment, you may have to change some configurations within your Office 365 tenant to authorize the deployment to take place without fail.

System Dependencies

The solution you are creating may need to interact with other solutions outside of Office 365. Any such dependencies need to be called out and the impact of not having them understood.

Deployment Package Contents

After the deployment environment has been set up, the person performing a deployment should confirm the contents of the deployment package. Each artifact that contributes to the deployment package, such as software modules, deployment scripts, or documents, should be clearly labeled with a version number so the user can be sure that they are deploying the correct version. A good way to document the deployment package is shown in Table 11-1.

Table 11-1. *Deployment Package Listing*

File name and path	Version	Date	Purpose
Happy People Intranet Deployment Guide.PDF	2.1	4/12/2018	Deployment guide for deploying the customizations to the new digital hub, including branding and the integration to the legacy HR system
Deploy.ps1	1.0	3/22/2018	Main deployment script to deploy the solution to the Office 365 tenant
/config/	1.0	3/20/2018	Folder containing the environment and configuration files used for the deployment
/config/Global.json	1.1	3/20/2018	Contains global information about templates to be provisioned and the package folder structure

Deployment Steps

Deployment steps are at the core of the deployment. They need to be descriptive enough so that it's easy to know what task is being performed and whether it succeeded or not. One way to achieve this is to write the deployment steps like a test plan. Table 11-2 provides an example of some scripts that the user will need to execute to connect to an Office 365 tenant, enable scripting, and enable content delivery network (CDN) on the tenant.

Table 11-2. *Documenting Deployment Steps*

#	Action	Notes
1	Open a PowerShell window as administrator on the deployment machine.	

2	Run the following commands after adjusting the tenant values to point to your tenant:
	`Connect-SPOservice -Url https://<tenant>-admin.sharepoint.com`
	`Set-SPOsite https://happypeople.sharepoint.com-DenyAddAndCustomizePages0`
		A login page may appear. If so, continue to log in as normal for your tenant

3	Run the following commands after adjusting the tenant values to point to your tenant: `Connect-SPOservice -Url https://<tenant>-admin.sharepoint.com`	A login page may appear. If so, continue to log in as normal for your tenant

4	Run the following commands to determine the status of the Office 365 CDN settings for this tenant:
	`Get-SPOTenantCdnEnabled -CdnType Public`
	`Get-SPOTenantCdnOrigins -CdnType Public`
	`Get-SPOTenantCdnPolicies -CdnType Public`
		These commands indicate the current CDN status of the tenant.

5	If the CDN is not already enabled, run the following command to enable the Office 365 CDN: `Set-SPOTenantCdnEnabled -CdnType Public`	It may take up to 15 minutes for the CDN to be enabled. You can check the status by running the GET commands from step 4.

Post-Deployment Activities

After the deployment has finished, there may be some additional steps required to complete the overall process, such as adding content or providing users with access to the new functionality. You should ensure that the deployment plan clearly states what these activities are, who performs them, and in what order they should be performed.

Back-Out Plan

As you will discover over time, not all deployments proceed as planned. There will be times when you are forced to back out of a deployed solution and restore the system to a previous stable state. Therefore, you must capture all the configurations, customizations, and content around the current state of the specific parts of Office 365 that your deployment is targeting and store this information in a way that you can use to restore the system to an earlier state.

Tip When possible, include version numbers in your solutions. This can help in case your team needs to dig into the inner workings of the specific version of the solution to resolve any issues.

Automating Deployments

Since the goal is to be agile, which involves multiple releases over a short amount of time, you need keep things as simple and quick as possible. The way to do this is to use some form of automation. In a perfect world, all deployment would be fully automated with the click of a button (such as in Continuous Deployments). However, often some steps must still be done manually.

Depending on the type of solution you are deploying, the number of steps and complexity can vary significantly. I have led deployments that were as simple as uploading a few new files that added new functionality to complex ones involving Azure, Flow, PowerApps, Power BI, and more for creating an entirely new SharePoint Online digital hub experience.

Since the early days of Office 365, Microsoft has invested heavily in providing administrators with management capabilities using PowerShell.[1] This scripting language lets administrators perform many common tasks without the need to interact with the user interface. As a result, the scripts can be combined into more complex sets of operations, including deployments in Office 365. Another important resource to consider is OfficeDev Patterns and Practices (PnP).[2] OfficeDev PnP is an open source initiative driven by community contributors to enhance the already-existing PowerShell functionality for SharePoint. There are even specific commands for provisioning SharePoint sites using the PnP framework.

With PowerShell and the OfficeDev PnP extensions, you have the freedom to automate much of your deployments.

SharePoint Site Deployment

Entire SharePoint site structures can be created and configured using the Office Dev PnP *Provisioning Templates*. The structures, or information architecture, can include the taxonomy, metadata fields, content types, lists and libraries, sites, and various settings for each of these elements.

Deploy Content

The apps in Office 365 are tools to help you store and manage your content. So, when a new solution is rolled out into an organization, it is often beneficial to start with some initial content and make it grow over time. How exciting would it be to see a new, flashy intranet that has no news, no events, no corporate updates? What would be the value of visiting an FAQ that is empty?

I will touch on the content itself in the next section, but for now, consider having the content deployed together with the solution.

---

[1]Manage Office 365 with Office 365 PowerShell, `https://docs.microsoft.com/en-us/office365/enterprise/powershell/manage-office-365-with-office-365-powershell`

[2]Office Dev Center Patterns and Practices, `https://dev.office.com/patterns-and-practices`

Office 365 Tenant Configurations

Part of a deployment may include making global changes to your tenant or specific ones to some of the apps. If those configurations don't change as part of the deployment process, then they only need to be set once. Still, it's a good idea to include them as part of the automated deployment process if possible.

I will touch on the content itself in the next section, but for now, consider having this content deployed together with the solution.

Accounts

If your deployment is to a new Office 365 tenant, you may be required to set up user accounts. Not a problem if there are only a few. But what if there are several hundred or thousand accounts to provision? The same applies if you need to make a change to all the user accounts, such as adding specific data into every user's profile or changing their Office 365 licensing. By combining PowerShell with simple Excel lists, you can automate this process to make it quick and reproducible.

Reporting

When your deployment is smooth and everything works as planned, it's a good day. But what if things go sideways during your deployment? How do you get down to the root cause of the problem?

In most Office 365 apps, when you encounter errors, you are typically presented with a short, sometimes cryptic message. Depending on the nature of the issue there may be some references to research and you can see what went wrong. If your deployment is leveraging some automation, you can often as part of the actual deployment capture these errors and request more details from the system. With such a deployment log in hand, the process of reviewing and validating the deployment becomes much easier.

As you can see, there are many benefits to automating deployments. Of course, there is a cost in building the automation process for your solution and validating it. If all you'll ever do is a single release, you can argue that the cost may not be worth it. However, best practices in application development and general IT management dictate that any change being done to a production environment should first be performed in an alternate environment to ensure that the changes will not have any negative, potentially catastrophic impact to your users or data.

Deployment Dry Run

Whether it is the first time you're preparing to put your solution into production or you have introduced some significant changes around the process of deployment, you should plan to perform a deployment dry run. A dry run in this context implies that the deployment is taking place in an environment that is different from where the solution was originally created (development environment) or the production environment.

Performing dry run deployments serves as an important step in your overall rollout planning and serves three main purposes. First, it allows you to validate the deployment process. Ideally, dry run deployments should be performed by someone outside of your project team who has the necessary technical skills to complete such a task but is not acquainted with the solution. Without the detailed knowledge around how a solution is built and deployed, the individuals who perform your dry run deployments can help ensure that the documented deployment process is clear to follow and no steps have been missed.

A second benefit to performing the dry run is for validating any prerequisites in the deployment environment or Office 365 tenant you are deploying to. Often, technical project members will have certain tools installed in their environment that can be used to complete their work. Inadvertently dependencies may be created for these tools, where they become a prerequisite for a successful deployment. This may not be much of a concern if you are working on an internal project and the team that is developing the solution is the same team that will ultimately be deploying it into production. However, if this is not the case, then you need to take into consideration that the technical environment for your clients may differ. To avoid this potential risk, always perform your dry run deployments using a pristine deployment system that mimics as closely as possible the simplest possible configuration of a deployment environment you may encounter. If you are aware of any potential limitations on deployment environments that you may encounter, you should aim to introduce them as well during the dry run deployments to work out any potential deployment kinks early on. This includes dependencies on an external system needed for the solution to work properly. Ideally, you should try to connect to those systems as part of your dry run deployments.

The third benefit to dry run deployments is making sure that the Office 365 tenant has not been tainted in any way with previous deployments that could result in different outcomes from what will be seen in production. For example, in the case of SharePoint, if you are deploying a new solution that leverages taxonomy or search, those services may already include content from previous implementations or other SharePoint solutions that may alter the behavior of what you are expecting.

Sample Data Deployment

Content plays an important role in this type of testing because it allows the user to verify the functionality and its influence on the content. For example, you may have some functionality that will be hidden unless there is content (such as an upcoming events calendar). Therefore, having the sample content is important.

Tip Include some sample content for each type of functionality that is being introduced or updated. This will help in verifying that the components have not only deployed successfully, but that they are also behaving as designed.

Smoke Testing

Smoke testing is a type of software testing to verify that important functionality is working as it should. It should cover most of the major functions that are being released, but none of them in great depth. Smoke testing is non-exhaustive and should be used to give the team some level of confidence that the build has succeeded but should in no means replace the thorough testing required during the agile development lifecycle.

Just as with other types of testing, smoke testing should have clear acceptance criteria defined. If your team has done a good job in building out acceptance criteria for the previous test phases (quality assurance, user acceptance testing, etc.), then you could leverage these acceptance criteria to determine proper system behavior.

The outcome of your smoke testing should help you decide whether the solution is stable enough and functioning as desired to deploy it into the production environment.

Smoke testing also helps expose integration issues early on in your overall project life cycle. Capturing integration problems early on can give you enough time to alter your technical approach or identify potential risks and mitigate them.

The tests themselves may be performed manually or include some type of automation. As with the deployment scripts, consider the effort involved in building these automated test suites vs. the number of deployments you're expecting to perform. If your team decides to do manual testing, then it is best to have someone who is not a core member of the technical team verify the release. Consider having one of the business stakeholders participate in this type of testing.

Release Planning for the Future

You already know that Office 365 is a dynamic environment that will change over time. This means that there is a real risk of a change in Office 365 impacting your release at any time. To mitigate this risk, you must keep up to date with the latest changes. There are two ways in which you can do this.

Office 365 Roadmap

The Office 365 Roadmap[3] is an important resource you should consider not just for release planning, but overall for your Office 365 journey. This website depicted in Figure 11-1 contains a detailed list of all the updates that are planned and their expected timelines.

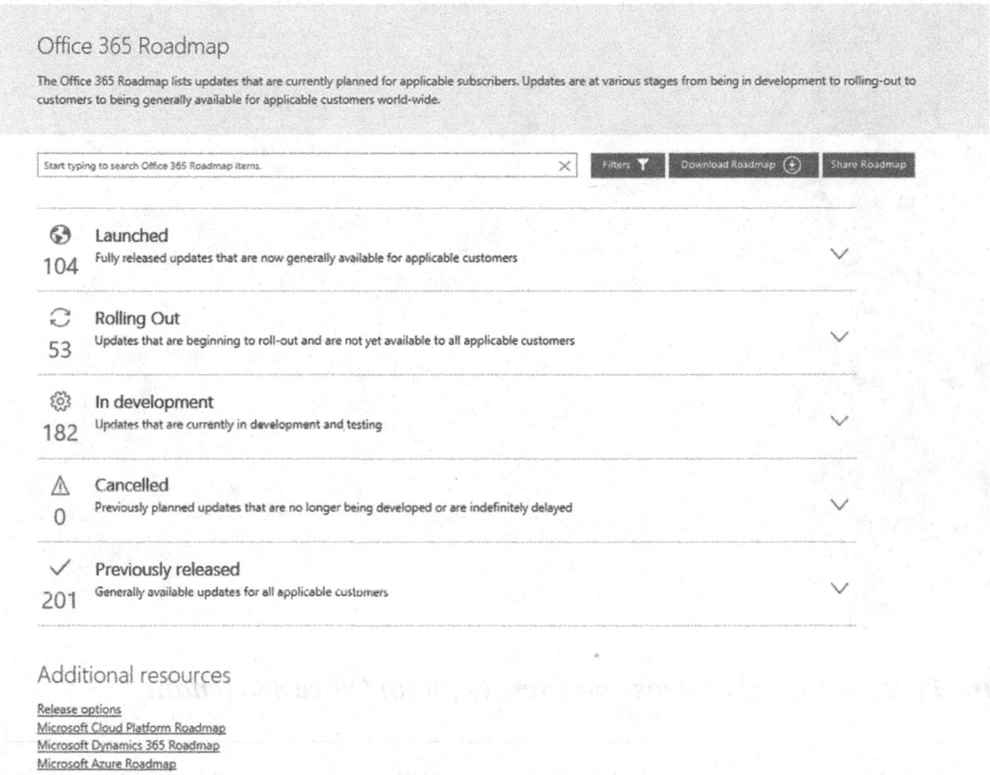
Office 365 Roadmap
The Office 365 Roadmap lists updates that are currently planned for applicable subscribers. Updates are at various stages from being in development to rolling-out to customers to being generally available for applicable customers world-wide.
Start typing to search Office 365 Roadmap items.
Filters
Download Roadmap
Share Roadmap
Launched
104
Fully released updates that are now generally available for applicable customers
Rolling Out
53
Updates that are beginning to roll-out and are not yet available to all applicable customers
In development
182
Updates that are currently in development and testing
Cancelled
0
Previously planned updates that are no longer being developed or are indefinitely delayed
Previously released
201
Generally available updates for all applicable customers
Additional resources
Release options
Microsoft Cloud Platform Roadmap
Microsoft Dynamics 365 Roadmap
Microsoft Azure Roadmap

***Figure 11-1.** Office 365 Roadmap showing number of updates and their progress*

[3]Office 365 Roadmap, `https://products.office.com/en-US/business/office-365-roadmap`

Release Preferences

As Microsoft works on new features and enhancements to Office 365, you can request to receive early releases as they become available. Turning on *Targeted release*, as shown in Figure 11-2, lets you select specific users to have access to the latest release features. Having an early release is a good way to plan for what's coming. However, at the same time, you should consider the overall impact to the organization of sharing new functionality that hasn't been fully documented and may not have sufficient resources available to support it.

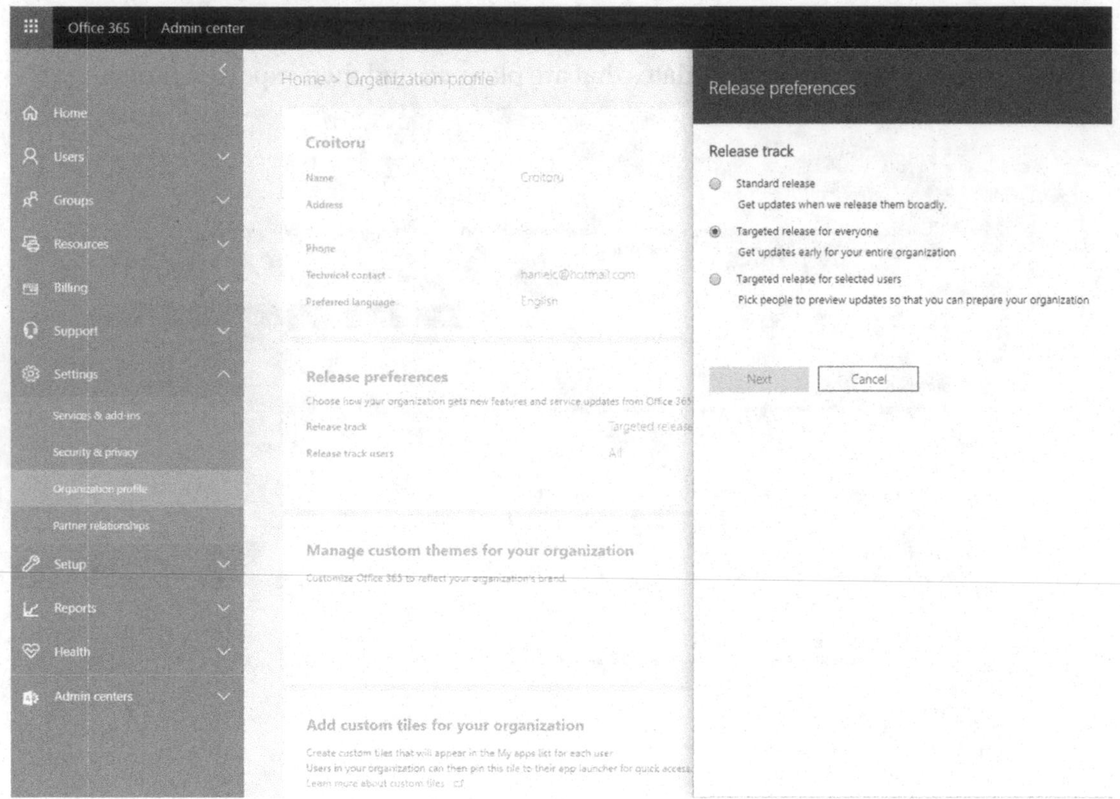

Figure 11-2. *Setting the release preferences for an Office 365 tenant*

Tip Consider having a small group of users within your organization have access to targeted release functionality. You can experiment with them to give you some time for proper change management planning.

With every release, you should review your deployment documentation and process to ensure that it is still valid.

Communicating Releases

Keeping your stakeholders informed about releases can help increase excitement. At the same time, communicating any potential issues early on can help gain support to overcome any blockers. Your stakeholders should have a clear understanding of what they should expect to see from a specific release and any deviations from that original plan. I will be discussing more on this topic in Chapter 15.

Summary

Building great Office 365 solutions is not enough if they don't function well when put into the production environment. Therefore, it is imperative that you carefully plan out a release plan that includes frequent releases. Document and verify the release process often and ensure that your stakeholders are informed about the progress of each release to get continuous buy-in and support.

As you progress with the early releases towards a solution that will be deployed into production, you need to plan how the solution will be transitioned to the operations team that will support the users. This is the topic of the next chapter.

CHAPTER 12

Transition to Operations

One of the last steps in the agile project life cycle that is often overlooked is the proper hand-off from the Scrum team to the teams that will support the project once it's finished and the Scrum team has disbanded. Without a proper hand-off, the operational teams may not be prepared to take on the new solutions and users could be confused about who to reach out to if they need help.

Products of agile projects will often be composed of more than one release. In those cases, it is imperative to mobilize a team that will be able to support the product throughout the various releases.

The focus of this chapter is to look at the activities and teams that are typically involved in this process and provide recommendations to avoid becoming "lost in transition."

Resources

One of the first steps is to identify the teams that will be responsible for supporting the product once it has been released. When you're choosing the team, you need to stop for a moment and think about the nature of the changes that are being rolled out.

Traditionally, in environments where you would have an infrastructure that supported a solution, there would be owners from IT that were responsible for managing the servers. Those roles were very involved and required a high level of expertise. Moving to Office 365 means your environment and support needs have changed. The infrastructure itself is supported by Microsoft's partner, 21 Vianet, and it guarantees an uptime of 99.9%. Based on that, the role of the IT team evolved from reactively working on issues in the environment to proactively managing the cloud services with planned changes. In general, your operations team will be made up of two groups, business operations and IT operations.

The business operations team will be tasked with answering questions around which tool should be leveraged for a particular purpose and why it was changed from a

H. Croitoru, *Agile Office 365*, https://doi.org/10.1007/978-1-4842-4081-6_12

previous tool (although these questions should have been communicated earlier on to the organization). The business operations team will also dive deeper into usage-related questions if they were not already covered in the existing training materials and will communicate the answers to the training team to enhance the existing training materials.

The IT operations team has several responsibilities. Using the Office 365 Message Center, accessible via `https://admin.microsoft.com/AdminPortal/Home#/MessageCenter`, the IT operations team gets informed of any possible service interruptions, as shown in Figure 12-1. This information needs to be shared effectively throughout your organization to avoid users reporting the same issue to IT several times. Such a situation can quickly overload a slim IT team and create a negative sense that IT is not doing what they should.

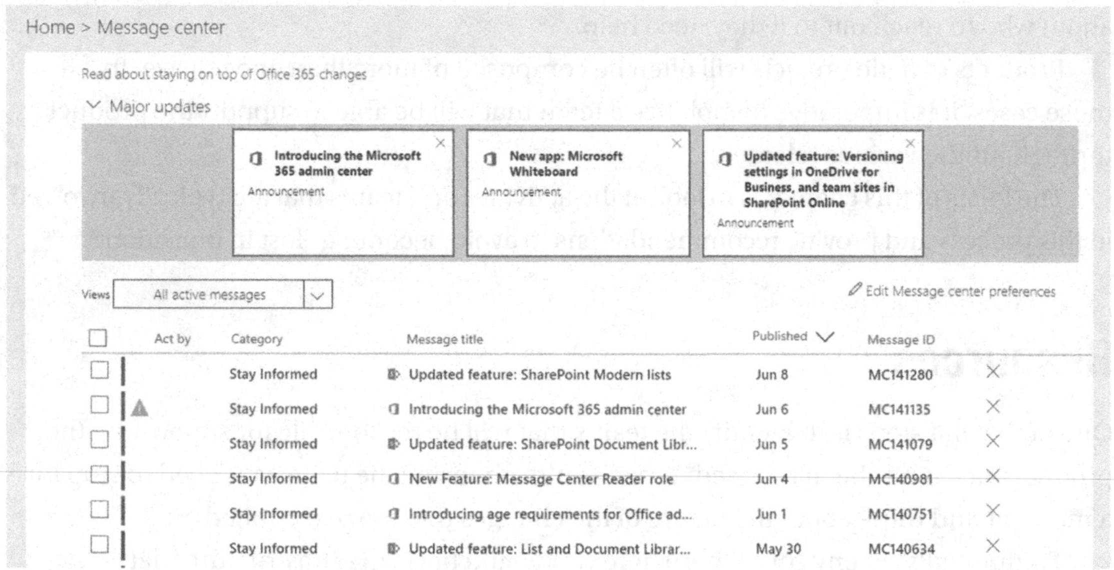

***Figure 12-1.** The Office 365 Message Center helps the IT operations team stay informed of any service issues*

Similarly, the Office 365 Roadmap, shown in Figure 12-2 (`https://products.office.com/en-us/business/office-365-roadmap`) is a great source for determining what functionality has recently been added by Microsoft or is currently planned. The information in the roadmap, which is publicly accessible to anyone, is an important tool throughout the entire project and operations life cycle. In one way, it helps you plan out your work. You may save you project team some time on delivering new functionality if you discover that Microsoft is currently working on releasing something similar.

Office 365 Roadmap
The Office 365 Roadmap lists updates that are currently planned for applicable subscribers. Updates are at various stages from being in development to rolling-out to customers to being generally available for applicable customers world-wide.
Start typing to search Office 365 Roadmap items.
Filters
Download Roadmap
Share Roadmap
Launched
156
Fully released updates that are now generally available for applicable customers
Rolling Out
71
Updates that are beginning to roll-out and are not yet available to all applicable customers
In development
189
Updates that are currently in development and testing
Cancelled
5
Previously planned updates that are no longer being developed or are indefinitely delayed
Previously released
226
Generally available updates for all applicable customers

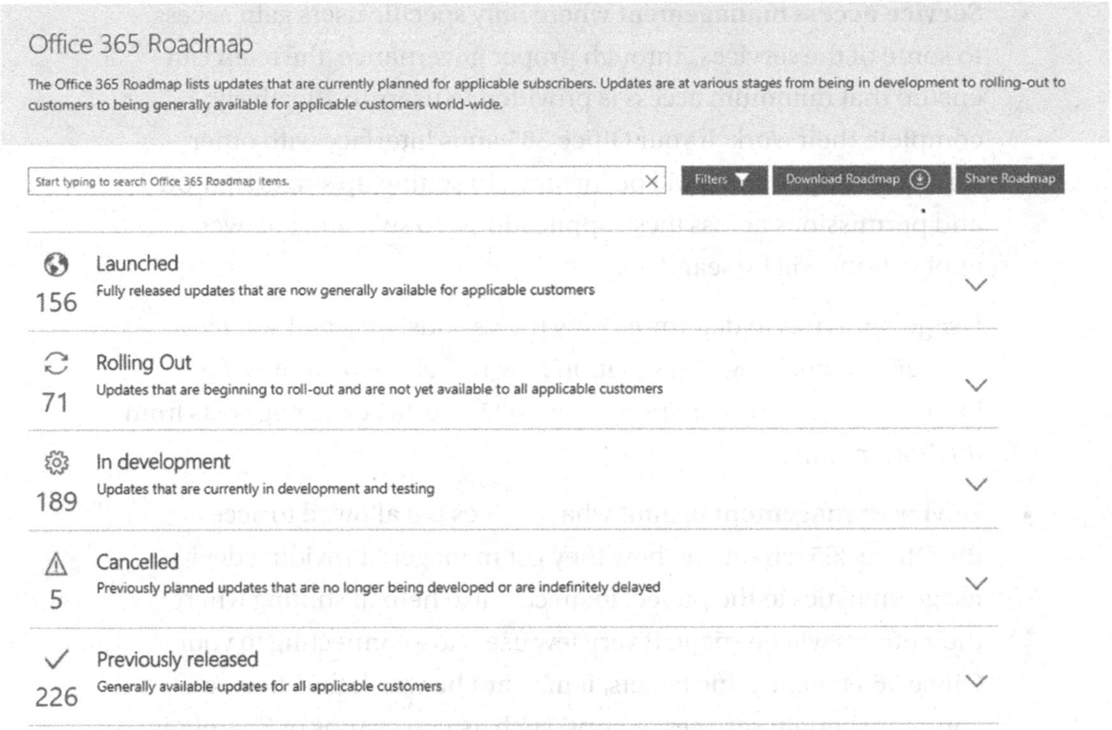

Figure 12-2. *The Office 365 Roadmap provides the IT and business operation teams and project teams with a clear overview of what Microsoft is planning for Office 365*

With a shift away from maintaining the servers and applications to managing services, the IT operations team can move closer to understanding how your users are using these services. This empowers them to look at areas of support, including the following:

- **Service administration** to understand the management of the various Office 365 apps and how they are configured in your organization. For apps that require some level of elevated permissions to create collaboration spaces, such as Office 365 Groups, Microsoft Teams, or Yammer, IT operations is often the gatekeeper tasked with managing these spaces.

- **User management** to manage the user accounts and password resets.

- **Service access management** where only specific users gain access to some of the services. Through proper governance, the team can ensure that minimum access is provided to users to effectively complete their work. If your Office 365 apps interface with other services, IT operations will be involved in setting up single sign-on and permissions across these applications, so switching between applications will be seamless.
- **Usage analytics** to determine how the various apps and services are being used. Usage information may reveal opportunities for increasing the return on investment of Office 365 or saving costs from the bottom line.
- **Device management** to limit what devices are allowed to access the Office 365 tenant and how they get managed. Providing device usage analytics to the project team can also help in shifting where their efforts will be spent. If very few users are connecting to your Office 365 tenant using tablets, it may not be worth the effort to configure certain services or apps, such as PowerApps or SharePoint customizations, to serve these devices.
- **Security and compliance** to ensure that a solid data loss prevention (DLP) policy is in effect and that corporate email policies are respected.

If the release includes any custom functionality, such as in SharePoint Online, it's a good idea to include someone from the development team to review the requests that are coming in. These individuals may not necessarily respond to user requests directly but will be able to provide guidance to the business and IT operations team on whether such customizations are working as designed or need to be changed.

Transition Meetings

The transition meetings should happen prior to but close to the launch date. This will (ideally) ensure that the operations team will be getting the most up-to-date information from the project team and will be prepared to deal with questions as they arise. During these meetings, the project team will share as much information as it can, which has been properly documented about the release, including the following:

- **New functionality** being rolled out and how it will affect users.
- **Deprecated functionality** that users were accustomed to and don't have access to anymore.
- **Known limitations** on how the functionality will work. For example, uploading large files may have been allowed in the past but is now governed and limited to 50MB.
- **Future functionality** that users may be expecting but hasn't been rolled out yet.

Managing Changes

As is common for many organizations, you need to establish a process for gathering the feedback from your users and managing the changes. As you already know by now, things are a little different in the agile world. Rather than having large releases that can last several months or more, releases will be typically shorter in duration and smaller in scope. You also know that the scope is subject to change more frequently than in traditional projects.

You should start by establishing a change control board for your releases. As the name suggest, this group of individuals is involved in determining and prioritizing what changes should be made in future releases. Luckily for you, you are one step ahead of the game if you've been maintaining the product backlog! All your releases and sprints should have been following a process similar to the one I introduced in Chapter 2. Therefore, the purpose of the change control board is to prioritize the feedback provided to the operations team against items that are already in the backlog.

Leveraging the Center of Excellence

In my experience, one of the best approaches for learning is to make your users as self-sufficient as possible. By empowering them to get answers quickly, you're not only giving them a sense that they can learn how to use Office 365 on their own, but you will potentially reduce the load on your operations team. This is particularly important when your operations team is made up of some of the same individuals who are working on future versions of the products being released.

For all of the Office 365 apps, there is a vast amount of information that is publicly available on the Internet. It's a good idea for the operations team to ensure that the Center of Excellence is up to date with the latest information and to point users to it. If something is missing, it's a great opportunity to review the questions/issues with the training governance team and provide answers in case the same question is asked again. You should periodically review the information offered by Microsoft directly, such as the Office 365 Training Center (`https://support.office.com/en-us/office-training-center`).

In cases where the release includes customizations, the operations team should ensure that the support content (such as videos or documents) is also available in the Center of Excellence.

FAQ Forum

Part of the Center of Excellence should include an FAQ Forum that will contain common questions and curated answers for the users. At first, such a forum will likely contain preset questions, but it should grow over time. Building a FAQ Forum can be achieved using a SharePoint list that is managed by the operations team, as shown in Figure 12-3.

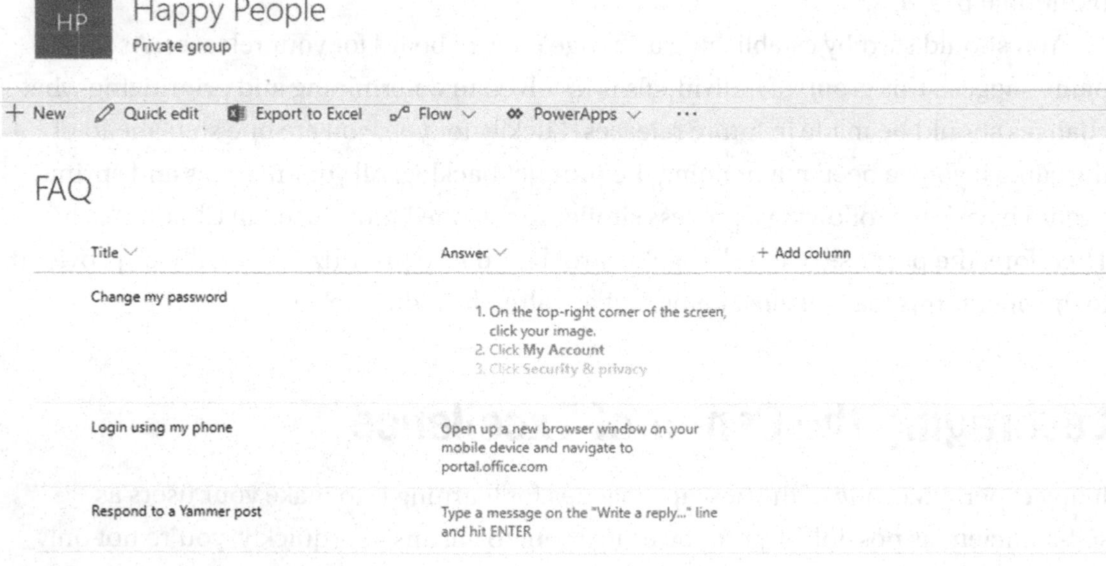

Figure 12-3. *A FAQ list that provides users with quick answers to questions*

There's nothing fancy about the FAQ list. All you need to capture is the question (title) and answer for it. This list should be accessible to everyone within the organization but only editable by the individuals or teams responsible for curating its content.

Now, having an FAQ list somewhere on your Center of Excellence is good, but what is even better is to make its content easily accessible from everywhere for your users. You should consider adding access to the FAQ on your organization's intranet so users can easily get to the answers they are looking for without having to move away from the work they are doing and navigate to the Center of Excellence. Using PowerApps, you can build an appealing user experience where users can pick from pre-existing questions and quickly get to the answers. Figure 12-4 illustrates such a form and how it can be used.

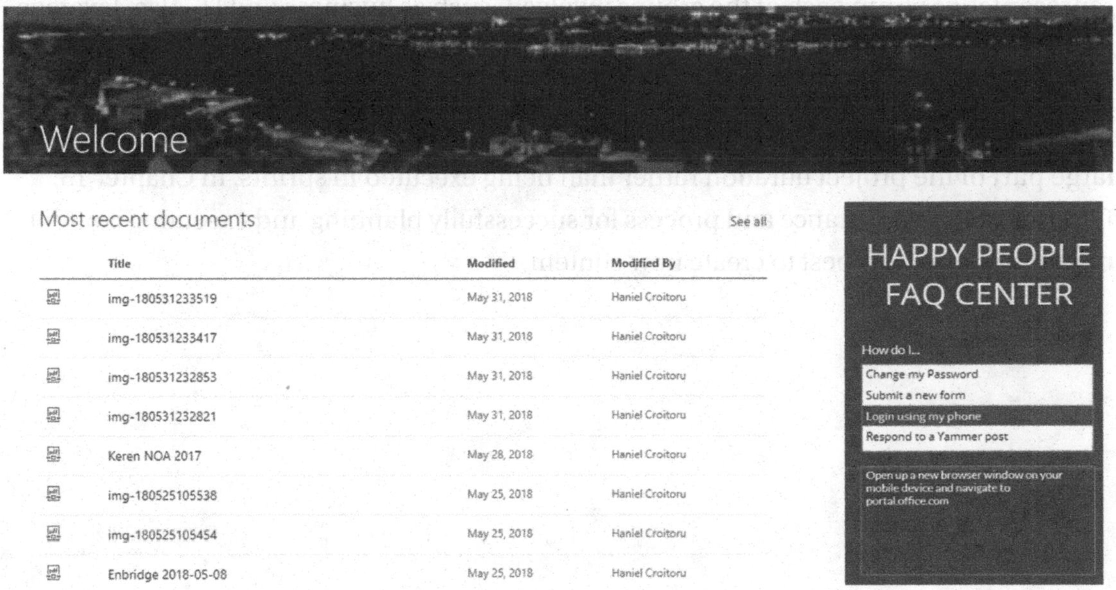

***Figure 12-4.** A FAQ access form made available to users directly on their intranet*

The form should also allow users to submit new questions if their question hasn't been asked before.

Tip When you build the FAQ submission form using PowerApps or a Form, it is also available to your users on their mobile devices.

If you really want to streamline the operational process, you can further enhance the form with some more questions to better direct the question to the correct operations team using and even providing notifications and approvals using Microsoft Flow.

Summary

Transitioning the responsibility of a product from the project team to the operations team needs to take place prior to its release. The operations team, which will be the first to respond to requests for support, needs to be equipped with plenty of information to successfully triage questions by the user community.

When planning the transition to the operations team, you must include representatives from each of the groups involved, such as business and IT. Also, leverage a Center of Excellence for your users to reduce the reliance on the operations team and make your organization more self-sufficient.

In the next section of this book, we'll look at the overarching activities that span a large part of the project duration rather than being executed in sprints. In Chapter 13, I'll discuss the importance and process for successfully planning and executing content migrations and how best to create new content.

PART V

Overarching Activities

CHAPTER 13

Content Migration

Imagine you just got married. It's time to move into your new posh condo downtown. Your spouse and you are very meticulous and organize all your wedding gifts and belongings carefully into the drawers, cabinets, and closets so you can easily find them. Fast-forward a few years. Your family has grown, as have your belongings. Things are not as organized as they used to be when you first moved into the condo. Eventually you realize that it's time to upgrade to a bigger place. You pack up all your belongings into marked boxes, often more than you need and maybe you even leave a few things behind.

Moving day has arrived. Your boxes are delivered to your new home. You begin to unpack and reorganize your belongings to match the layout of your new home. Things are organized once again. At least for now.

This example has nothing to do with Office 365 or SharePoint but serves as a great example of everyday situations where we have to deal with content migration. The example is meant to convey that such situations are not unique to content management systems but are common in life as a whole.

Let's see how the Happy People staff is preparing for their big move. Today, they are keeping important information on static web pages and paper, while corporate documents and records are stored on the network and local drives. There is little governance or visibility on who is doing what, which makes the task of planning such a migration that much more difficult.

Content Migration Defined

Content migration may mean different things to you depending on your background and the domain in which you're working. In the most fundamental way, *content migration* can be defined as the process of taking information (content) from a source system, modifying it to fit the structure of the target system, and finally loading the information to the target system. Information can be a collection of digital assets such as documents

H. Croitoru, *Agile Office 365*, https://doi.org/10.1007/978-1-4842-4081-6_13

or multimedia files stored on a content management system (CMS) or network drive as well as web page content which includes HTML files, script pages, or content stored in some type of HTML/JavaScript-based system and can be either static or dynamic content.

The migration process is similar to the *extract, transform and load* (ETL) process process in database usage and especially in data warehousing that involves

- **Extracting** data from outside sources
- **Transforming** it to fit operational needs (which can include quality levels) and
- **Loading** it into the end target (a database; more specifically an operational data store, data mart, or data warehouse)

In most of the Office 365 implementations I have worked on in the past, the vast majority of content migration included adding content to SharePoint Online for corporate information and OneDrive for Business for user content. In some cases, there was a need to also add content directly to Office 365 Groups.

In the SharePoint world, content is defined as either *documents* or *items*. Documents are essentially files, similar to those stored on a network drive or a desktop computer. Content types can be derived from the basic content types to include additional metadata. Items can be thought of as rows in an Excel table or records in a database. Like the documents, there can be derived content types with unique metadata.

Although the common term for this activity is "content migration" I'll use it carefully because the word "content" is also used to describe what's inside a web page or file. This chapter is going to be a bumpy ride. So, hold on tight and follow along closely.

Why Content Migrations Fail

If you look at the definition of content migration above, you might think that doing a content migration is straightforward and simple. Download a bunch of documents or files, have a look at them and tweak them as necessary, and then push them to another system. If things were so simple, there would be many more successful Office 365 and SharePoint implementations and happier employees.

Not a Technical Limitation

Technical implementations (and the content migrations associated with them) are typically performed by IT to meet the business' needs. That is often enough of a reason to blame IT or technology when implementations fail. This, however, is a misconception. In reality, it is the correctness and validity of the content that will ultimately determine the success or failure of the migration.

Lack of Understanding

Understanding the impact of a content migration is critical. Even if the IT department delivered a perfectly-functioning Office 365 environment with all the bells and whistles, unless all the required content the business needs to operate is available, the project would be deemed a failure and the system would be useless.

Content migrations are often misunderstood and thus underestimated. On several occasions where I joined in-flight SharePoint projects I found that there was little or no time, budget, and resources allocated to the migration.

Caution When content migrations are required, you will find yourself playing a dual role of Scrum master for any sprint-based development pieces and project manager/lead for the migration piece. As the project lead for the migration, your goal is to provide the content owners the tools and guide them through the process. Be careful not to assume responsibility for doing thc actual work described below for the migration.

If you ever see a project plan like Figure 13-1, you should let the project sponsors and stakeholders know that there's a gap in the project plan. They should create new tasks and checkpoints in the plans that are specific to content migration planning and execution that begin right at the start of the project or as early as possible.

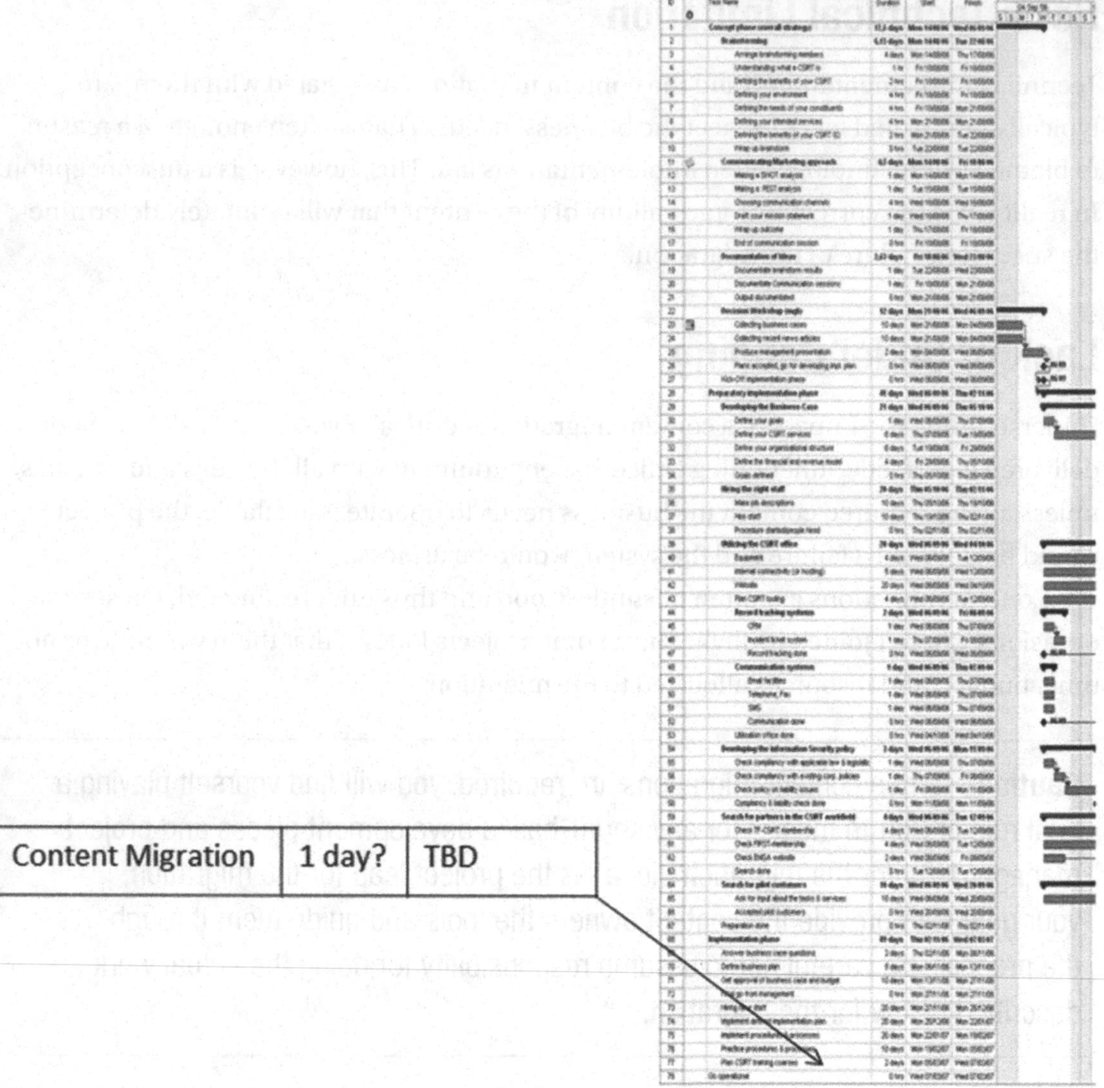

Figure 13-1. *What a project plan should not look like*

Tip Plan your content migration kick-off right after the project kick-off. Chances are that some of the same stakeholders will be involved in both. It also sets a tone for the importance of the content migration.

As discussed in Chapter 3, unlike the development that occurs in sprints, content migration should follow a traditional method to give the content owners ample time to prepare the content for the migration.

Lack of Ownership

The content migration kick-off should involve as many of the content owners as possible. This means that at a macro level the content to be migrated should be identified together with its owners. There's a good chance that some of those owners will delegate the work to someone else in their group. If you are aware of such situations, invite them as well. Make sure everyone involved in the migration process is engaged and rewarded for their efforts.

It's Ugly!

Let's face it, if you had the choice of working with some new technology and features (like SharePoint) or sifting through endless documents, which would you choose?

Content migrations can be extremely tedious and are not fulfilling. You can find yourself looking at lists and doing mundane manual tasks ad nauseam. Sometimes you may develop scripts to help migrate some of the data but even those may be for small subsets of the overall content set. Great attention to details is required in these tasks. Even the smallest error can result in a document not being migrated over or being misclassified. What if there are some items that are marked as personal information on a secure intranet site and you inadvertently tag them for everyone's consumption on your intranet? Such cases could have significant business ramifications.

Things can go wrong for many reasons. That's why it's important to create a strategy and plan early on. The remainder of this chapter will cover these aids.

Content Migration Strategy

Like any other project, a strategy needs to be developed for its execution. To develop a strategy for content migration, answer the following questions:

- **Why?** The reasons to migrate content vary between projects. Here we are discussing SharePoint implementations and the drivers for such implementations differ from one project to another. Thus, it's still important to ask why content is being migrated because it helps reinforce the point to make sure all the bases are covered.

- **What?** Of the five questions, this one is the most important one to ask. The answer to this question will dictate what's in and what's not, and help in understanding the complexity of the migration.
- **Who?** Build your migration team.
- **How?** Will you be using some tools or doing it manually?
- **When**? Are you bound by any black-out times or restrictions by the business or IT?

Get answers to these questions early on, ideally within the first few days following the migration kick-off meeting.

Drivers of Content Migration (Why)

The needs for content migration can spawn from many events. They can typically be grouped into three categories.

Consolidation

As organizations grow, the systems need to grow with them. An organization with a few employees can use a network drive for most of their needs. However, as this organization grows, additional systems will be introduced to meet the ongoing business needs for centralized control, governance of content, and better knowledge management and sharing.

Reorganization

In addition, mergers and acquisitions will require systems and content to be assimilated to create a unified look and feel.

Conversion

As discussed earlier in the book, information architecture (taxonomy, naming conventions, navigation, content types, etc.) play a key role the organization and findability of content. Over time, content that has grown organically either in a CMS or flat HTML structure needs to be reviewed and aligned to unify the formatting and structure of the content.

Migration Scope (What)

Treat a migration just like any other project. This means that scope should be set early on and locked down. Content sources can vary in time and size and will impact the complexity of the project. Having vastly different content sources may mean that different migration methods, tools, and individuals are required.

Depending on the migration method used you may elect to divide the work into several migration *iterations* (similar to agile iterations but not the same).

Building a Migration Team (Who)

Content migrations are not a one-man show. Rather, they often require a large number of individuals who need to work closely together in an orchestrated fashion to ensure that all the work is complete. Attention to detail is very important for this. Selection of the migration team members is discussed later in this chapter.

Migration Methods (How)

Figure 13-2 depicts five scenarios in which content migration typically occurs with SharePoint. Remember that SharePoint is the basis of Office 365 Groups, OneDrive for Business, and Microsoft Teams. So, by association, the same methods can be applied.

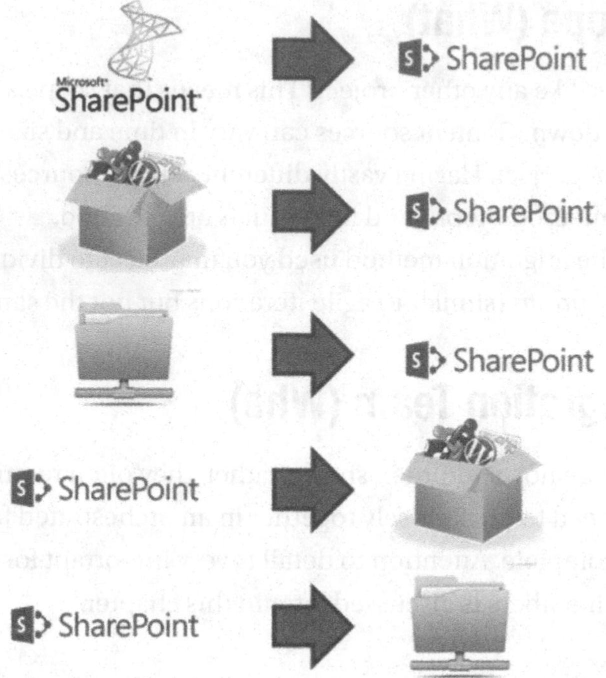

Figure 13-2. *Content migrations involving SharePoint*

The first three scenarios involve migrating content from older versions of SharePoint, other content management systems, or network file shares (including flat web sites) into SharePoint. The latter two scenarios involve moving content from SharePoint to other systems. Those two scenarios are not discussed in this book.

These types of migrations are not mutually exclusive. A single SharePoint implementation may include several content sources. Things get more challenging when content from multiple sources are migrated to the same document library or item list. Such scenarios may result in items with duplicate metadata such as file name or title.

If you followed the steps in order, then you should know the content sources involved in the migration, what items are to be migrated, and what the metadata mapping is. The next step is to think about the approach used to move the items. There are three types of approaches and you may choose to employ a combination of them based on your needs.

Automated

If a content owner manually uploads files or pages to a SharePoint site, their name appears as creator and the creation timestamp is when they added it. This does not accurately reflect the metadata and reduces the quality of the search results if these fields are searched on.

There are many third-party tools on the market today that can help overcome this problem and offer other advantages such as updating entities like external links within content. Such tools can be used to move content from a myriad of sources into SharePoint.

Another option is to develop scripts (such as PowerShell) to modify the original content and populate the new site if the original content is well structured.

Manual

In some cases, content is disorganized to begin with and the changes necessary will vary. In such scenarios, a manual copying/pasting of content and updating of metadata may be required. This approach is obviously less favorable because it is more time-consuming but may be the only option.

Hybrid

When migrations involve multiple content sources, a hybrid automated/manual approach may be taken for the different portions of the new SharePoint site.

Migration Planning

Content migrations tend to take on a life of their own and often run on different schedules than the technical implementations do and have different stakeholders, risks, and (hopefully) budgets assigned to them.

Content migrations should be developed using a phased approach with regular checkpoints, as they are very involved and require a lot of steps in order to succeed. Table 13-1 outlines a five-phase approach that I use for various types of SharePoint implementations.

Table 13-1. Migration Plan Overview

Initiation	Current state analysis	Future state planning	Execution	Closing
Kick-off meeting	Inventory analysis	Content security	Training	Support
Stakeholder identification	Content review	Governance	Trial migration and validation	System retirement
Scope definition	Content enhancement	Migration tools	Actual migration	
Timing		Scheduling	Validation	
Budget		Validation planning	Reporting	
		Fall-back planning		

Communication is key when it comes to projects. This is especially true when talking about moving content to a large system such as SharePoint. You want to make sure that everyone in the organization is fully aware of the progress and implications of the data move. At a minimum, your communications should include information about when the migration will be taking place, instructions for end users on what they need to do to prepare (e.g. closing applications, logging off), advice on when files will no longer be backed up, and information about how to resolve data problems or retrieve files that are no longer accessible.

In the remainder of this chapter, the migration phases will be discussed in detail.

Phase 1: Initiation

The purpose of the initiation phase is to define in detail the typical tangibles of a project: scope, resources, timing, and budget. At the end of this phase you and your team should know what work lies ahead of you, who will be doing it, and when it will be completed.

Kick-Off Meeting

As mentioned, holding the migration kick-off meeting together with the project kick-off makes sense because there will be common stakeholders and you will not be repeating the same information twice about the purpose of the project. While you will focus on the project scope and timelines in the project kick-off, the content migration kick-off should serve as an introduction into what content migrations are, what they entail (at a high level), the benefits of doing them right, and the drawbacks of not doing them.

It's important that the stakeholders understand the relationship between requested functionality and content migration. Interestingly enough, content migration kick-off meetings may inadvertently result in scope reduction once the business users realize what effort is required by them to complete the work. While some SharePoint implementations may introduce new functionality with little or no impact to content (such as a new workflow to automate manual processes), others could be content-intensive (replacing network drives with a site structure and document libraries).

Stakeholder Identification

At the start of your project you should make an effort to identify many of your migration team members. Get to know them well because you'll be relying on them heavily.

Building the migration team should include individuals from various parts of the organization. The core team will be comprised of the content owners who will analyze the content and validate the migrated content and communicate the progress of the migration to the rest of the organization because the migration will touch a majority of users. Finally, IT will help determine the best execution paths for the migration, provide necessary access to the content sources and new SharePoint environment, evaluate third-party tools, and develop scripts where applicable.

There's a good chance that someone may have the idea of outsourcing this work because no one really wants to do it. This should be avoided at all costs because it distances the organization from taking ownership of its content and allows someone else to make decisions that could have a big business impact. Furthermore, it denies your content contributors and owners the opportunity to learn the new SharePoint system inside and out prior to launch.

Keep some budget for recognizing their hard efforts. As the migration leader you should plan to give out little prizes to people who exceed their target, are really good at helping others solve problems, or exhibit great leadership skills. Let them be champions to help create a positive attitude within the team. Keeping team morale high is important, particularly in lengthy migrations.

Scope Definition

The overall project may require content from numerous sources to be migrated over. When possible, the migration should be broken down into smaller units. Your migration team will appreciate it because it won't be as overwhelming. You need, of course, to assess the business needs to ensure that such an approach is feasible.

Table 13-2 should help you describe to the content owners the three groups of content that they need to classify their content into.

Table 13-2. *Overview of content classifications for migrations*

	Vital content	Valuable content	Idle content
Size of content	Small	Medium	Large
Content types	Specific content types (e.g. HR policy, travel request form)	Generic content types (e.g. document, picture)	"Loose" (file shares)
Information architecture	Strong IA, detailed libraries, versioning	General IA, default libraries	Weak IA, flat structure, duplicate files, folder structure
Effort in content analysis and update	High: Careful review of content and its metadata, modify target structure as needed to meet the needs of the content	Medium: Modify existing or add some new metadata fields	Low: Little or no changes made to content
Migration approach	Use third-party tools or scripts to migrate data to ensure the current state of the metadata is maintained.	Use a combination of third-party tools, scripts, and manual copying.	Bulk copy/paste of content into libraries

Assessing the source content against this table will help you get an initial sense of what sort of work lies ahead for the team, prerequisites for the migration, and some of the challenges that they may encounter.

It's not uncommon to have the content owners request to migrate all their content over as-is because they need all of it. It's the least effort for them but may result in a new system where content will be disorganized and poorly classified from the get-go. Search results may not be optimized as the system will carry the extra burden of crawling content that is not needed.

Content sources will need to be carefully analyzed based on the file types, size, creation/modification dates, content types, record retention policies, and content. Those are some of the main drivers that will help identify the fate of each content item. Use this two-step approach to filter out the content in the Inventory Analysis step of Phase 2 of the migration project.

Macro-Elimination

Macro-elimination can result in significant reductions of content that needs reviewing. In a recent project, my client was able to reduce the content from about 65GB to just over 400MB through this method. Some common examples are

- **Multimedia files**: Unless you're in the digital media business, having large video files or entire albums of pictures (yes, I mean vacation pictures, stag parties, and the likes) should not be migrated. They probably shouldn't have been stored on the corporate systems to begin with.
- **Binary files**: This includes DVD images (.ISO), or similar images that were downloaded and stored. Again, unless there's a specific need, they should not be stored on the server.
- **Age**: At a macro level, the content owners could agree that any content over a certain age is obsolete. It's important to remind them that even after the migration is complete, the old content will not necessarily be deleted and can always be brought back from an off-line archive if required.

Micro Elimination

Micro-elimination requires more attention and time. The remaining items need to be carefully assessed based on their metadata and content. In this step, the content reviewers have the opportunity to map the content to new locations and assign it new metadata such as file names, content types, and new owners.

Timing

There are two types of timing in migrations. The first relates to the timelines of when preparation of new material or modifications to existing content is complete. The second one focuses on the schedule to move content from the content sources to the new SharePoint environment. Factors that play into the schedule include prioritization for specific business units or content sources, allowable downtime for any systems, expected duration of migration, approaches used for moving the content from source to destination, physical distance between source and destination systems, and network traffic.

When developing your migration schedule, determine if there are any key milestones within the SharePoint implementation that require content to be ready. One such example is in the final round of user testing (e.g. user acceptance testing or UAT). Asking the user to validate that the new system is functioning properly without content will be difficult.

Not all your resources will need to be engaged full-time during the migration. However, whether full-time or part-time, you want to make sure that they are available when needed.

Many third-party migration tool vendors offer solutions that work with SharePoint on-premise, hosted by a service provider or Office 365. Although the strategy and plan would be similar, the timing may not. If you are dealing with large amounts of data, and the source and target systems are geographically dispersed, your migration may be slowed down by the network traffic.

Budget

Migrations are not cheap. If you calculate the time of all your migration team members and tools required, some migrations may end up costing of more than the SharePoint implementation itself! If there is any custom code that was developed for the old content such as web parts, it will have to be updated. Development costs may be higher when you plan on migrating to SharePoint Online and need to convert existing web parts into new apps. You may also need to buy new versions of third-party solutions to work on your new SharePoint platform.

Phase 2: Current State Analysis

This phase of the migration project is the longest and most resource-intensive one. Your team will need to do a deep dive into the content to review specific items and their metadata. By the end of this phase you should have a good understanding of the number and sizes of document and pages that need to be migrated, what content types are used in the new SharePoint environment, all the metadata associated with these items, and the changes required to the content of these items such as links or branding.

Inventory Analysis

Let's go back to our example of Happy People. During the migration kick-off and through some conversations you were able to identify the content sources. In this case, let's assume there is a network file share (`\\iis-tor1`) hosting pages for a website including HTML, CSS, and JavaScript files. The content in these pages will invariably change as URLs will take on their new form and the new site will capitalize on the rich content offered in SharePoint such as web parts and content parts. The second source is another network file share (`\\nas-tor2`) where documents are stored that are surfaced via the website. Some of these documents are for public viewing such as press releases, reviews, and resort descriptions. Other documents are in a private section and should be available only to users with specific privileges.

Now that the content sources are known, the next step is to build a map of the content. It will help in visualizing the content repositories and how they relate to the final state. Such a map can be built using a number of tools. I recommend using mapping tools such as MindManager or MindMapper.

During the inventory collection, try to capture as much information as possible about the content. The more you capture early on, the less will need to be recreated later. Begin by creating a list of all the files and pages you need to migrate. To get an inventory of files that are stored on network shares or content management systems that store their content directly in a file system, you can use a tool or develop your own scripts using PowerShell. Ideally, try to create a dump that will contain all the available metadata fields associated with all the files destined for migration. You can then use Excel to view the results, as shown in Figure 13-3.

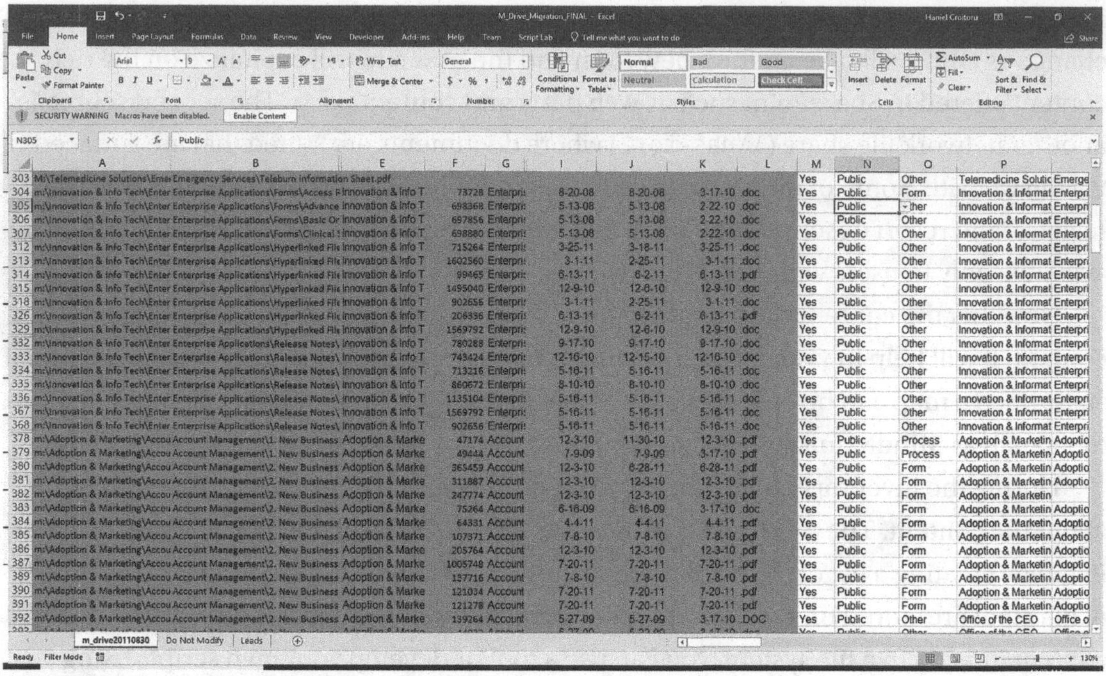

Figure 13-3. *Content inventory viewed in Excel*

Directory scanning tools do not work for content management systems like SharePoint where the content is stored and accessed via a database. As an alternative to this, PowerShell scripts can be used to crawl the content sources (e.g. specific SharePoint site collection) and generate an inventory list.

When creating a list of source web pages targeted for the migration you need to also look at dynamic fields that make up the page (e.g. web parts or content parts), associated formats, and any file permissions and access to ensure that dependencies remain intact.

At the end of the inventory gathering exercise you should have a report of all the items that need to be reviewed by the team. In addition to the metadata associated with these items, capture the overall structure (e.g. site/folder hierarchy), number of documents per content type, pages with no references to them or broken links, and access and modification statistics.

These reports may not reflect exactly the content as your owners see it. The file system or content management system in place may contain multiple copies of the same data. For web pages, getting the count may not be accurate because some pages contain plain data while others are dynamically generated from content coming from somewhere else. The analysis needs to include a review of both the front end (e.g. site map) and back end (e.g. CMS) to ensure full coverage. Finally, there may be unpublished content or metadata that will appear in the inventory results which may need to be excluded from the migration.

Content Review

Now that the content has been identified, it is time to begin reviewing it. The content listings should be divided up such that each content owner will only see their content. It will be less overwhelming for them and they won't have to worry about inadvertently reviewing someone else's stuff.

Before any review can begin, you must ensure that permissions have been granted to all the content reviewers to read and edit the files.

The review will serve to categorize each item into one of the following groups:

- **Don't migrate**: Self-explanatory. It will be archived with the backup of the old system but will not exist in the new SharePoint site. Make sure to remove any references to it.
- **As-is migration**: Here the page or document is moved with no modification to its content or metadata. This should be used either if the document is already in the right structure and contains all the necessary information to be used in the new SharePoint site or if it's idle content that is unstructured and will be copied to a dumping location.
- **Enhanced migration**: In this case the source page or file has existing metadata fields updated and additional metadata fields added to fit into the new content type structure.
- **Standardization migration**: Here the source pages are broken down into smaller levels of granularity to fit into "templates" that are defined in SharePoint.
- **Restructure migration**: This method is similar to the standardization method but pages are also updated to reflect the new information architecture.

It's a good idea to provide each reviewer with a worksheet that contains all the metadata about each item as well as additional metadata fields they need to complete. For example, if you use the Excel worksheet in Figure 13-4 as an example, the first new column (column H) should be a Yes/No question on whether this content is still required. If it's not required, then the reviewer is not required to do anything else with the file. If the answer is Yes, then the remaining columns representing metadata should be completed. Where possible, metadata fields should be based on pick lists so that the chance of errors in data entry is reduced. This is also an opportunity to identify new owners for specific items where the original owner is no longer with the organization or has changed roles or departments.

As you review and reorganize the information you need to remember that SharePoint imposes certain limits on the size and count of items stored. Table 13-3 lists some of these limitations.[1]

Table 13-3. *SharePoint Online Boundaries and Limits*

	SharePoint Online
Storage per tenant	1TB
Site collection limit	25TB
Maximum file size	15GB
Items in a single folder view	5,000
Items in a document library	30,000,000
Items in a list	30,000,000

When mapping the content to the new location, you may realize that the new content structure will exceed the limits imposed by SharePoint. To overcome this, look at the current folder structure and see if the content can be divided across multiple sites or libraries. An added benefit of spreading the data over multiple sites/libraries is that it will give the users more granularities about what data they can take offline when synchronizing SharePoint with their desktop system. If you migrate everything into one big document library (not recommended), it means that all users will need to synchronize everything, which can have a severe impact on your network bandwidth.

[1]SharePoint Online Boundaries and Limits: `https://support.office.com/en-us/article/SharePoint-Online-software-boundaries-and-limits-8f34ff47-b749-408b-abc0-b605e1f6d498?ui=en-US&rs=en-US&ad=US`

Content Types

So far I've been talking a lot about the metadata. Another aspect to consider in migrations is the content types. As in the house moving example at the beginning of the chapter, when a new system is put in place things start out well organized. In the case of content types, there are usually no more than necessary to meet the immediate business needs and potentially a few more for future plans. Over time, content types tend to change due to organizational or business changes. Suppose a small company is acquired by larger one. There may be some duplication of documents but both are required. The existing content type for documents may now be altered to capture the owning organization.

Although there's nothing wrong with changing content types, there are often cases where new content types are created and old ones are left in the system. A scan of a system may reveal a large number of content types while in reality only a small set are used.

Also, improper restrictions in a system or the creativity of content editors can result in misuse of content types (or entry of metadata) or new unnecessary content types.

When reviewing and mapping content types, each one should be classified as one of the following:

- **No change:** A → A
- **Merged:** A + B → C
- **Retired:** A

Content Enhancement

In addition to mapping the pages and files to the new structure, this is a good opportunity to make enhancements to it. Some key documents such as policies or procedures may be due for a review or overhaul. If the branding of an organization has changed, this is a good time to update logos, contact information, and other graphic templates. Other types of content enhancement include the following:

- **Translation**: Often times, file names are created such that they encapsulate information such as creator's initials, version, date stamps, language, and more. When content is moved into SharePoint, this is all handled by the document library, assuming that the document content type is configured with the necessary metadata columns. This is an opportunity to rename documents or pages (HTML, XML, CSS, etc.) to correct naming convention and structure.

- **Deletion**: Remove erroneous or unused tags, scripts, and unwanted code.
- **Transform**: Transform any old XML to match the XML required by SharePoint.
- **Restructuring**: Change the structure of the content to conform to the new structure.

Beware of long path and file names. Try to keep file names shorter than 50 characters and paths to less than 260 characters. This can pose a problem if a file was copied to a network location using a mapped drive but needs to be accessed using the longer UNC file share name. 260 characters may sound like a lot but remember that URLs in SharePoint often have encoding applied to them, which increases their length. For example, a space character would be translated to %20 in Unicode, which is three characters long.

Note SharePoint blocks certain file types that can be uploaded to lists and libraries for security reasons. The restrictions for the on-premises deployments are stricter; however, the SharePoint administrator can modify some of these restrictions. Check out `http://office.microsoft.com/en-ca/office365-sharepoint-online-enterprise-help/types-of-files-that-cannot-be-added-to-a-list-or-library-HA101907868.aspx?CTT=5&origin=HA102694293`.

SharePoint also poses some limitations on the characters that can be used in site names, folder names, and file names. A full list of these of the characters is provided at `http://support.microsoft.com/kb/905231`.

Phase 3: Future State Planning

During future state planning, the goal is to take all the knowledge you have gathered about the current state and the goals for your new environment and combine them to recommend where the content will live and how it will be managed in the new environment.

Content Security

In planning the migration there are two types of security you need to be concerned with:

- **Source repositories**: Open source repositories for analysis and to view the content of the records. Enable accounts and access levels to the migration team and tools to access the source repositories and copy the records over to SharePoint.
- **Target (SharePoint)**: Finalize access and security levels and groups in SharePoint. Review migration worksheets and new information architecture with the content owners to identify the groups and individuals who need to have access to the new repositories.

Governance

There's a lot to be said about governance when it comes to SharePoint as a whole. When talking about the content migration you need to focus on usage and process monitoring and ongoing maintenance. Ensure correct permissions are applied and adjust roles and permissions as people change jobs. Monitor the volume of content stored within SharePoint. Content that is not actively used adds an extra burden to the system and will slow down the search crawler and indexing. It will also make it harder to find things that are needed and can slow down searches and performance.

Execution Approach

Several factors can influence the type of approach taken for the migration.

- **One time**: As the name implies, it happens all at once, typically over a weekend.
- **Phased**: Allows for a gradual transition whereby you turn on only parts of the new system at one time.
- **Synchronization/integration**: Both old and new systems run together. As content is added to one system, it is synchronized to the other system. When the content is loaded and thoroughly tested, a cutover is made.

Several factors can influence the type of approach taken for the migration. When it is not possible to have both old and new systems available at the same time, a one-time migration is undertaken. An example of this is when you wish to upgrade SharePoint from an older version to a newer one that will reside on the same physical server. The downside to this method is if delays occur, or if the new system doesn't work as planned, there may be a negative impact to your business' top and bottom line.

Phased and synchronized approaches are used when content supports mission-critical 24/7 applications. The phased approach has the advantage that results are achieved sooner; it's easier to test smaller, incremental datasets; and it's possible to back out before committing to the new system. The synchronization/integration method requires synchronization software to keep both systems running in tandem and can be costly but has the advantage that there is little likelihood of problems because the systems will run together until the new one is proven.

Migration Tools

Selecting migration tools takes time and resources (cost). There are many great third-party migration tools available on the market today. At the core they are similar but differ in cost and some features they offer. When selecting a tool you should consider the following:

- Based on the analysis, what would be the cost to migrate all of the content? Some tools are purchased at a fixed price while others have a cost model that is based on the amount of data being migrated.
- Whether the price is high or low, you should ask yourself what would be the cost of doing it internally, either developing your own scripts or moving the content manually.
- From a cost perspective, it would be great to have a single tool that can do all the migrations for you. This may not be possible because different tools work on a different set of content repositories.

Open with Explorer and OneDrive for Business

In addition to third-party tools or scripts, consider using the *Open with Explorer* option on a library or OneDrive for Business on a desktop computer to upload the content into a SharePoint library, as shown in Figure 13-4. However, neither of these options is optimized for large volumes of data being copied into SharePoint. At the time of writing, it doesn't check for illegal characters or file types, path length restrictions, etc. Another drawback is that neither of these options preserves the metadata of the files and folders that come from the file shares. Modified Date and Creator fields are set to the time of migration and the person performing the migration, respectively. If these fields are of importance, then neither of those options should be considered.

Figure 13-4. *Open with Explorer is not an ideal option for content migration to SharePoint*

Scheduling

Migrations tend to place a heavy burden on the infrastructure as large amounts of data need to be moved over the network and there are a lot of disk read/write operations taking place. Thus, migrations should be scheduled at times when there is much more bandwidth for moving the data (usually at night).

To get a sense of the time it would take to move all the content from the source to the destination SharePoint site, test your migration speed upfront by moving about 1% of the data. This should be done for each data source because different systems may have more overhead to read/write files than others. Multiply your results by 100 and that will give you a rough estimate of the total migration time.

In general, the more complex and larger the migration, the better it is to execute it in smaller, logical groupings (such as by content source or department) in an agile manner.

Caution Office 365 throttles the upload bandwidth. One way to overcome this limitation is to use machines in parallel to speed up the migration process.

Your organization may have black-out periods during which migrations can't take place. These could include statutory holidays or regularly-scheduled maintenance windows for the IT infrastructure where servers may need to be taken offline.

Content Freeze

Included in the migration plan should be a freeze period during which users are prevented from adding new or modifying existing content to the old repository.

During this time, a snapshot of the content is taken and any new files added since the original inventory are reviewed following the same process.

In the event that a freeze is not feasible, remember the timestamp of when the first inventory was taken. After the migration, subsequent inventories should be collected where the creation or modification dates of the content are newer than the last one. A new migration called delta migration is when only the difference in content between the original migration and the current time should be migrated.

Validation Planning

Just as in the technical implementation plan, you need to develop your validation plan. The plan should outline what subsets of content will be used for the validation, what are the pass/fail criteria, who will be validating, when validation will take place, on which servers/infrastructure it is going to take place, and what are the triggers to invoke the fall-back plan (see below). Remember that the content is ***the*** core piece at the heart of any SharePoint project.

Fall-Back Planning

With validation planning comes fall-back planning. Despite best efforts, things can go wrong. It could be that the new production SharePoint site was not configured exactly as the staging environment and is missing some metadata fields or there was some data corruption that happened during transmission. The fall-back plan will describe what steps will be taken to return the previous systems to a state where the business can continue working with minimal interruption. The most complex fall-back plans are ones where the future SharePoint environment will be deployed to hardware used by one of the content sources. In these scenarios, a full backup should be taken of the system so if a fall-back is required, restoration is easier than having to build the server and then restore the content.

Phase 4: Execution

Follow the steps outlined in the following sections.

Training

Just prior to beginning the trial migrations the users who were identified as frequent contributors and readers of the content as well as power users should be trained on the new SharePoint solution. These individuals can help with the uptake of SharePoint and become internal champions.

Since the technical implementation project is running agile, you can identify these power users from early sprints, particularly if part of their work was to create new content.

Trial Migration and Validation

A staging environment will be created where a subset of the content can be migrated to and validated. Each repository needs to go through at least one trial migration.

Additional trials should be happening if there are any changes to the files being migrated or the structure of the new SharePoint environment that will house them.

Users should have been identified at this point to assist with the validation of the selected content using the validation plan.

Locked Files

Users need to understand that open files are likely to interfere with the migration procedure. While it's possible to work around these issues, during critical times, it might be a good idea to encourage users to close unused folders and documents.

This is especially true for files open in MS Office because it not only locks the file but also creates an auto-recovery file starting with ~$ that can't and shouldn't be migrated into SharePoint.

Performing the Migration

At this time all the content for migration should have been collected, enhanced, cleaned and updated, migration tools configured, trial migrations finished, and the various content owners informed.

Migration execution can begin.

Validation

Once the migration is complete, the content owners should do a final review to ensure that all the content is there as it should be. The reviewing should be done directly on the SharePoint system, which will combine validation with testing of new SharePoint functionality (e.g. search)

In the event that there are serious flaws that can't be fixed, the team needs to assess whether to implement the fall-back plan discussed in the "Fall-Back Planning" section in Phase 3.

Reporting

Just when you think you're done, there's always one more report. It's good practice to generate a report of all the content as it was entered into the new system and keep it for future reference. Even with robust site governance, there should be control over who can modify or delete files. However, in case a file or page falls through the cracks, it's a good idea to have something to look at and find out if it was migrated to begin with.

Support

Despite best efforts to migrate all the content correctly, inevitably questions will arise that will require support, such as:

- How can I get some content in that wasn't migrated?
- How can I modify metadata that is incorrect?
- Where can I find information that was previously located somewhere else?
- Why am I not able to modify/read files that I was able to prior to the migration?

If you prepared a solid communication plan, these questions should have been covered. Still there are those users who require personal hand-holding. A team of users (typically a subset of the content reviewers) may be able to assist in answering some of these questions.

System Retirement

Once all the data has been migrated from the content repositories to SharePoint and verified, a strategy needs to be executed to retire the old systems.

There are often cases when users missed a few items in the migration which are required after all. Thus, keeping a full backup of the old systems is prudent. Since there is usually an added cost to keep the old system online (software licenses, hardware/software, human resources, utilities, real estate), the plan should aim to have these systems taken offline as soon as possible. However, before doing so, check with your legal/compliance department to determine if there are regulatory reasons to keep the old systems online for longer periods of time.

The process should begin by removing access to all users to the system. You will be able to tell quickly if people are missing something if they ask for access to be granted again. If that's the case, make sure to provide only read access so users cannot store anything new on the old system.

Any links pointing to the old system (e.g. on an intranet site) should be modified to point to the new source.

Once you're confident that the system can be permanently retired, you should proceed with the system retirement procedure for the organization, which may include physical destruction of permanent storage devices and repurposing, destroying, or returning leased hardware. Any software licenses and support contracts should be terminated as well.

Summary

Content migrations are complex and resource intensive. They should be treated as separate projects running in parallel to the technical implementation. There are a number of key activities that need to happen to ensure that the content to be migrated is properly identified, modified according to the new site structure, and migrated successfully to the new SharePoint site.

CHAPTER 14

Change Management and Adoption

In the days preceding the cloud, changes often affected a single system. This simplicity made it easier to train users to help in the adoption of the changes. Today's Office 365 rollouts are much more complex. They often involve a number of communication, collaboration, and productivity tools that are rolled out at once. In this chapter, I will discuss how combining traditional change management practices with innovative ways to deliver the required support can greatly improve this process.

Setting Goals

Changes to working environments are introduced for a number of reasons. In general, changes aim to address some known gaps or issues in the existing systems or introduce improvements that will enhance the user experience or functionality. So how do you know whether the changes are hitting the mark? One way is to collect specific metrics over time which will help you determine whether you've reached your goals or not. These adoption metrics can be based on user behaviors as well as intrinsic changes. Some of these metrics could include the following:

- **Reduce internal emails**: By leveraging Office 365 communication and collaboration apps, you can measure whether the volume of internal emails being sent is shrinking over time.
- **Reduce time for travel approvals**: Replacing paper-based forms with online ones will not only reduce the overall time it takes to approve travel requests but will also help optimize the business process by automating the approvals and escalations, sending notifications on late responses, and informing the requestor on the status of their request.

H. Croitoru, *Agile Office 365*, https://doi.org/10.1007/978-1-4842-4081-6_14

- **Eliminate use of network drives**: Apps such as OneDrive for Business, Office 365 Groups, and Microsoft Teams will let the users store, share, and collaborate with others inside the organization and outside without relying on network drives.
- **Increase employee satisfaction**: With apps like Yammer, sharing communications company-wide is a lot easier and can help users stay engaged with what is happening inside the organization and participate in conversations, thus making them feel that their voice matters.

You can set goals for any change that is being introduced. Adopting changes can take different levels of effort depending on their scope and impact on the users. Imagine that a new alert widget, depicted in Figure 14-1, is getting added to an intranet. There's no user interaction required and informing users of its introduction can easily be done via normal corporate communications.

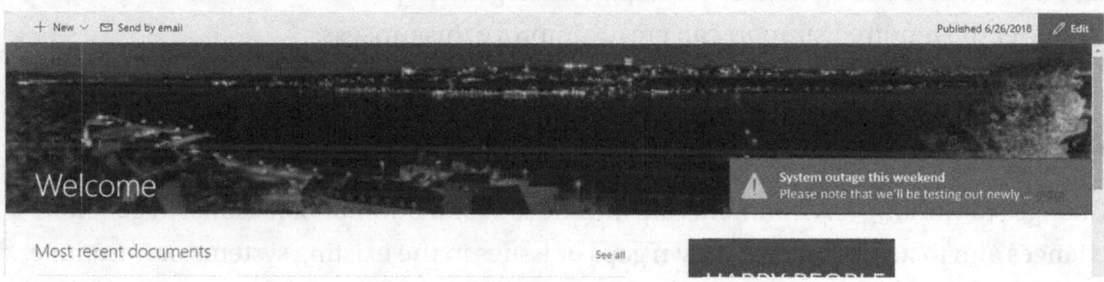

Figure 14-1. *Adoption of a new alert feature*

On the other hand, a more complex change will take more time and will require continuing communication and training. For example, rolling out Microsoft Teams across the organization for all departmental, project, and client collaboration work will require users to pivot on how they work today. At first, adoption will be slow as users learn how to use Teams and slowly start using it. This will likely result in reduced productivity for a given period until they become more proficient in it and recognize its value. Figure 14-2 is a typical change graph that shows how the productivity level dips initially when a large change is introduced. After some time, the productivity exceeds the current state.

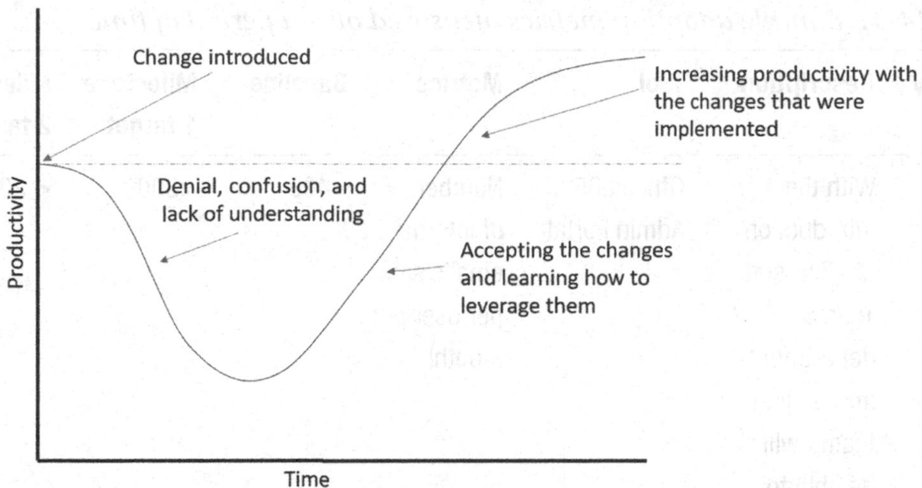

Figure 14-2. *Change management graph showing the impact of changes on productivity*

As you can see from Figure 14-2, adoption happens over time and is not a one-time event. You should therefore identify metrics for each of your goals for specific milestones and plan on capturing adoption metrics at different times to determine whether you are trending towards your adoption goals. The first set of metrics should be captured prior to deploying the changes and will be used to determine the current state baseline, as shown in Table 14-1.

***Table 14-1.** Sample adoption metrics measured over a period of time*

Category	Description	Tool	Metrics	Baseline	Milestone 1 target	Milestone 2 target
Email	With the introduction of Microsoft Teams, departments and project teams will be able to communicate and collaborate directly within the tool rather than through emails.	Office 365 Admin Portal	Number of internal emails sent per user per month	~400	<300	< 200
Automation	Leverage forms and workflows to digitize and automate business processes	Microsoft Flow, Microsoft PowerApps	Number of travel requests submitted online	0	20%	35%

(*continued*)

Table 14-1. *(continued)*

Category	Description	Tool	Metrics	Baseline	Milestone 1 target	Milestone 2 target
Sharing	Leverage OneDrive for Business for all personal files	Office 365 Admin Portal - OneDrive Usage, Power BI Adoption Content Pack - OneDrive for Business Usage, OneDrive User Activity	Number of active accounts, Number of files	50% active accounts, 20% of total personal files (OneDrive for Business plus file share personal home drive)	100% active accounts, 50% of total personal files (OneDrive for Business plus file share personal home drive)	100% active accounts, 75% of total personal files (OneDrive for Business plus file share personal home drive)
Sharing	Leverage Office 365 Groups, Microsoft Teams, and SharePoint Team sites for all collaborative content	Office 365 Admin Portal - OneDrive Usage, Power BI Adoption Content Pack - SharePoint Usage, SharePoint User Activity				

Make sure that when you capture the metrics that it is done in a consistent manner. Office 365 offers two great tools to help you with gathering these metrics, Office 365 Usage Reports and Power BI Adoption Content Pack.

Office 365 Usage Reports

The Office 365 Usage Reports provide your admins with information on how your users are leveraging the various apps and services in the platform. Reports can be filtered for the last 7 days, 30 days, 90 days, and 180 days. As shown in Figure 14-3, you can capture metrics such as the following:

- **Email activity**: Emails sent, received, and read by each user
- **OneDrive for Business usage**: Number of files used by each user and last activity
- **SharePoint usage**: How many files are viewed, synced, and shared internally or externally
- **Skype for Business**: Number of calls organized, participated in, and peer-to-peer chats
- **Office activations**: How many users have activated Office 365 ProPlus on their PC or mobile devices
- **Yammer activity**: Number of messages posted, read, and liked by each user
- **Microsoft Team activity**: Number of channel messages, chats, calls, and meetings each user participated in

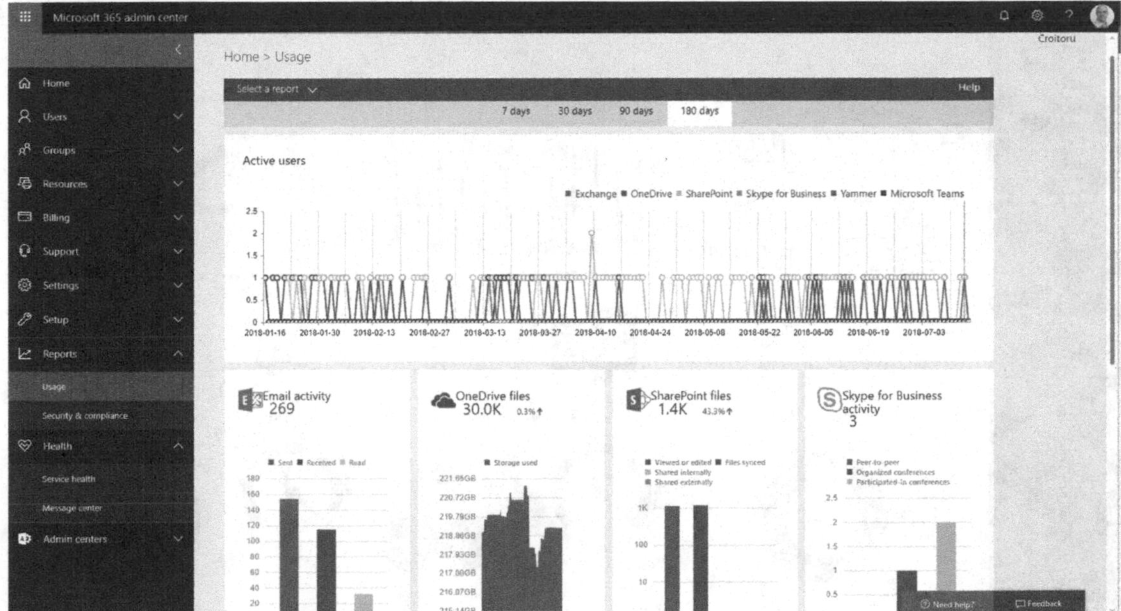

Figure 14-3. *Office 365 Usage Reports*

You can export each of these reports in Excel format and leverage them in your adoption metrics.

Power BI Adoption Content Pack

The Adoption Content Pack in Power BI connects to your Office 365 to provide further insights into how your organization is adopting Office 365 to communicate and collaborate. The visual report shown in Figure 14-4 allows you to drill down into the various metrics to better understand how specific departments and regions are using the various apps.

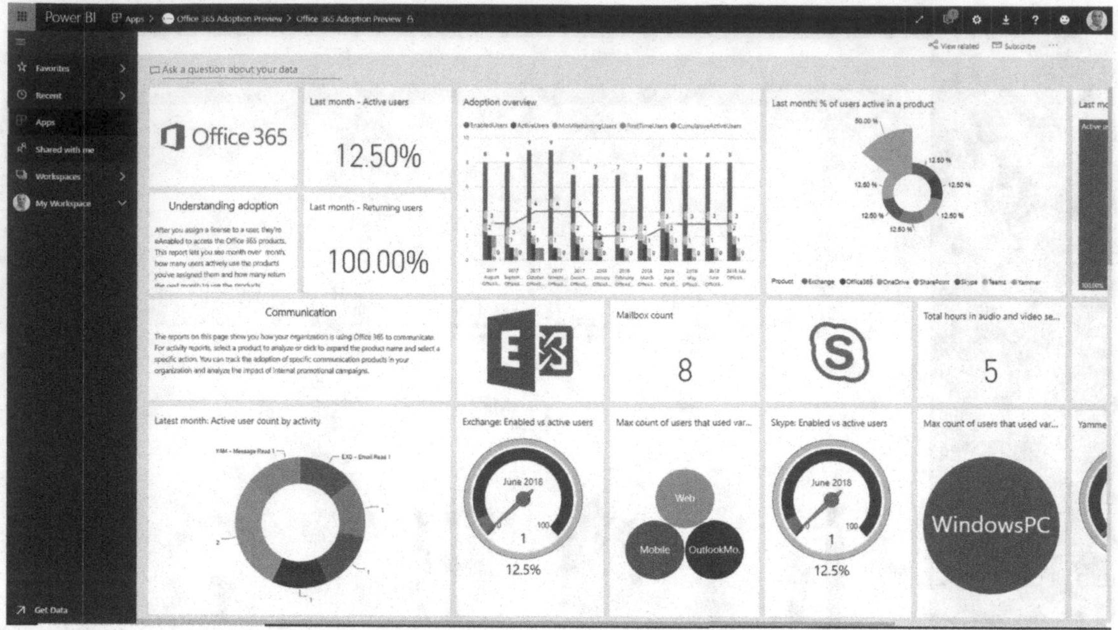

***Figure 14-4.** Power BI Adoption Content Pack provides visual reports of how Office 365 is adopted within your organization*

The data captured from your tenant is used by Power BI to provide you with the following reports:

- **Adoption overview report**: Summary of overall adoption trends in your organization to help you learn how your users have adopted Office 365 as well as how overall usage of the individual services has changed month-over-month.
- **Product usage report**: Summarizes key activities for each service.
- **Storage used report**: Track cloud storage for mailboxes, OneDrive, and SharePoint sites.
- **Communication report**: Find out whether your users have adopted Teams, Skype for Business, and Yammer for their internal communications or whether email is still the preferred means of communication.

- **Collaboration report**: Find out how your users use OneDrive for Business and SharePoint to store and collaborate on documents (internally and externally) and how these trends evolve month over month. You can also see how many SharePoint sites or OneDrive accounts are actively being used.
- **Office activation report**: Track license activations for Office 365 ProPlus, Project, and Visio.
- **Access from anywhere report**: Find out which clients and devices people use to connect to email, Skype for Business, or Yammer.
- **Individual service usage reports**: Usage reports are available for certain individual services.
- **Individual service user activity reports**: Determine user activity for certain services.

These two tools provide a wealth of adoption-related information to help you assess how well your organization is adopting Office 365 and any other specific changes you may have introduced. Depending on your scenario, you may need to rely on other information that may be extracted from your Office 365 tenant via Power BI, PowerShell, or other third-party tools.

Maturity

One question that may come during your adoption conversations is whether the adoption goals are realistic. One of the worst things that you can do as a project lead is to set unachievable goals. This will not only demoralize the team but may actually slow down adoption as users are faced with changes that are too complex to adjust to. When you work with your business sponsors to identify goals, I suggest that you begin by building out the maturity model for your organization to determine how advanced you are in various categories. This will help you determine your project.

Moving your business to Office 365 will require a certain level of business, process, and IT maturation to best leverage the functionality that it offers.

- **Level 100, None**: Your organization is lacking knowledge or structure in the particular area. The activities in that area are mostly ad-hoc with little long-term benefit of the work performed.

- **Level 200, Basic**: Your organization has adopted some fundamental structure to create more consistency and contains the knowledge to continue building and improving the processes.
- **Level 300, Standard**: Your organization is functioning in an efficient, reproducible manner with the proper support structure. Processes are well defined to minimize waste.
- **Level 400, Transformational**: Following established processes and keeping with the structure is not enough for your organization. You are currently reassessing the performance and innovating for further improvements.

Table 14-2 provides a few examples of key maturity categories and a description that matches the various maturity levels listed above.

***Table 14-2.** Office 365 Maturity Model*

	Level 100, None	Level 200, Basic	Level 300, Standard	Level 400, Transformational
Social collaboration	Users are working independently, leveraging traditional collaboration tools for document sharing. The organization is change-resistant. No well-established policies exist.	Users leverage autonomous group-based collaborative tools without a common platform. There is intra-departmental group collaboration. Users are becoming receptive to change. High-level policies are established, but may not be enforced.	Collaboration tools are leveraged at higher organizational levels (divisions, practices). Policies are actively enforced and applied by IT.	Collaboration is occurring at all levels of the organization, both internal and external. Policies are aligned with core strategy, and enforcement is not limited to IT.

(*continued*)

Table 14-2. (*continued*)

	Level 100, None	Level 200, Basic	Level 300, Standard	Level 400, Transformational
Document management	No organizational data management strategy is defined. Users store documents in private folders. Sharing of documents occurs via emails. Naming conventions don't exist. A high level of data duplication exists.	Documents are stored in centralized locations. Guidelines exist on types of documents and where they should be stored as well as naming conventions. However, these guidelines are not often followed and seldom enforced. A moderate level of data duplication exists.	A document management system is used to control shared content. Versioning and check-in/check-out functionality exist but is not enforced. Data duplication is significantly reduced through proper use of centralizing DMS.	A document management system is fully integrated into daily activities. Policies are in place to manage document lifecycle. Workflows are implemented to archive final/approved versions of documents. Little corporate data is stored in any non-DMS locations.
Enterprise mobile	There is no support or capabilities for mobile devices. A mobile strategy does not exist. No mobile policies exist.	There is corporate agreement on the need for a mobile strategy. Some policies and reactive governance exist. There are limited mobile device capabilities. There is limited usage of unmanaged mobile devices in the organization.	There is a published roadmap and strategy. Proactive governance, cross-platform security, device management, and policies exist. Enterprise mobile enabled email, calendar, corporate directory, and IM options exist.	Mobile support is a key strategy driver. Mobile governance is integrated as part of overall governance. Centrally-managed device management, security, and policies exist. There is enterprise communication and collaboration including enterprise social computing.

Maturity Assessment

Leveraging a maturity model allows you to evaluate your organization's baseline and readiness to adopt changes. One way to present the information is by using a radar chart, as shown in Figure 14-5.

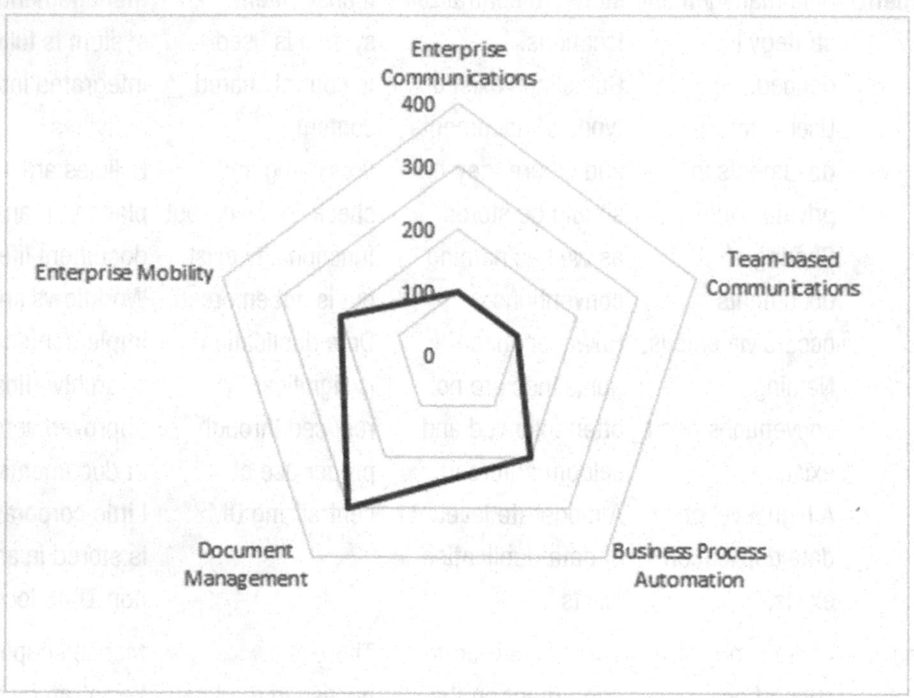

***Figure 14-5.** Radar chart showing maturity for various categories within an organization*

By grouping related categories close to each other, you can get a sense of the general areas of maturity that your organization excels in. Over time, you can capture the same maturity levels (as compared to the goals) and determine in which area the progress is trending, as shown in Figure 14-6.

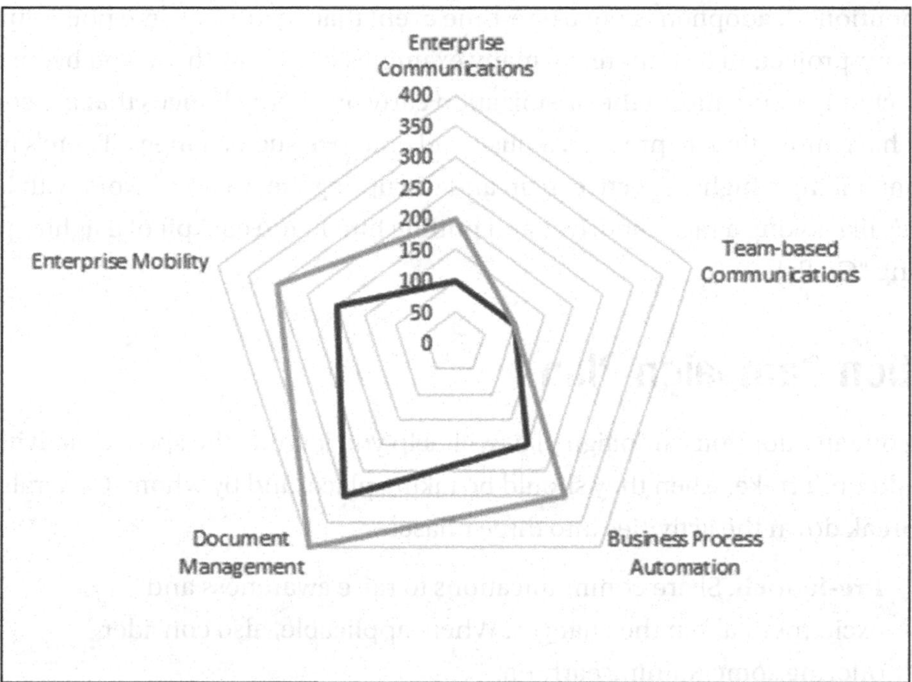

***Figure 14-6.** Radar chart showing maturity progress over time*

In Figure 14-6, you can see that most categories have advanced in their level of maturity, except for team-based communications, which remained the same. This would indicate that the changes that were introduced were focused more on areas such as enterprise communications, collaboration, mobility, and business process automation. Therefore, the adoption goals for the changes introduced should not focus on showing an increase of team-based communications but rather focus on the other areas that are in fact impacted.

Adoption Campaigns

So far, I've been talking about adoption goals and how to measure them. In this last section, I'll present you with some examples of activities or campaigns that you can use to drive user adoption. The real campaigns you'll introduce will vary based on the changes that are being introduced.

As mentioned, adoption is not a one-time event that occurs at some point during or after your project. In fact, there are many examples that show that if you begin to socialize changes and inform the organization early on about changes that are coming, they will have more time to prepare, adjust, and embrace such changes. There's nothing worse than taking a highly effective team and disrupting the way they work with little notice. It's like taking a race car driver and putting him in the cockpit of a fighter plan and saying "Go fly!"

Adoption Campaign Plan

Building out an adoption campaign plan will help you identify the specific activities you should undertake, when they should be taking place, and by whom. Generally, you should break down the activities into three phases.

1. **Pre-launch**: Share communications to raise awareness and excitement about the changes. Where applicable, also consider offering some training early on.

2. **Launch**: During this hypercare period, there should be an increased amount of communication to get participation from the users. As this will be the first time that many users will see the new product or enhancements, make sure to have extra support available to answer questions and react to issues being raised.

3. **Post-launch**: In an ongoing basis, review the adoption goal metrics discussed earlier in this chapter and identify specific areas that need additional attention. You should plan regular user engagement activities to take place.

The ongoing attention will ensure that as new capabilities are released into Office 365 and the organization, change continues to be managed effectively. Table 14-3 provides some examples of adoption campaigns you can include as part of your own change management activities.

Table 14-3. *Adoption Campaign Plan Detailing Various Activities Throughout the Project Phases*

What type of activity?	How will it be delivered?	When will it be delivered?	Who will it be delivered by?	What purpose will it serve?
Name your intranet	Online survey	1-2 months pre-launch	Marketing & Communications	Let users feel that the intranet is theirs and they have a say
Intranet goals and purpose	Yammer/email	Periodically, pre-launch	C-suite and key leadership	Raise awareness of new intranet
Highlight of Office 365 resources	Yammer/email	Pre-launch	Training team	Provide resources for users to come up to speed with the new changes
Training sessions notifications and sign-up	Yammer/email	Pre-launch, launch, post-launch	Training team	Provide ongoing training to users
Intranet treasure hunt	Yammer/email	Launch	Marketing & Communications	Give users reasons to dive into the different parts of your intranet to discover new content
YamJams	Yammer	Post-launch	C-suite and key leadership	Open forum for anyone to ask questions to senior leadership and get their responses answered to a broad audience
Picture contest	Yammer	Launch, post-launch	Marketing & Communications	Break down mental blocks of posting content on the corporate Yammer group by encouraging users to post their pictures

(*continued*)

Table 14-3. *(continued)*

What type of activity?	How will it be delivered?	When will it be delivered?	Who will it be delivered by?	What purpose will it serve?
Tips and tricks	Yammer/email	Pre-launch, launch post-launch	Training	Each tip will include answers to a common question and a "Learn more" link that will redirect users to the organization's Training Center of Excellence

As you can see, there are many areas of communication that can help drive adoption for Office 365 and specific new features. Experiment to see what works best in your organization.

Summary

To increase the chances of success for new Office 365 features or products being rolled out into your organization, you need to plan for their adoption. It's not enough to send out a message mentioning what change is being made and when. Successful adoption requires careful planning and delivery of adoption campaign activities to determine whether the adoption goals are being met.

In the next chapter, I will dive deeper into various forms of communication that can be leveraged for adoption activities and other areas of your agile project delivery.

CHAPTER 15

Communications

Communication is one of the most important activities a project lead performs. This is particularly true in agile project management where there is a heavy reliance on verbal and informal communication in lieu of structured documents. As discussed in Chapter 2, agile projects thrive in an environment where team members interact face-to-face on a regular basis. However, today's project teams are becoming increasingly disparate. So how can you still effectively communicate at a level that will make your agile projects successful?

In this chapter, I will discuss some strategies and mediums to best communicate progress on your Office 365 projects using Office 365 itself as a medium.

The Importance of Good Communication

We often hear about the importance of good communication in project management. But have you ever stopped to wonder what makes it so important? One of the big factors has to do with stakeholder management. When someone trusts you and your team to deliver what was committed, your communication will help reassure them of the progress or bring forth any important information they need to know. In fact, effective communication plays such an important role in project delivery that it can mean the difference between success and failure.

Figure 15-1 provides a great visual summary of a study[1] performed by the Project Management Institute (PMI). It showed that 80% of projects delivered by highly effective communicators met the original goals vs. only 52% by their minimally effective counterparts. The same study showed that highly effective communicators are also more likely to deliver projects on time (71% vs. 37%) and within budget (76% vs. 48%).

[1]PMI's "Pulse of the Profession™ In-Depth Report: The Essential Role of Communications"

H. Croitoru, *Agile Office 365*, https://doi.org/10.1007/978-1-4842-4081-6_15

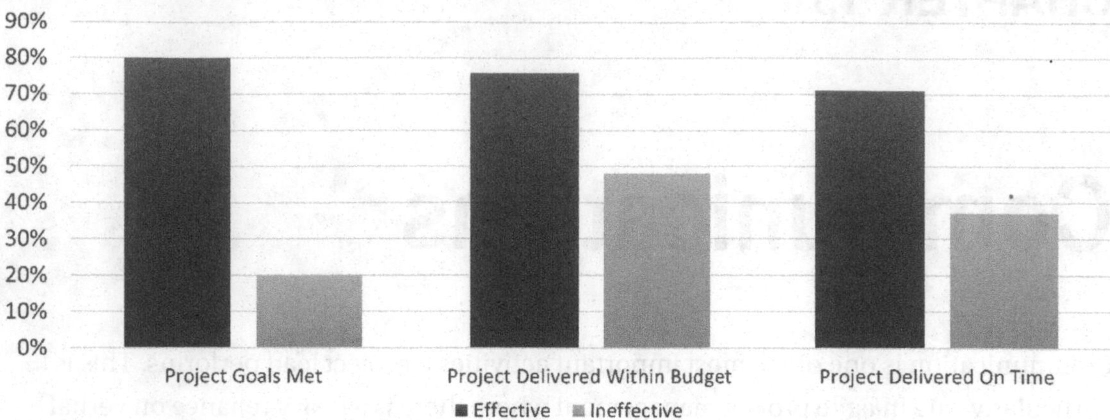

Figure 15-1. *The impact of effective communications on a project*

When you plan your work, you must allocate sufficient time to clearly capture and share key information about the progress of the project.

Communicating Up, Down, and Across Your Organization

As a project lead, you will undoubtedly need to interact with numerous individuals and teams within your organization and outside. Depending on their level of involvement and stake in the project, the type, frequency, level of detail, and medium of the communication will vary. In Table 15-1, I provide you with a high-level overview of the recommended communication types for your agile Office 365 project.

Table 15-1. *Communication Types Used in Agile Projects*

Type	Purpose	Medium	Timing	Audience
Vision statement	Communicate the overall project vision to the organization	Presentation or announcement	Onset of the project	Project sponsors and stakeholders, including anyone within the organization who is impacted by the project or its outcome
Product roadmap	Communicates long-term view of features that will be available for the various releases that make up the project	Presentation or announcement	After initial planning	Project sponsors, stakeholders, and steering committee
Release plan	Communicates what will be included within a specific release	Presentation generated from backlog	At the end of each release planning activity	Project sponsors, stakeholders, steering committee, project team
Product backlog	Captures the features and functionality in the form of user stories and epics	List (e.g. Excel or SharePoint list)	Continuously updated by product owner	Project sponsors, stakeholders, steering committee, project team
Sprint backlog	User stories that were committed by the project team for the sprint	List (e.g. Excel or SharePoint list), including the backlog items being committed, details around the user story, and estimates	During sprint planning	Product owner, project team

(*continued*)

Table 15-1. *(continued)*

Type	Purpose	Medium	Timing	Audience
Sprint planning daily Scrum	Short (15-min) meetings to help the Scrum team coordinate the priorities of the day and identify any challenges	In person or via audio/video conferencing. Summary of the meeting should be published in a location accessible to anyone who is part of the project.	Daily during project execution	Project lead/Scrum master, project team, product owner
Sprint review	Live demo of the working product to the team to convey progress	In person or via audio/video conferencing. Summary of the meeting should be published in a location accessible to anyone who is part of the project.	At the end of each sprint	Product owner, project team, stakeholders
Sprint retrospective	Discuss how the Scrum team performed and identify ways to improve for subsequent sprints	In person or via audio/video conferencing. Summary of the meeting should be published in a location accessible to anyone who is part of the project.	At the end of each sprint	Project lead/Scrum master, project team
Project updates	Provide a general project update to the organization	Presentation or announcement	At key milestones throughout the project lifecycle	Anyone within the organization who is impacted by the project or its outcome

Communicating with Dispersed Teams

An agile team that is geographically dispersed requires additional communication because the team members cannot benefit from the osmotic learning of being directly or indirectly exposed to discussions surrounding the project. There are, however, some steps you can take to ease the communication gap, including

- Work items that are closely dependent on each other should be developed by team members who are co-located as much as possible and/or speak a common language.
- For larger projects with different user groups, try to co-locate the business users in the same region where the solution is being developed.
- Communicate frequently using several mediums, such as e-mail, OneNote, Microsoft Teams, and audio/video conferencing.
- When teams are in vastly different time zones, rotate the meeting hours out of basic courtesy and consideration for everyone.

Office 365 Apps for Remote Meetings

Everyone has their favorite set of tools they use for everyday tasks. Working within a remote working environment for over half a decade has helped me develop my own preferred ways to facilitate meetings and communicate successfully with my team members. Here are some of the main tools and practices I use on a regular basis:

- **Audio/video conferencing**: Microsoft Teams has recently become my Office 365 app of choice for internal communication and collaboration. It enables me to easily schedule single or recurring audio/video calls with my teams and capture information in the Team meeting channels. Similarly, I commonly use Skype, particularly when working with external users. Using audio and video allows me to not only get the core information but also to perceive information that may not be shared in written communication. Is a team member frustrated? Do I sense concern about the progress? Also, it's great to have the ability to record a meeting, such as when important decisions are being made or I don't have time to capture notes. If you choose to record meetings, just make sure to get permission from the other attendees on the call.

- **Live note taking**: This is a technique in which I share my screen during an audio/video session and show the users the notes that are being captured. It allows the attendees to provide immediate feedback so when they receive the meeting minutes, there are no surprises. As well, live note taking enables me to send out meeting minutes almost as soon as the meeting is over (assuming there are no follow-up items).
- **Collaborative note taking**: Leveraging OneNote lets the various attendees all edit the same content, thus making sure that each individual validates their own information.
- **Instant messaging**: Microsoft Teams and Skype both let you instant message your peers. It's quick and easy, and when users are online, it provides them with a notification immediately. While some users love the reactiveness, others find it distracting while they are focusing on work. Find out from your team members what works best for them. The etiquette I recommend to my teams is that if they are busy with work, they should mark themselves in Do No Disturb mode or even close their Microsoft Teams and Skype applications.
- **Yammer**: This app is great for sharing and discussing information outside of the immediate project group. Use Yammer to provide project updates to the organization, including images and links to some of the information.

Leveraging Communication for Product Direction

The role of the project lead is to identify the features and functions for the product and prioritize them against each other. However, there may be times when even they could use a little help from others. Consider the scenario where your project team has completed all the planned work for the releases but there's still some time and budget left. Wouldn't it be great to have a poll to ask your users what functionality *they* would like? Imagine how pleased they would be to know that their opinion mattered. In fact, Microsoft adopted a similar approach in recent years where users are able to submit requests and vote on requests posted from others. These requests, submitted on a site called *User Voice* shown in Figure 15-2, are reviewed internally by the Microsoft product management teams as feedback for future enhancements.

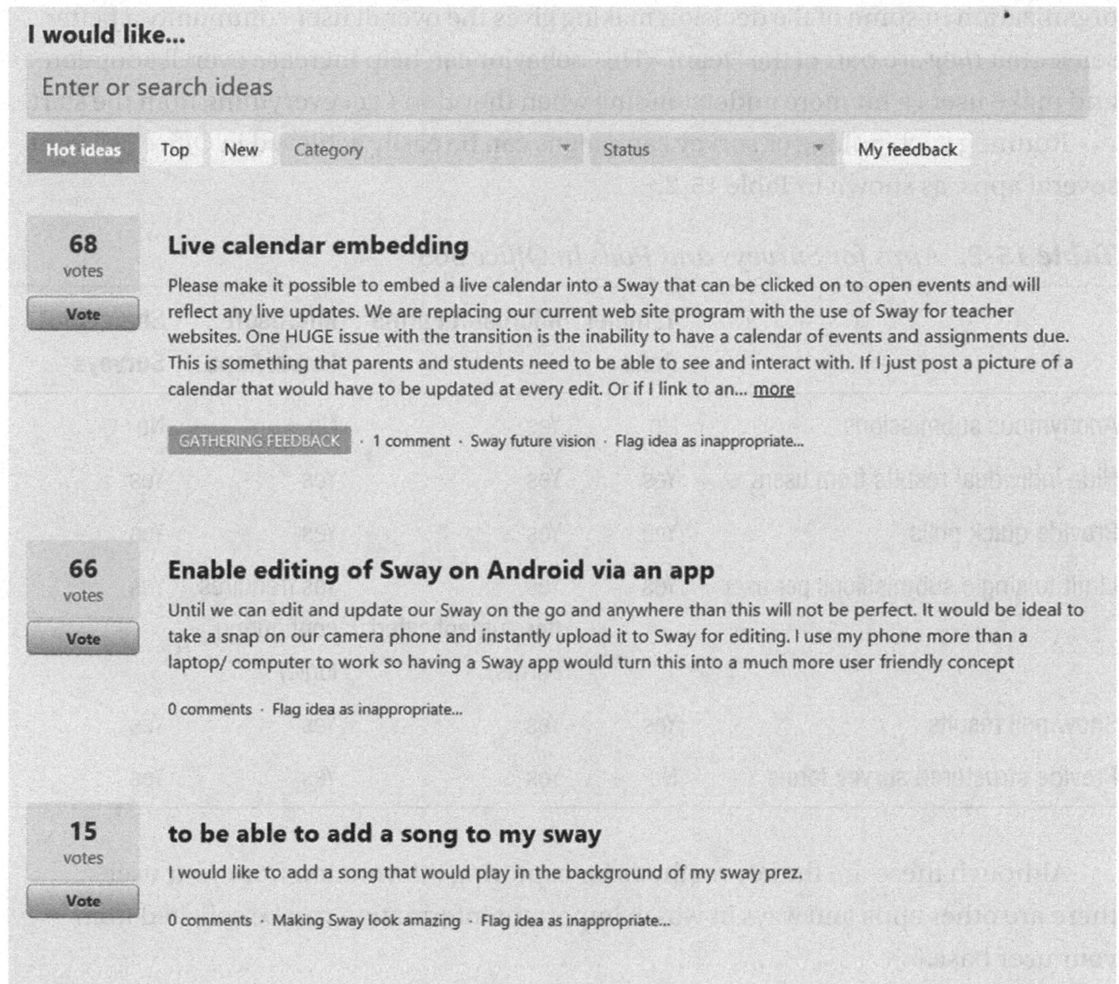
I would like...
Enter or search ideas
Hot ideas
Top
New
Category
Status
My feedback
68
votes
Vote
Live calendar embedding
Please make it possible to embed a live calendar into a Sway that can be clicked on to open events and will reflect any live updates. We are replacing our current web site program with the use of Sway for teacher websites. One HUGE issue with the transition is the inability to have a calendar of events and assignments due. This is something that parents and students need to be able to see and interact with. If I just post a picture of a calendar that would have to be updated at every edit. Or if I link to an... more
GATHERING FEEDBACK · 1 comment · Sway future vision · Flag idea as inappropriate...
66
votes
Vote
Enable editing of Sway on Android via an app
Until we can edit and update our Sway on the go and anywhere than this will not be perfect. It would be ideal to take a snap on our camera phone and instantly upload it to Sway for editing. I use my phone more than a laptop/ computer to work so having a Sway app would turn this into a much more user friendly concept
0 comments · Flag idea as inappropriate...
15
votes
Vote
to be able to add a song to my sway
I would like to add a song that would play in the background of my sway prez.
0 comments · Making Sway look amazing · Flag idea as inappropriate...

***Figure 15-2.** User Voice is used by Microsoft to gather product feedback and requests from the user community*

Another common scenario for gathering feedback from your user community is to have naming contests for a new intranet, for example. There are different ways in which you could run such a campaign. In an open campaign, every name submission could be seen by everyone within the organization and users could have the option to vote on someone else's submission or add their own submission into the mix. In a closed campaign, users could still submit a name and a smaller group (typically marketing or corporate communications) would select the winner or even open the voting to a second round for users to pick from one of the finalists. Regardless of the approach taken, the fact that the project leadership team is reaching out and involving the entire organization in some of the decision making gives the overall user community a better sense that *they* are part of the "team." This behavior can help increase overall adoption and make users a bit more understanding when they don't get everything from the start.

Running such polling or survey campaigns can be easily achieved in Office 365 with several apps, as shown in Table 15-2.

Table 15-2. *Apps for Surveys and Polls in Office 365*

	Yammer Polls	Microsoft Forms	Microsoft PowerApps	SharePoint Surveys
Anonymous submissions	No	Yes	No	No
Hide individual results from users	Yes	Yes	Yes	Yes
Provide quick polls	Yes	Yes	Yes	Yes
Limit to single submissions per user	Yes	Yes (for authenticated Forms)	Yes (requires configuring logic)	Yes
Show poll results	Yes	Yes	Yes	Yes
Provide structured survey forms	No	Yes	Yes	Yes

Although these are the key methods for capturing information from your users, there are other apps and ways in which important information can be solicited from your user base.

Summary

Communication plays a key role in successful projects. The need is amplified by the nature of agile projects, where there is more reliance on frequent verbal and written communication over heavy documentation. You need to pay special attention if your project team is not co-located because it adds another level of complexity. Luckily, Office 365 offers a number of tools than can help you address your communication needs.

In the sixth and final section of this book, you'll dive deeper into how the Office 365 apps can be used to manage your agile projects. Chapter 16 will look at some of the common needs for a project lead working on Office 365 projects, while Chapter 17 will introduce Office 365 as its own project management information system (PMIS).

PART VI

Tools for Managing Office 365 Projects

CHAPTER 16

Information Requirements

Having managed projects for over 15 years, I can tell you that there really isn't such a thing as "standard" project management practices. Organizations leverage their own unique blend of project management-related processes, artifacts, and governance. Yet, you'll likely find that there is a lot of overlap between project management practices across organizations. But rarely will you be able to reuse the same practices you're accustomed to as you move from place to place.

Whether you have a PMI, Prince 2, Scrum Alliance, or any other project management body background, one thing is common to them all. They provide you with a best practices framework that you'll build on and refine to your own processes and procedures needs. Let's have a look at the common information requirements you will likely encounter when leading projects.

Information Requirements

Throughout the project, you and your team will be creating vital information, which will ensure the successful progression and outcome of the project. The information produced generally falls into four categories:

- **Communication**: All the audio, video, written, and in-person forms in which your team communicates with others
- **Logs**: Information gathered during the project to help manage certain events and decisions
- **Reports**: A form to capture a moment in time on the progress of your project
- **Files**: Artifacts that are the deliverables or supporting the overall outcome of your project

H. Croitoru, *Agile Office 365*, https://doi.org/10.1007/978-1-4842-4081-6_16

Communication

If you put aside any form of methodology or framework you use, you will likely agree that one of the most important values you provide to your team is communication. No matter how good your processes or methodologies are, if you are not communicating well, your project is bound to suffer. In fact, as discussed in Chapter 15, studies have shown a strong correlation between communication and project outcomes.

As a project lead, you will have frequent communication up, down, and across your organizational levels. The medium, frequency, and content of your communications will vary based on who you communicate with. Within your project team, it is up to you to ensure that all your team members are well informed to perform their duties; conversely, your team should share with you their progress, needs, and any impediments they need your assistance with. Outside of the team, you inform your sponsors and stakeholders on the progress and provide important data back to your team.

Before videoconferencing, email, and intranets entered the workforce, project teams needed to be co-located in order to work effectively. Today, however, many of us are working with colleagues who may be sitting next to us or half-way across the globe in a different time zone. Working in geographically-dispersed teams adds a level of communication complexity that is important to consider in agile teams because the sense of eavesdropping or learning by osmosis is lost.

Your tool set should allow for synchronous as well as asynchronous communication to take place and ensure that others can easily access the content in case they were not able to participate in real time.

Logs

Project logs help you capture, track, and communicate important events and decisions that occur throughout the project. Common logs include risk, issue, decision, change logs, and action items. The value of logs is often overlooked because they are perceived as overhead that provides little value to the outcome of the project.

In some cases, you will track risks or issues that may never materialize for the remainder of the project. Yet, this information can help plan future projects and preempt similar situations from happening.

Decision logs help the team keep track of important decisions that were made and why. With Office 365 evolving quickly, it will help you recap why your team went down a given path. For example, if you are implementing a solution that requires collaboration on documents between various team members, you can use either Office 365 Groups or SharePoint team sites. There are advantages and disadvantages to both, and your decision log will capture why your team chose to proceed with an option in a point in time.

Change logs help you track important changes that were introduced since the onset of the project. Given that your project is following an agile methodology, change is something you should expect to manage on a very frequent basis. For a large part, you'll be managing the scope changes through the product backlog and reviewing it with the product owner and stakeholders on a regular basis. However, other types of changes will not be captured in the backlog, and they should be noted in the change log. Changes to budget or overall timelines will not have a direct impact on each sprint you execute, but will impact how long your team will need to be allocated to the project and whether the team needs to shrink or grow. There are also scope changes that may appear in the product backlog that can have a large impact on the overall delivery and should be captured separately. For example, if your minimal shippable product included 10 items from the product backlog and now there are 20 items, it will impact other factors, such as number of sprints required to deliver the work.

Some of the logs mentioned above will often include action items which, depending on your approach, may be tracked as part of the logs themselves or in a separate action log. In my experience, getting into the practice of tracking all action items in one place will save you from hunting for information in multiple logs.

The amount of information that you track in your logs will depend on the PMO practices and governance in your organization. I have seen risk logs that have very little information, such as title, status, and a short description to more extensive logs that include probability, impact, mitigation steps, mitigation probability, accountable person, updates, and more. At the end of the day, consider the use of these logs to determine how much information you will track in them and how.

Updates on log entries will typically be reviewed during project updates or when your project proceeds through major milestones, such as implementation or transition from your project team to the support team.

Reports

Reports are used to provide project updates to key stakeholders for a given point in time. As with logs, you will find a lot of variety in the format and content used for reports and you will need to assess what works best in your organization (Table 16-1). Reports will often include a combination of text and graphical content to convey the status. Some common themes you would expect in reports are shown in Table 16-1.

Table 16-1. *Common Project Report Information*

Data	Format	Example
Sprint goals	Free form text	Overview on progression of sprint against sprint goals
Constraint KPIs	Color indicators	Visual indicators (e.g. green, yellow, red) on various project parameters, such as cost, timelines, scope, risks
Product backlog burn-down	Chart	Graphically depicts how much of the product backlog has been completed and how much remains
Sprint backlog changes	List	Any changes that were introduced throughout the sprint
Risks/issues updates	List	Updates on all open or new risks/issues identified
Change request updates	List	Updates on all open or new change requests
Action items updates	List	Updates on all open or new action items
Decision log updates	List	Updates on all open or new decisions made

I've worked with some organizations where reports were presented with real-time dashboards (Figure 16-1) so that any stakeholder could get an up-to-date picture of the project's progress at any time. If you decide to use this approach, consider the audience for the reports. Some stakeholders may review your status reports days or even weeks after you've sent it to them and ask for clarifications on certain items. You want to make sure that you can determine all project parameters at a specific point in time.

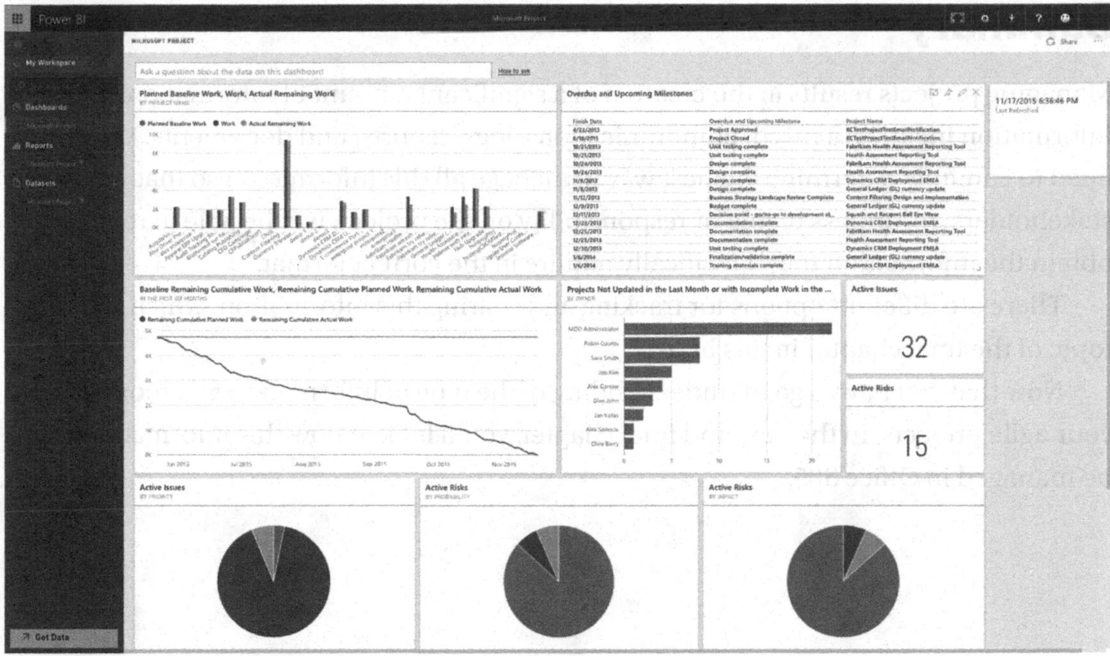

Figure 16-1. *Project dashboard (courtesy of Microsoft)*

Files

When working in Office 365, most of the intellectual property created by your project team will be files of some sort. These files constitute part of the deliverables as well as supporting documentation that lives on after the project is closed. The files that get created can be a mix of source code, training and user manuals, technical and business speciations, and various guides.

There is often a clear division on the creator and consumer of certain files. For example, you would expect your architects and developers to be working on the source code files and tests, and your business analysts on test plans and adoption plans. Because of the differing audiences and how the files are managed, you will likely also deal with multiple sources for the files. Source code and related files are commonly stored in a source control and versioning repository system such as Microsoft Visual Studio Team Services or GitHub. Documents like manuals and guides should be in a shared workspace where team members can collaborate on them.

To leverage past work and create a sense of consistency between projects, you should generate templates for your documents and standardize naming conventions for files.

Summary

Managing projects results in the creation of a significant amount of information. This information includes a mix of communications, logs, reports, and documents. You will need to carefully determine the best way to manage all this information so that your stakeholders, regardless of role or responsibility on the project, will be able to readily obtain the information they specifically require in the correct format.

There are different options for tracking and sharing this information, which is the topic of the final chapter in this book.

Now that you have a good understanding of the type of information you require for your agile projects, in the next and final chapter, you'll look at how this information can be managed in Office 365.

CHAPTER 17

Office 365 as a PMIS

If you have ever purchased a new car, you probably went through an agonizing experience to find just the right one for you. You know your new ride will help you get places and pick up your buddies, but what else? Are you a thrill seeker who likes to feel the road under your feet? If so, then a roadster will be your vehicle of choice. Do you like going camping deep in the woods and bring your canoe along? Then consider an SUV or cross-over. Is your family growing and do you need more space? You'll probably want a minivan in that case. To complicate things more, each specific model has its own features and bells and whistles, like leather trim, sunroof, and GPS. The point is that it's not easy to know what is right for you. And it doesn't help to be overwhelmed with all the car manufacturer advertisements on TV, radio, websites, and magazines that try to sway you to buy their cars.

Opening up the Office 365 app launcher may leave you scratching your head, asking yourself which app you should use to achieve a given task. Often a specific scenario will dictate the optimal choice for the task. The key is to provide the right information to the right person, at the right time, and in the right format.

To meet the diverse needs of different organizations, Microsoft introduced a number of great project management-focused tools for both agile and waterfall-based projects. In this final chapter, I will review what tools are best for managing your agile projects. The review will cover the tools that fall into the categories introduced in the last chapter: communication, logs, reports, and files.

H. Croitoru, *Agile Office 365*, https://doi.org/10.1007/978-1-4842-4081-6_17

Project Communication

Since its purchase by Microsoft in 2012, Yammer has become one of the main social communication offering for Office 365 users. With the ability to create specific groups, embed a Yammer feed into a web page such as SharePoint, and a dedicated mobile app, Yammer is one of the most popular options for project communication (Figure 17-1).

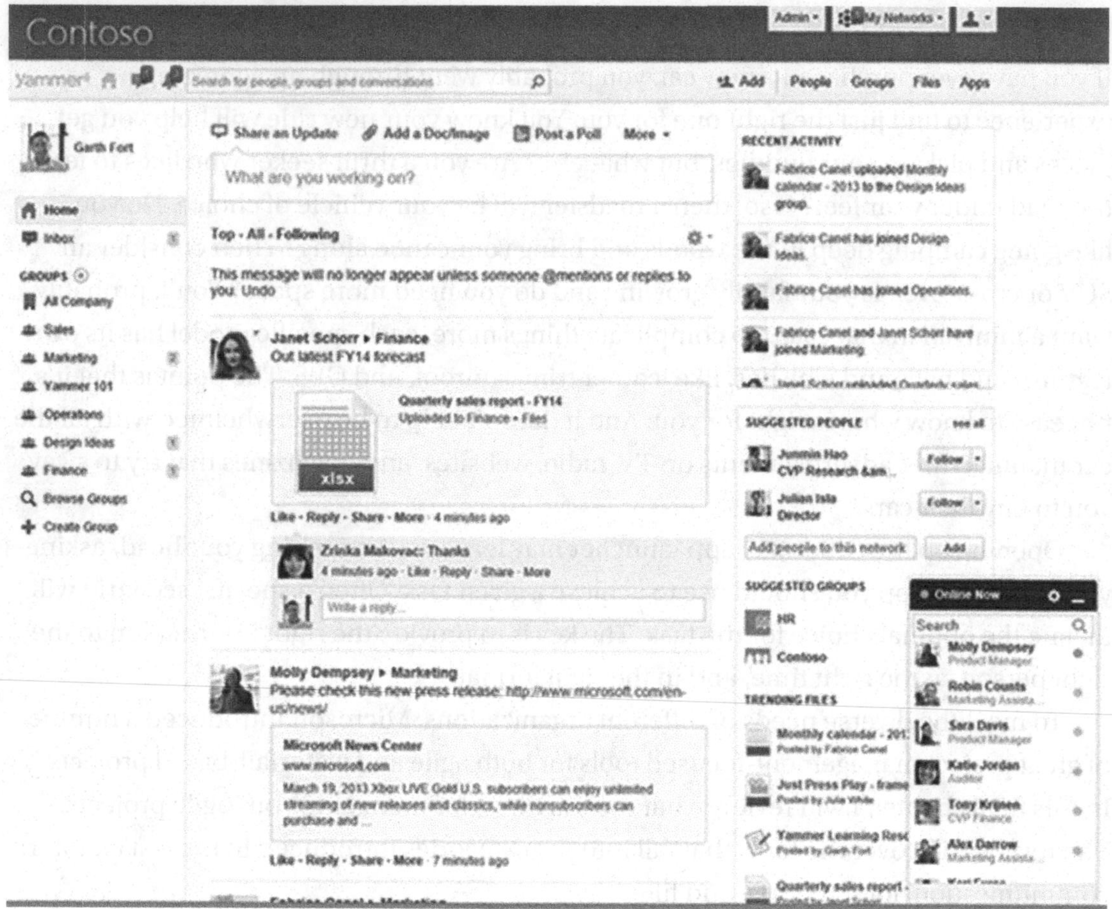

Figure 17-1. *Yammer is one of the most popular otions for project communication*

Another popular choice for project communication is through Office 365 Groups. The groups offer a dedicated email address that project team members can leverage to keep others in the loop.

Microsoft Teams offers a great mix of feeds and email-based communications through the creation of channels that users can use to directly send messages or email content.

Skype for Business and Microsoft Teams audio/video chats are great for conducting real-time conversations. But keep in mind that others who are not attending these meetings may have a hard time getting this information.

Logs

When a single project lead manages risks or other list-based information, Excel lends itself well to the task. However, it is best to have this type of information readily available to all team members and other stakeholders.

SharePoint Online and Project Online lists are the preferred way to manage such logs because they provide you with the flexibility to track the items and alert users immediately of any changes to the various logs with little effort.

When it comes to tasks, there are many options available to you. If you are tracking the tasks and no one else will need to review or collaborate on them, Excel is a decent option. If you want to have the ability to assign tasks to others and let them provide updates, you may want to look at Outlook or Office 365 Planner tasks.

Planner provides a simple board-based interface for managing unstructured tasks. Figure 17-2 shows an example of a plan, including image-rich task content. Each plan is associated with an Office 365 Group, which includes a document library, calendar, conversation mailbox, and OneNote. Planner tasks are managed in the cloud and can easily be collaborated on by multiple users. You can also use Planner to manage other types of logs, such as risks or action items.

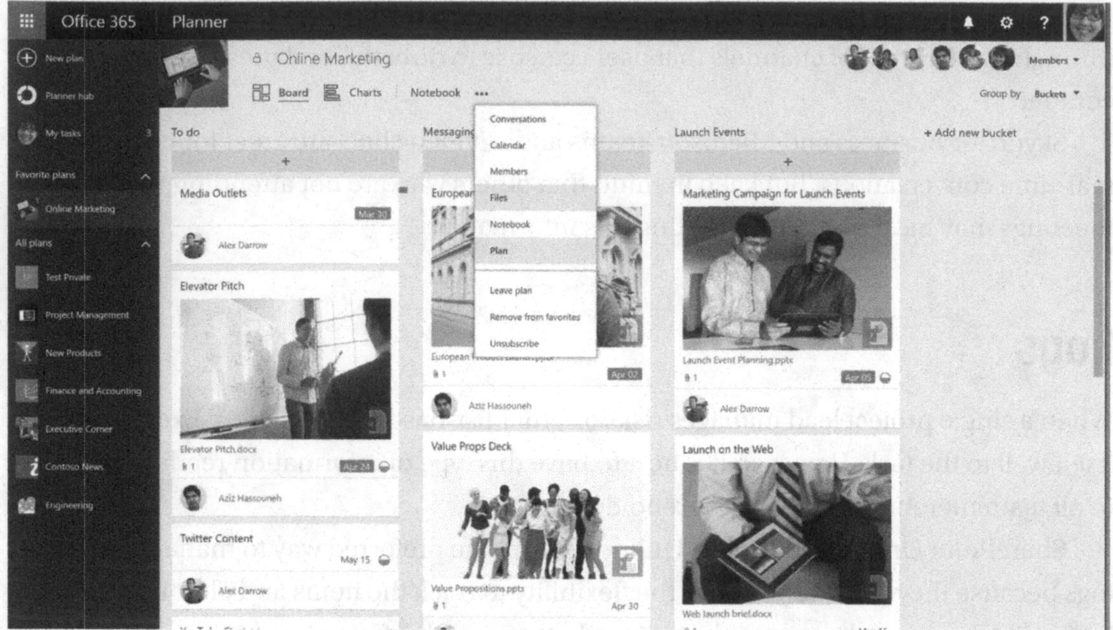

***Figure 17-2.** Office 365 Planner is used to track unstructured tasks*

SharePoint Online provides you with a Tasks list that integrates with Project, Project Online, and Outlook tasks. Once configured, your team can update their tasks directly in any of these apps.

Microsoft Project and Project Online are your fully-featured task management apps, which are used to provide great details on each task. Although in the agile world you manage your deliverables from sprint to sprint, project plans and tasks are still helpful for tracking some of the overarching tasks and release dates.

Reports

As mentioned in Chapter 16, reports are unique to each organization and can even vary between functional groups within an organization. The good thing is that in most cases, reports are based on information that has already been captured in your project plan, logs, and other communications. So, preparation of such reports will involve copying the information over. If you're lucky, you may have some workflows or other options to pull the data from the various sources to automatically generate the reports for you. If not, you'll have to manually copy the information over.

Regardless of the means of generating the report, the sources for the information will not change. Any list-based information, such as tasks and the various logs, will come from a SharePoint list or other tables stored in some document. The charts will likely be generated by Excel or Power BI, while the general overview description for the report can be added directly into the report or tracked in various other ways, such as a SharePoint list or OneNote.

Because of the large variety of reports, I typically don't consider building a project management solution around them. Rather, I ensure that the content gets managed in such a way that it can easily facilitate the creation of such reports.

Files

By using Office 365, much of the hard work is done for you when managing your project files. For documents, whether you're using SharePoint Online sites, Office 365 Groups, or any other app that is built on these two (such as Microsoft Teams and Project Online), the enterprise document management functionality is available to you. Depending on how you wish to structure your files, you can easily segment, group, and filter them in various ways.

Source code files are best managed using dedicated code repositories, such as Visual Studio Team Services (recently rebranded to Azure DevOps) or GitHub. These two services are not a part of Office 365 but integrate nicely with it.

It is possible to store documents on a network drive. However, this is not recommended because it segregates your information. When someone is not in the office, they may not have simple access to the documents. Other reasons to not use network drives are that content is typically not version controlled and it is more difficult to manage metadata associated with the documents.

Putting It All Together

Now that you've seen how the various pieces of the puzzle can fit together, let's look at some common ways to manage all aspects. Keep in mind that the recommendations below are only a few examples. There may be other ways that would work more effectively for your organization and projects.

SharePoint Sites

SharePoint Online sits at the core of several apps in Office 365, including Office 365 Groups and Project Online. For that reason, it makes sense to consider it as one of the viable options to meet your needs.

SharePoint Online comes with several templates that can be applied when creating a new site. Two of these templates, Team Site and Project Site, are most conducive for managing projects.

Team Site

The new Modern SharePoint Team site depicted in Figure 17-3 allows you to create multimedia-rich pages that can be easily viewed on desktop and mobile devices. You can easily add documents, videos, images, site activities, Yammer feeds, and more into these pages. Whenever you create a SharePoint Team site, an associated Office 365 Group will be created for it.

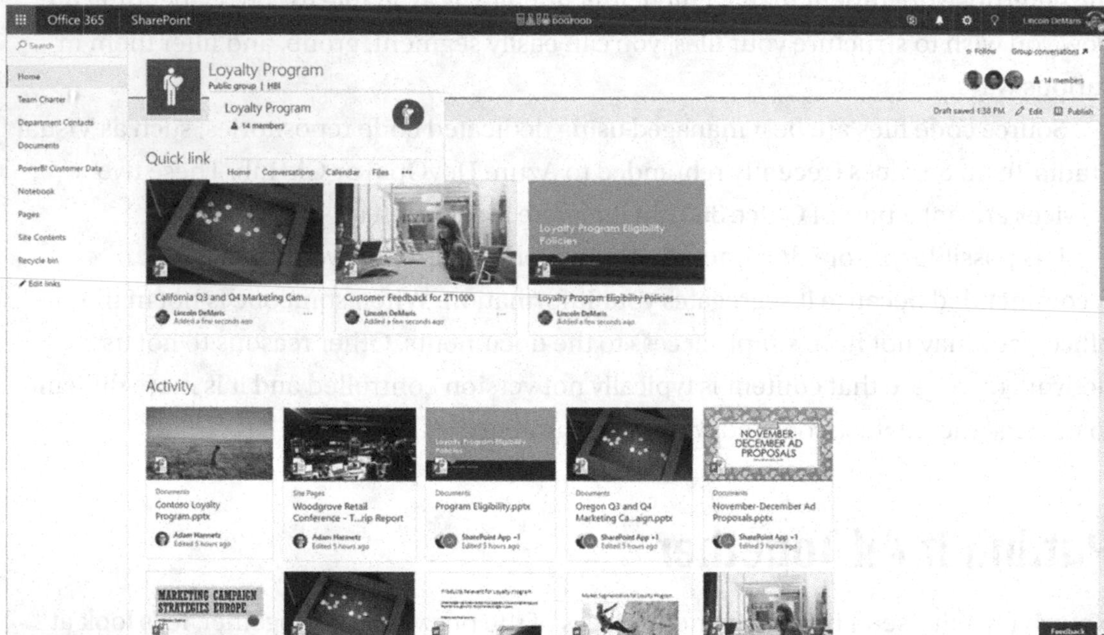

***Figure 17-3.** The new Modern SharePoint Team site provides much of the content needed to manage projects*

The items included in the new Team sites are explained in Table 17-1.

Table 17-1. *Common Team Site Content*

Items	Description
Quick links	Links to files, pages, or apps from within the site or anywhere on the Web
Activity	Find out what is happening on the team site by viewing the activity feed.
Lists	Leverage the lists for tracking the structured log data. Through the integration with Microsoft Flow and PowerApps, you can automate business processes and create mobile business applications for these logs.
Libraries	Libraries can be used to co-author, share, and organize documents.
Notebook	A OneNote is available to track your unstructured notes and meeting minutes.

Project Site

The Project site (available in Classic SharePoint only) can be looked at as an extension of the Team site with additional functionality that is specifically geared towards project management. The additional functionality includes a Tasks list and a Project Summary, as shown in Figure 17-4.

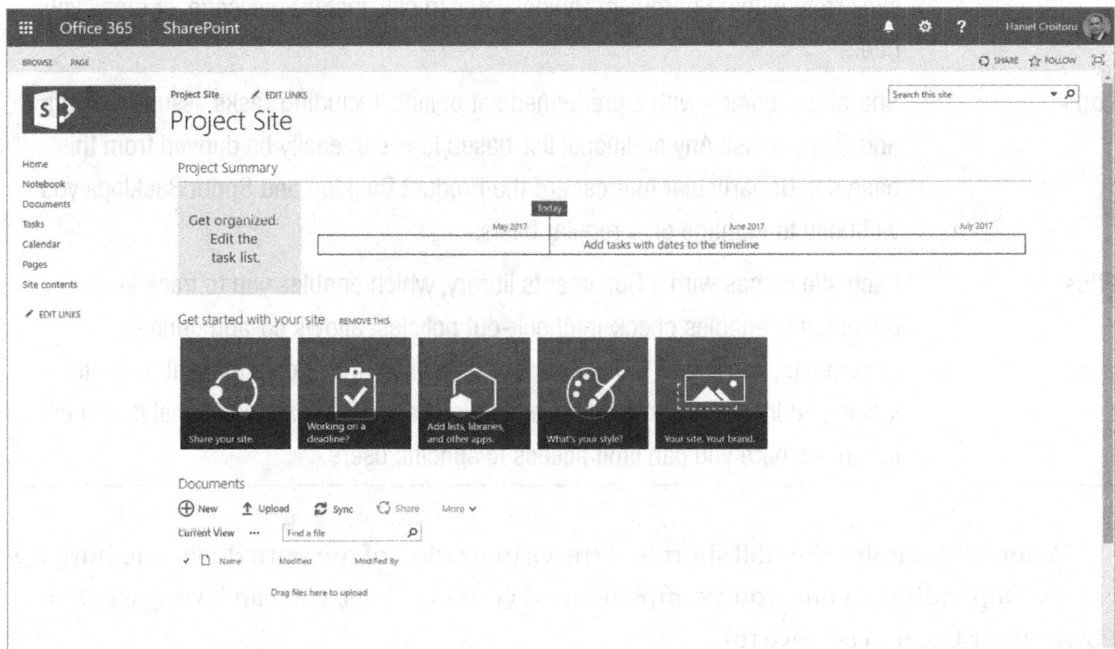

Figure 17-4. *Project site template used in SharePoint Online*

The Tasks list, as its name suggests, is used to track tasks. Each task has a number of important metadata fields associated with it, including the name, start and end date, % Complete, Assigned to, and more. When you synchronize your Microsoft Project or Microsoft Project Online project plans with SharePoint, the task list will automatically get updated with all the information. This makes it easy to track and allows your users to review progress without needing a license for the other tools to access it.

The Project Summary is a visualization control that provides two views into the tasks. The first view is a graphical representation of tasks and where they are relative to today's date. The second view provides a summary of late, upcoming, and future tasks.

Out of the box, SharePoint sites provide you with the necessary functionality to manage most of your project information. Where functionality is missing, other apps can be easily integrated, as shown in Table 17-2.

Table 17-2. *Additional Functionality That Can Be Added to SharePoint Sites*

Communication	Each SharePoint site can have a site mailbox set up to capture emails. A better option is to leverage Yammer groups and integrate the conversations directly into the SharePoint site. Skype for Business integrates directly with SharePoint Online and provides presence indicators to see if someone is online or busy. Using a single mouse click from within SharePoint Online, you can call, instant message, or email your peers.
Logs	SharePoint comes with a predefined set of lists, including Tasks, Issue Tracking, and Custom List. Any additional list-based logs can easily be derived from this base set. Of particular interest are the Product Backlog and Sprint Backlogs you will need to manage on a regular basis.
Files	Each site comes with a Documents library, which enables you to track your documents, enables check-in/check-out policies, allows co-authoring of documents, and more. You can further customize these document libraries to include additional metadata. If needed, you can also create additional document libraries where you can limit access to specific users.

Where SharePoint sites fall short is in the visualization of the burn down and burn up charts. Depending on how you've implemented your backlogs, you can leverage either Power BI or Excel to achieve this.

Office 365 Groups

Office 365 Groups are a close cousin of SharePoint Online. In fact, Groups are built using SharePoint Team sites. What distinguishes them mainly is their canned nature. When you create an Office 365 group, you are provided with a predefined set of features.

Microsoft Teams

In Chapter 1, I briefly described Microsoft Teams as being a new chat-based app that allows your team to communicate via private or team conversations, meetings, email threads, and multi-person audio and video conversations so you can stay abreast of what is happening. That is only the tip of the iceberg. In fact, although it's very new, Microsoft Teams today has all the necessary functionality to allow teams to effectively communicate from a single place. You can think of Microsoft Teams as your hub for managing all (project) team-related conversations and artifacts stored in Microsoft Office 365 Groups and other line-of-business systems (Figure 17-5). Let's have a look at how Microsoft Teams can help you manage your agile projects.

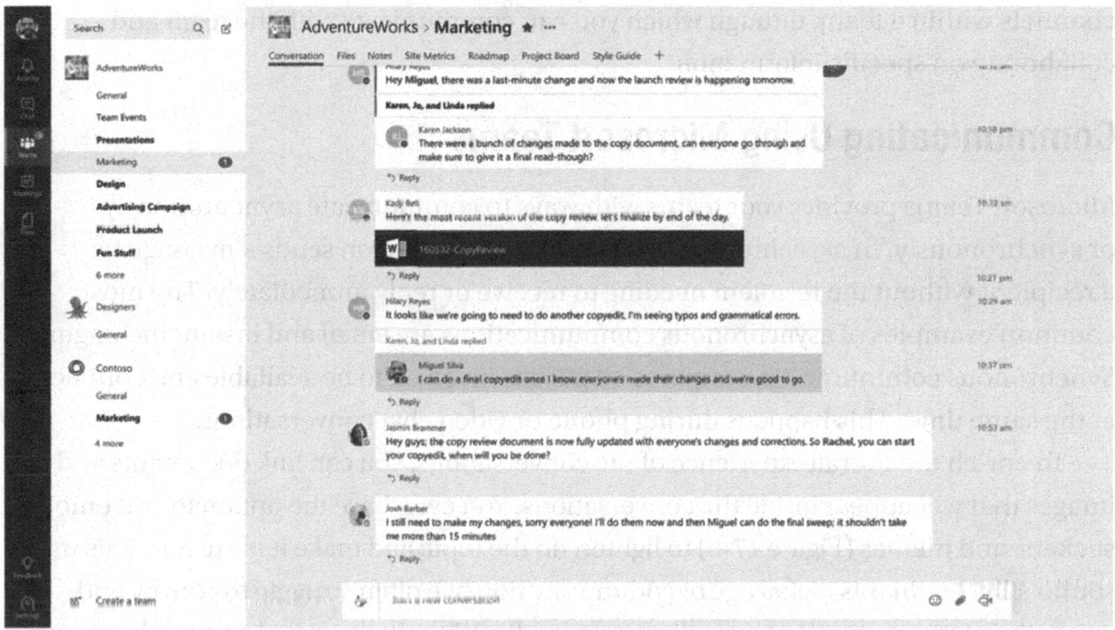

***Figure 17-5.** Communicate and collaborate with your teams from a single location using Microsoft Teams*

At the time of writing, Microsoft Teams is available in the following formats:

- Office 365 Commercial Suites
- Office 365 Business Essentials
- Office 365 Business Premium
- Office 365 Enterprise E1, E3, and E5 plans (E4 before retirement)
- All Office 365 Education Suite licensing
    - Office 365 Education
    - Office 365 Education Plus
    - Office 365 Education E5
    - Office 365 Education E3 customers who purchased E3 prior to its retirement

If the license you use for Office 365 is not on this list, you may have to wait or use the alternatives that I listed in this chapter.

What makes Microsoft Teams particularly appealing is the ability to create specific channels within a team, through which you can communicate with the team and collaborate on specific information.

Communicating Using Microsoft Teams

Microsoft Teams provides your teams with ways to communicate asynchronously or synchronously. In asynchronous conversations, one person sends a message to a recipient without the recipient needing to receive or reply immediately. The most common examples of asynchronous communications are email and instant messaging. Synchronous communication requires all parties involved to be available and connected at the same time. This happens during phone or video chat conversations.

To enrich the overall experience of the conversations, you can link documents and images that will appear inside the conversations. You even have the option to add emojis, stickers, and memes (Figure 17-6) to lighten up the topic and make it more fun. This may sound silly, but in this digital age of communication, we often struggle to convey and correctly interpret emotions over electronic media. Without the visual or audible queues we get from a voice or visual conversation, it can be tough to differentiate sarcasm from seriousness, busy from angry, or other similar emotions. Adding visuals such as emojis are not the answer to all such situations, but can definitely help, so let's use them.

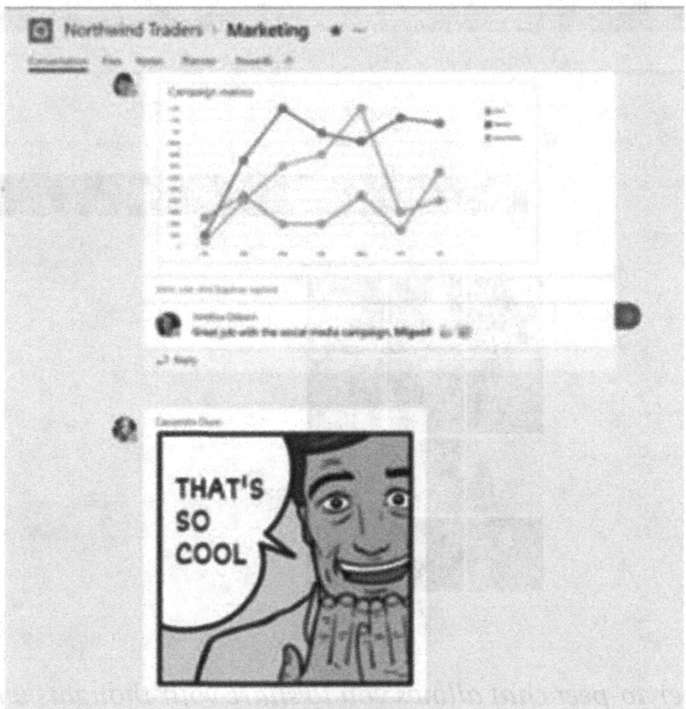

Figure 17-6. *Memes, stickers, and emojis are helpful ways to convey emotions in eletronic communication*

Peer-to-Peer Conversations

Like Skype and many other instant messaging (IM) technologies that are prevalent on the market today, Microsoft Teams lets you conduct peer-to-peer private chats with up to 20 individuals at a time (Figure 17-7). These conversations are not visible to anyone outside of the chat itself, even if they belong to the team.

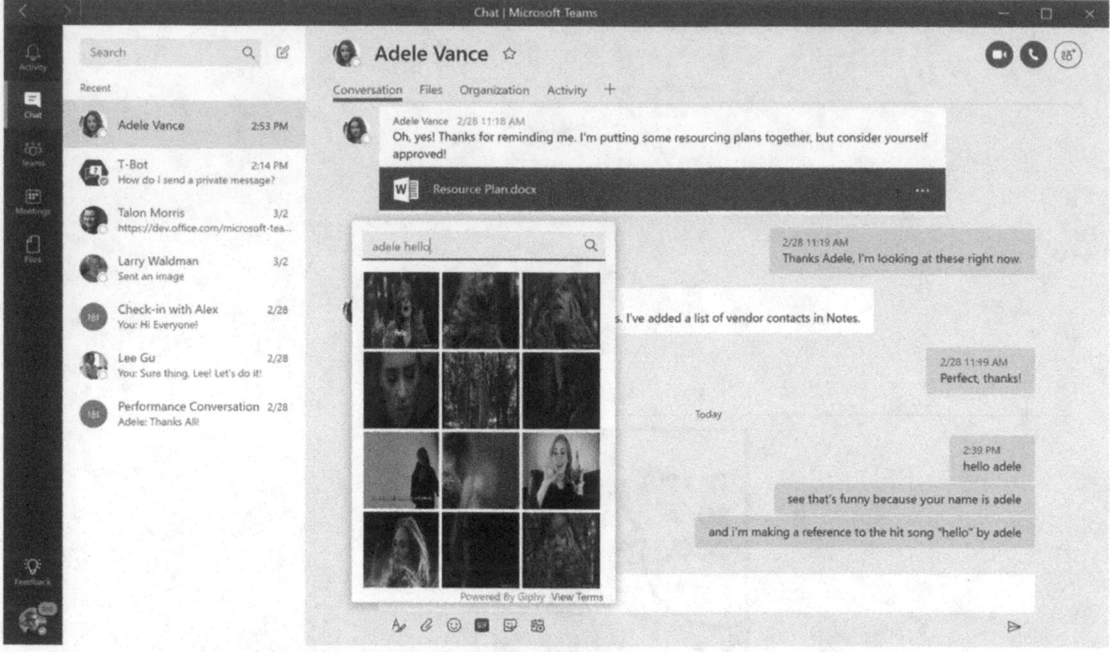

Figure 17-7. *Peer-to-peer chat allows you to share your thoughts with specific individuals only. Others will not be able to see these converstaions.*

Channel Conversations

As mentioned, Microsoft Team introduced the concept of *channels*. Each channel has its own conversation stream. In an effectively-communicating project team, the number of conversations can be quite high. Using channels, you can keep the conversations focused by sprint or other logical groupings.

An organization or project team that has effectively adopted the use of Microsoft Teams can benefit from a significant reduction in internal emails. There may, however, still be legitimate reasons to use email, such as when communicating with individuals outside your organization. To ensure that the channel is being kept in the loop, each channel has its own unique email address that can be included. Any email and its attachments get stored separately in a SharePoint site associated with the team.

Audio/Video Conversations

Microsoft Teams enables you to conduct real-time audio or video meetings with up to 80 individuals at a time. You can see the video feed from several attendees simultaneously, as shown in Figure 17-8. When scheduling meetings, the organizer can pick specific individuals who should attend or invite the entire team. In either case, invitees will get a calendar invitation. If they accept, the event will appear in the Microsoft Teams as well as Skype for Business Meetings list.

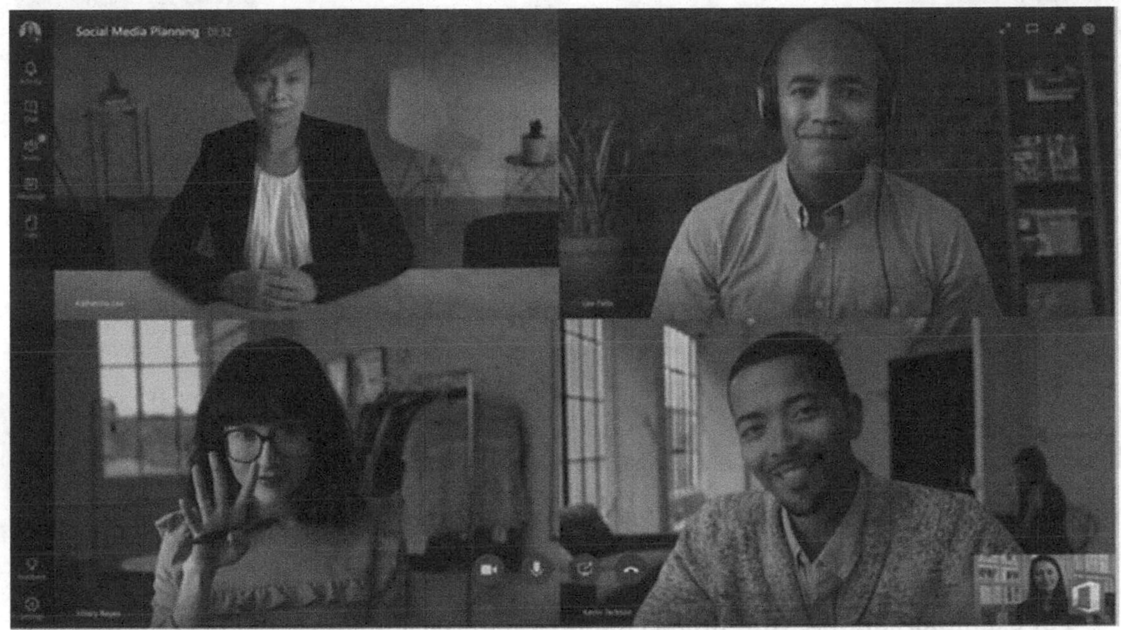

***Figure 17-8.** Teams allows you to conduct audio or video conversation with your team in real time*

Connectors

Connectors are used to monitor for specific events and provide updates to your project team when such events take place. Many Microsoft and third-party cloud-based services, such as the ones shown in Figure 17-9, provide some sort of connector today. If they don't, a common connector interface called *webhooks* can be used to provide such information. With webhooks, you don't have the full freedom to format the result to your liking, but the information is still provided.

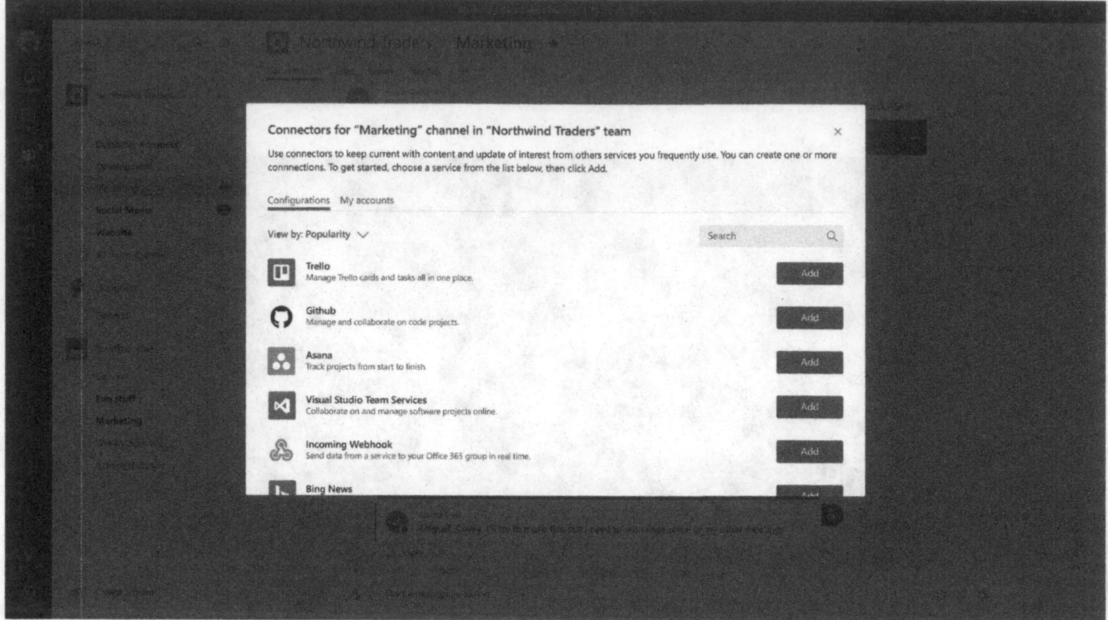

Figure 17-9. *Connectors are used to display information from other services in conversation feeds*

For example, suppose your project requires some custom development and you are running regular software builds throughout the sprints. It's important for you to know when a build was generated and whether it succeeded or not. A connector can listen to the build system (e.g. Visual Studio Team Services) and when a build takes place, send a message to a specific channel conversation feed on the outcome (Figure 17-10).

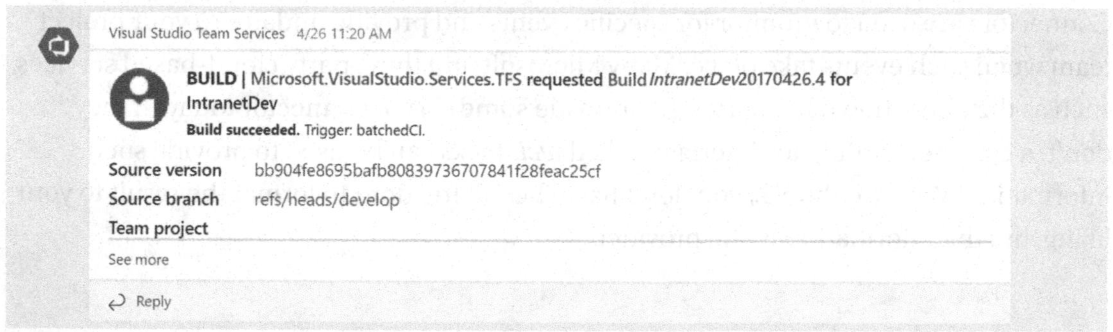

Figure 17-10. *Visual Studio Team Services Connector provides updates on a build*

What is great about the connectors is that not only do you get near real-time updates, but the updates are all provided to you within the Team channel, so you don't have to switch applications.

Bots

Bots are semi-intelligent apps that are designed to help you perform tasks you would usually do on your own, such as booking a flight, adding an appointment to your calendar, or fetching and displaying information. Bots tend to simulate real conversations and should feel like you're chatting back and forth with a human, as shown in Figure 17-11.

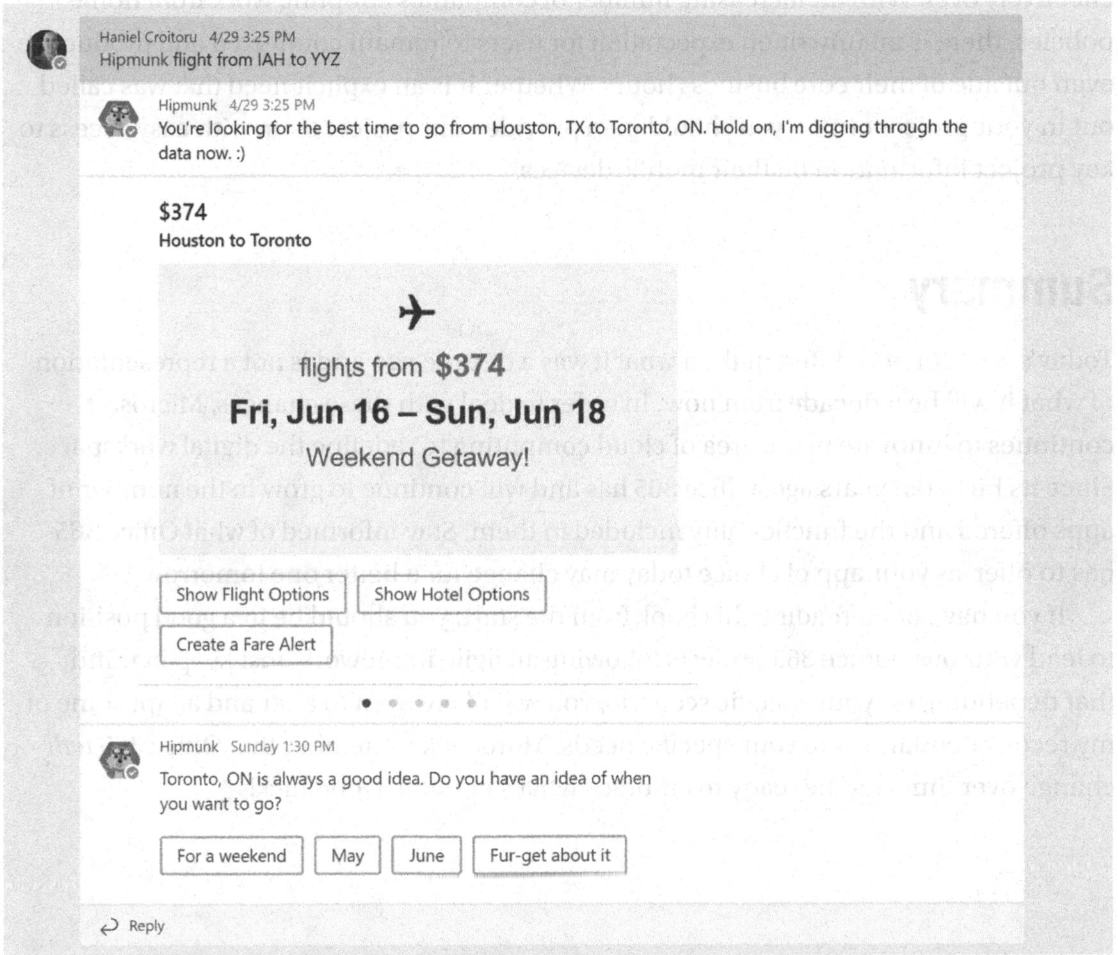

***Figure 17-11.** Bots are meant to provide the user with information through the use of dialog-like conversations*

More advanced bots are capable of learning and improving their responses over time based on the questions and feedback they receive. For example, when you ask a question, the bot will provide you with an answer. By indicating whether the answer was correct or incorrect, the bot will know the next time when prompted with a similar question whether to provide the same answer to the user.

Accessing Information on the Go

Ubiquitous connectivity and a surge in personal mobile device proliferation have given users the ability to work from almost anywhere, anytime. The era of the 9-to-5 job is effectively over. With an increasing number of companies adopting work from home policies, there is an unwritten expectation for users to remain connected and productive even outside of their core business hours. Whether it is an explicit need that was called out in your project or not, you should plan provide your project team with easy access to key project information on their mobile devices.

Summary

Today's workforce is different than what it was a decade ago and is not a representation of what it will be a decade from now. In order to deal with these changes, Microsoft continues to innovate in the area of cloud computing to redefine the digital workspace. Since its birth ten years ago, Office 365 has and will continue to grow in the number of apps offered and the functionality included in them. Stay informed of what Office 365 has to offer, as your app of choice today may change for a better one tomorrow.

If you have been reading this book from the start, you should be in a good position to lead your own Office 365 projects following an agile framework. Just keep in mind that depending on your specific scenario, you will likely want to alter and adapt some of my recommendations to your specific needs. Moreover, remember that Office 365 *will* change over time and be ready to embrace what's coming. Good luck!

Index

A

H. Croitoru, *Agile Office 365*, https://doi.org/10.1007/978-1-4842-4081-6

B

C

D

P, Q

R

S

T

U

V

W, X

Y, Z

Printed in the United States
By Bookmasters